Chiron was a centaur, half man half horse, symbolising the joining together of humans and animals. Is this close relationship what is happening, or what could happen, between people and .... circuses and zoos?

Dr Marthe ....ington, one of the world's for ....imal ...aviour experts, was c ....ed by the RSPCA and UFAW (Universities Federation for Animal Welfare) to carry out an independent, scientific study of circus animals, in comparison with animals in zoos and in the wild. The results of her 18 month investigation are in this book.

● Do animals in circuses and zoos suffer psychological ill-health?
● Is handling and training cruel?
● Does transportation cause stress?

After 3000 hours of scientific observation of animals and many visits to circuses and zoos, including training, travel and performance, Dr Kiley-Worthington concludes that, while there are improvements that must be made, circuses do not by their nature cause suffering and distress in animals. She states, "On balance, I do not think that the animals' best interests are necessarily served by money and activities diverted to try and ban circuses and zoos either locally or nationally. What is much more important is to continue to encourage the zoos and circuses to improve their animal welfare along the lines recommended."

Arguing against animals and people having no contact ('Animal apartheid'), Dr Kiley-Worthington looks towards a symbiotic animal management system in circuses, zoos and elsewhere, so groups of animals and people can live and work together, respecting each other's needs but each gaining from the relationships - CHIRON'S WORLD.

MARTHE KILEY-WORTHINGTON, B.Sc., D.Phil., was one of the first ethologists to go and live with and study wild African animals, and to recognise behavioural problems of captive and domestic animals. She has done research and taught at the Universities of Makerere, Sussex, Pretoria and Edinburgh. Her work includes studies of many large mammals, animal welfare and training. Since 1971, she has been an Animal Behaviour consultant, and she also runs experimental Eco-farms, currently in Devon. She has three sons and is the author of five books and numerous scientific papers.

Dedication

To all the animals in circuses and zoos. May your lives be long and happy. May your human handlers and associates learn to understand and respect you better, and may the conditions under which you live improve.

By the same author:

The behavioural problems of farm animals
    (Oriel Press, Stockton 1977)
The behaviour of beef cattle, with S. de la Plain
    (Verlag Birkhauser, Basel 1983)
The behaviour of horses in relation to management and training
    (J.A. Allen, London 1987)
Food First Ecological Agriculture
    (in press, 1990)

Introduction

After the mist clears in the early morning at Liloni, if you are lucky and the day is clear, you can see the white snow-covered pudding top of Kilamanjaro some 250 or so miles away. Looking west from the verandah one looks down into the Rift Valley, and again on a clear day, herds of zebra, and wildebeest, kongoni, impala, Thompson's and Grant's gazelles and groups of elegant giraffe can be dot-picked on the flat, hot plain. Closer to home, the little 'animated plums' - the Kenyan highlands answer to the robin - leaping, chattering and cursing among the moonflowers and red hot poker plants in the garden. As Gye, my duiker friend, tiptoes across the Kikuyu grass taking an odd nippet of this and that; stepping adroitly over the cocker spaniel puppy, already spreadeagled on the lawn for his morning sun-nap.

An idyllic scene perhaps; it is the story of my raising in the clean, brisk air of Kenya. Inevitably such an upbringing - and this does not have to be something of the past - leads not only to an appreciation of the wonder and beauty of the living world, but to an intense realisation that we, *homo sapiens*, are part of it. My closest associates and friends were not other little kids, but the young and old of other species. As well as learning appropriate social behaviour from humans; individual horses, duikers, giraffes, dogs, cows, and bulls among others taught me (as they do many other children worldwide).

Inevitably my interests, as I grew, were not confined to humans and their activities, nore to admiring other species from a distance. They were obsessed by trying to learn more about all my different intelligent tutors. My quest took me to studying biology at school, to university in England, and back to East Africa to research and study waterbuck. Then back to Europe to learn more in universities about how animals behave and communicate, to farming, keeping and training domestic animals, to a consultancy on Animal Behaviour and to being commissioned by the RSPCA to study circus animals.

In 1965, Ruth Harrison's *Animal Machines* (99) began the awakening of the urban public to what had happened to animals in the country. The watershed in recent years was perhaps in 1976, when Peter Singer's book *Animal Liberation* (21) was published. It hit a raw nerve, and set many people thinking.

Since then, animal welfare has grown in importance - even the Ministry of Agriculture has had to bend a sympathetic ear, and some small advances have been made for the animals' benefit in farms and laboratories, at least, although stables, and kennels are very slow to change. In the last decade, boosted by public opinion, zoos have had to rethink what they are doing, why, and how.

The easiest target for the ever-growing band of Animal Welfarists has been circuses. They are a minority with no very articulate or powerful representation, and they have wild animals as well as domestic ones. They exist only to entertain, not to feed people or to save endangered species, and they make the animals do 'undignified' things. It was, unlike fishing, or intensive farming, or certain types of pet keeping, a simple case: circuses were just **'wrong'** and ought to be stopped. However, it proved difficult to argue that the animals were physically in poor health, so it seemed that information must be accumulated on their psychological ill-health in order to strengthen the case against them.

The debates proved more complex than one supposed. To do a proper scholarly job it was not enough to restrict such an investigation to empirical scientific results. There is another fund of knowledge that must be bought to bear on the questions raised. The knowledge and understanding of those who live and work with animals should not be dismissed as just 'anecdotal' or 'opinionated' and therefore of no relevance.

Also, since the decisions are moral ones, the debates and ideas current among philosophers must be assessed carefully and the intellectual habit of critical thinking developed. Finally, we must assess the pros and cons of the existence of circuses and zoos on individual animals within them, on global and local ecology, and on other species, including human animals.

This work is an effort to put together accumulated knowledge from all these areas in order to asses what our attitudes should be to animals (vertebrates at least) and how we should live with them, use them and be used by them. It contains the result of the report written for the RSPCA in 1989, but it also examines all the various arguments in more detail.

Circuses and zoos are not the centre of multi-national industries.They serve people by only feeding their spirits (if at all), and have wild animals in captivity.

These are used as a springboard to examine what is or is not appropriate animal husbandry.

Do circuses and zoos **inevitably** cause prolonged suffering and distress to animals? Are they **by their nature** unacceptable, or is it just that some of them are badly operated? Are they worse than other animal husbandry systems?

Many people now argue that we should leave all animals alone, and not use them in any way. Is this either necessary, or desirable? What are the costs and benefits to the animal and the human of doing this? Should we not rather work out some criteria and codes of human conduct that would make association with animals morally, ecologically and ethologically acceptable for animal and human? If so, what would this involve?

I believe we can do this. All vertebrates, at least, should have a Bill of Rights. I suggest what should be included in such a Bill.

Make no mistake, Oh! Ye of little faith, I am on the side of my tutors, colleagues and friends, the animals. But this does not lead me to condone 'dis-association' between humans and other animals, rather to promote mutually beneficial relationships between us all... symbiosis.

Chapter 1

Background

In the last two decades or so, circuses in Britain have been on the decline, and some of the best known circuses have sold up (e.g. Bertram Mills) or given up travelling shows. This has been for many reasons. One of them has been the declining gates as the result of competition in entertainment from television and video. Another reason has been the public's changing attitudes to animals, particularly wild animals and their welfare. Conflicts (sometimes bitter and violent) with animal liberation activists have occasionally been the outcome. The RSPCA have been successful in sometimes lobbying local councils to ban circuses from their traditional tenting grounds.

Various television personalities with zoological interests have also come out against having animals in circuses, but not zoos. Zoos have come under criticism from some quarters but for various social reasons they have been successful at countering critical arguments; it is often argued that zoos are **not necessarily** cruel and wrong (but there are bad zoos), whereas circuses are **by their nature** cruel. This, perhaps more than any other single factor, has tended to make many from the middle classes consider that circuses are bad things where animals are exploited, badly looked after, badly treated, and **inevitably** suffer physically and mentally. On top of all this, they have to do unnatural acts to entertain human beings. It is widely believed by the 'nature loving' urban dweller that in order to perform these acts the animals must have had to be goaded, shocked, burnt and hit.

The circus people in Britain find themselves somewhat bemused by the public's change of attitude to the circus. Even in Switzerland, which has the strongest of all animal welfare legislation, the circus trainer and presenter is someone who is famous, and is a respected and admired artist. Here in Britain he or she may find themselves among people who despise them, and consider them almost criminal. Not only have the British circuses come up against hard times economically, but those which retain their animals have had to examine their motives and try to justify their profession in a way which the conventional horse trainer or zoo-keeper has rarely had to do. Some proprietors have decided that continuing with the travelling circus is not worth all the unpleasantness and have gone into other businesses.

Yet there remain perhaps a couple of dozen families in Britain who are circus people. The circus world and profession is all they have ever known and loved, and they not only keep going, but keep educating their children into it to ensure that their life will continue somehow. Economic difficulties will, one feels, always be staggered through; ingenuity and self-reliance are the circus people's middle names. Even if there was only one member in the audience: *THE SHOW MUST GO ON.*

The only real threat to the end of British circuses, and therefore to a uniquely different way of animal and human living, is the outlawing of circuses. This could happen should the government consider that circus people should not be allowed to live their lives as they wish; or that their animals should be kept no longer. Circuses are not really circuses without animals - they have been tried unsuccessfully (e.g. Circus Hassani on tour 1980, Gerry Cottle's Circus 1984-85). Over sixty percent of the circus-going audiences who returned our questionnaire said they would not go if there were no animals (Appendix 3).

The circus people are a close-knit, worldwide, nomadic sub-culture who are dependent on their animals; not for breeding, slaughter or experimentation but for their skills. Their children are brought up and usually educated within what effectively is a multi-species community. Like other minority nomadic cultures - such as the Lapps, the Bedouin, the Masai, the Aborigines and the Inuits - their way of life is under threat. This is not primarily because of human population increase and environmental threat, changes in land tenure or political boundaries, but because they have performing animals.

Whether or not the disappearance of minority human cultures is a good or a bad thing is not the point in question here. However, we must recognise in considering the banning of circuses that there are serious implications for a minority human culture as well as for individual humans and animals. We must be quite sure that the amount of pain and suffering that the animals must sustain in circuses outweighs that in other animal enterprises, and we must consider the anguish sustained by the humans, who will no longer be able to live their lives as they wish and are accustomed to, before they are singled out and outlawed. On the other hand, zoos are not a sub-culture or human community who live and work together. The zoo personnel may be united in their interest in zoos, but it is a job they go to at certain hours. They do not live within it or bring up their children within it.

The first question to ask then is: Is there more cruelty and suffering sustained by animals in circuses than in other animal husbandry systems? Even if it is found that there is **no more nor less** animal suffering in circuses than in other animal husbandry systems, this does not allow us to assume that all is acceptable within the circus. What we must do first is:

a) consider if this suffering is endemic to the circus: that **by its nature** there will inevitably be unavoidable high levels of animal suffering, or

b) consider ways of reducing or eliminating this animal suffering within the circus, and

c) consider if there are any important and unique contributions to the living world as a whole that circuses do, or could make.

Points a, b, and c must also be considered for other larger and more common animal husbandry enterprises such as zoos, farms, kennels, stables, pets and so on if we are to be consistent. Of course, human attitudes to animals are generally very inconsistent. The same people who demonstrate outside circuses will often happily chump their way through a pig that was conceived, born, raised, transported and slaughtered in conditions that are much more restrictive and 'unnatural' than one would see in a circus where hundreds rather than millions of animals' lives are at stake. We knowingly tolerate 'cruelty' on a massive scale where it affects our personal comfort, but God help one if one rides a lion, or has a pet bear (South West BBC TV News, 16 December 1989). Perhaps we should be more consistent. By examining the vexed question of the acceptability of zoos and circuses carefully, we can begin to think more rationally about animal welfare and ethics in general. The question of whether or not there should be animals in circuses raises all the questions pertinent to the animal welfare debates: ecological, ethological and ethical.

It has been argued by many [1;2; 3; 4 and 5] that if animals are subject to prolonged suffering then the husbandry system is unacceptable: the husbandry is 'cruel'.

The first question addressed therefore is 'Are the animals in British circuses subject to prolonged suffering?' Physical suffering is relatively easy to assess: it involves malnutrition, inadequate veterinary attention to wounds, disease, and

14

normal prophylactics (e.g. worming) or feet trimming. It also involves assessing the frequency of occupational disease, for example evidence for strains or wounds as the result of the animals' work.

If an animal or a human being is stressed for prolonged periods, then there are various physiological changes. One of these is often a reduced resistance to disease [6]. Thus the frequency of diseases, or the widespread use of prophylactic drugs to control the common occurrence of disease (such as feeding antibiotics to intensively raised livestock) is indicative of 'stress' or 'suffering'.

In addition, surgery is sometimes used not only to preserve life or cure disease, but also to overcome behavioural problems that interfere with a particular form of management; for example, the widespread castration of male animals, or neck surgery in horses to prevent a stereotypic behaviour known as 'crib-biting'; or debarking of dogs and declawing cats. Surgery is also used for cosmetic reasons; for example, ear clipping and tail docking certain breeds of dog, or the cutting of the vibrissae of horses for the show ring.

An assessment of the frequency of the use of drugs and surgery for these reasons will be relevant to an assessment of suffering in those animals in that environment.

It has been argued [7; 8] that whether or not animals breed in the environment is another index of their wellbeing. Whether this is a sufficient indicator is highly disputed as animals and humans may breed in extremely deprived and confined environments but zoos often argue that the breeding of endangered species is their main *raison d'etre* [9; 10]. Lack of breeding, on the other hand, can be used as one indicator of environmental inadequacy. Thus the amount of breeding in circuses must also be assessed.

Even if there is apparently little or no physical suffering demonstrated by these assessments, this does not mean that the animals may not be suffering psychologically. How can this be assessed? This has been debated heavily in the last decade and a half, particularly because of questions over the adequacy of farm livestock enterprises [1;11; 12]. There is much controversy among applied ethologists on how to measure psychological suffering, but there is also some agreement. I feel it is high time we made a real effort to apply some of the ideas that have come out of these debates to assessing practical examples of animal welfare.

The controlled environment of circuses and zoos: animal husbandry systems that are considered 'human luxuries', and therefore where the animals should be most sympathetically treated, is an ideal place to begin.

How much suffering is **too** much? This is a difficult problem since inevitably a living being will feel distressed and suffer sometimes, and without this he or she may not be able to feel joy and pleasure. But there is another approach that can help here - this is the assessment of **behavioural restriction.**

The idea that the animal should have the opportunity to perform their normal behavioural repertoire [13] has come under attack as a result of our lack of understanding of motivation. How do we know if the animal really **needs** to perform all the behaviour in its repertoire? Evolution tells us that the animal has evolved to live in a particular range of habitats and social organisations and has also evolved various behaviours which have helped them to survive. The species has also evolved a brain with specific types of expertise and abilities. Thus from the studies of the wild or feral animal who is unrestricted, we have considerable *a priori* knowledge about how and where the species evolved to live and how it behaves. Thus we can assume that an animal's well-being depends upon:

a) his being in this kind of environment, and

b) his being able to perform these behaviours.

Hence, if we wish to ensure he is in an environment to which he is well adapted (and therefore less likely to show evidence of prolonged distress), we should ensure that he is in such an appropriate environment.

In the 'wild', the animal may, by some of his behaviour, cause prolonged or acute suffering to others (e.g. hunting and killing). While he is under human jurisdiction, we should, perhaps, not cater for this part of behavioural repertoire as we also have duties to the hunted. On the other hand, since it may be that chasing and hunting may be particularly important to that animal, we should provide some form of substitute for this.

If we take this line of argument, the amount of behavioural restriction as a result of the animal's environment will give us an indicator of the degree to which it might be suffering. For example, a leopard is a relatively solitary forest-living creature which loves to climb. Keeping it in a large social group with nothing to climb on and no cover is likely to cause the leopard discomfort and probably also to suffer, although this would not necessarily be true for lions.

Of course, animals in the wild also suffer. They may suffer physically from extremes of temperature: heat or cold, from hunger, thirst and disease. They may also suffer mentally as a result, for example, of the death of their mother or infant or social partner. At least in these respects, provided the husbandry is good, domestic and captive animals should not have to suffer as much. In an assessment of behavioural restriction we must not ignore these features of the natural wild environment.

In these ways I have attempted to assess the relative amount of suffering of animals in circuses and other husbandry systems, particularly zoos. However, if animals can have unpleasant emotions (pain, fear, anxiety) then equally they must feel positive emotions (pleasure, joy, affection). How can we assess these? We have some idea from everyday observation of the demonstrative dog and horse. Using the detailed quantitatively recorded behavioural observations reported here - and previous work on displays and their meaning - I have made a first tentative step in trying to assess this for zoo and circus animals (Chapters 4 and 5).

This brings us to the subject of training animals for circuses. How is this done? Is it 'cruel' (i.e. does it cause prolonged suffering)? Do animals lose dignity by doing certain acts? If so, what acts are they, and are they respected less by human beings as a result? Are there any positive effects of training? If so, what are they, and do the animals and/or the humans benefit? (Chapter 6)

One group of arguments against zoos and circuses is that, even though their theoretical aims (eg conservation, education and research) may be acceptable, they inevitably cause suffering to animals, and are therefore cruel and wrong. Is this the case?

Another argument is that whether or not they cause suffering or pleasure to animals, they are by their nature wrong because, for example, they keep traditionally 'wild' animals in captivity, or display animals in unnatural ways.

Most of the various arguments for and against zoos and circuses also apply to all other animal husbandry systems so this debate encompasses our treatment of and attitudes to animals in all types of animal enterprises. Zoos and circuses act as a springboard because:

17

a) they exist primarily to entertain human beings, and

b) they keep wild animals in captivity (under human jurisdiction).

All the arguments must be examined carefully. The next four chapters do this, starting at the beginning: the degree to which we differ from or are similar to other higher mammals, and as a result the type of consideration that should be given to animals. Then the problems with the total respect for life approach are pointed out. One of the consequences of this position, and one which society seems to be working towards, could be an **'animal apartheid'**. Is this a good or a bad thing? Then there is the problem of the behavioural effect of domestication and whether wild animals should be given special status, and considered differently from domestic animals. This gives rise to the problem of what is 'natural' and whether **only** natural actions are acceptable for any animal, or human being.

We then look at the arguments that have been, or could be, put forward **for** zoos and circuses and examine them to see if they could be, or are in fact, put into practice. There are conservation arguments that are pertinent, but also those to do with education, research and our understanding of other living beings are discussed.

When we have, all be it briefly, examined how circuses operate in practice and the various arguments for and against them and zoos, it is clear that the issues are more complex than one might have supposed, and that we need some sort of series of guidelines or a blueprint to help in designing environments that will be acceptable to animals so that we can live with them in a mutually beneficial way: symbiotically.

I have attempted to do this, and conclude that **provided these criteria are met then no animal husbandry system is unacceptable,** including zoos or circuses, even though they do not at present exist necessarily in this form. It only remains to point out the most urgent changes needed in zoos and circuses in order to reduce or eliminate animal suffering, and to make constructive suggestions and recommendations as to how this can be done.

Animal welfare debates are growing up slowly, and those who take part in them, even the extreme radicals on both sides of the argument, are beginning to realise the value of rational debate.

Scientists are not educated, as a rule, to ask questions concerning the nature of their science, but rather they believe that what they consider 'good science' is FACT.

18

By contrast, philosophers are taught to be critical thinkers - everything is subject to question and debate; on the grounds that it is only by such open-minded debate that we can progress in our thinking and understanding of the world. On the other hand, equally important in this progress is the absorption of new, different, or long-forgotten information, some of which may well have been accrued from many sources, including empirical studies; that is from 'science'.

Only if these two approaches to understanding and knowledge are put together can we avoid the trap of spending a lifetime 'inventing the wheel' - learning 'commonsense' knowledge [14].

Science is society's present deity, and the general public as well as scientists themselves are in awe of the 'scientific fact', the 'truth'. Yet, at the same time, there are murmurings and mutterings of intuitive dissatisfaction with this approach from some thinking people. An illustration may clarify this point. Richard Dawkins is a populariser of 'scientific truth', whose publisher on the flyleaf of one of his latest books [15] was bold enough to say: 'Paley's case (for the existence of God on the grounds of the purposefulness and complexity of living things) is totally wrong'. Dawkins himself says concerning fairies (page 292 in the same book):

...we can never prove that fairies do not exist. All that we can say is that no sightings of fairies have ever been confirmed, and that such alleged photographs of them as have been produced are palpable fakes... Any categorical statement I make that fairies don't exist is vulnerable to the possibility that one day I may see a gossamer-winged little person at the bottom of the garden.

These statements I find truly awe-inspiring in their blind faith, their conviction that, in the first place, God (in the second case, Truth) is on their side and that the existence of fairies **must remain in doubt until they are confirmed, by some empirically measurable means.** How cosy it must be to have so little doubt, such religious fanaticism!

Perhaps many of us intuitively find such an approach slightly lacking. By such statements not only is a douche of cold water being metaphorically thrown in the face of fun, but fantasy, imagination, ideas, perhaps even feelings, are being denied.

Few of us have the knowledge or training in critical thinking to challenge such statements which are so close to the edifice of our technological society. One who does is Stephen Clark [16], a philosopher and for many years one of the major thinkers concerning animal welfare issues. He sums up this attitude (page 353):

> ...If fairies *[or dreams? - my addition]* are regularly, even if eccentrically seen, then fairies are as real as any other ideas... To believe in fairies is to acknowledge, and even to make real to oneself, the intermittent presence of spirits that enter our ordinary consciousness as moods of love or alienation, wild joy or anger... To doubt or disprove their existence it is necessary to do more than dredge Loch Ness or dig up every haunted mound.

Surely what science is about is the assessment of knowledge and ideas from all possible sources, **one** of which is empirical measurements. Other sources may also provide information or knowledge.

It is in animal welfare debates where such differences in approach are constantly clashing. Often each side does not recognise why their differences are so gross, each believing that they are the reasonable rational human, the others ludicrous cranks or non-feeling mealy-mouthed automatons. Their differences are fundamental in relation to their different view of the world, and it would seem sensible that the first stage is to examine the premise on which the edifice stands, not to bat the ball on the periphery.

There are a large number of societies and individuals concerned with animal welfare who reflect society's slightly ambiguous attitude: giving lip service to Dawkins' type of science, yet at the same time not prepared completely to deny the existence of fairies...of dreams, of imagination, which they **know** exist.

To keep the 'sensible rational debate' in the hands of the empirical scientist, and thus to avoid examining the foundations of the argument, 'Animal Welfare Science' [17; 18] has been invented and professional chairs instituted in it. Yet such is a contradiction in terms, unless we understand by 'science' an interdisciplinary search for knowledge.

Animal Welfare, inevitably, is fundamentally concerned with moral judgements; empirical measurements are useful **only** in so far as their results can be used to inform the ethical arguments.

Even those often considered to be representing the epitome of empirical scientific knowledge, the sub-atomic physicists are now concluding that it is sometimes the observer who affects the behaviour of sub-atomic particles [19]. It sometimes seems that modern biological thinking is stuck in the age of Newtonian mechanics; can we not progress towards applying Quantum theory and a more holistic approach in our thinking about living systems?

It would seem that Animal Welfare, which inevitably throws us into examining our own view of the world, is an ideal area to try out such thinking.

To date, the philosophers have started the ball rolling, and made the greatest contribution in this area [e.g. 20; 2; 22; 23; 24; 25].But the philosophers do not necessarily have great knowledge of the scientific work that has been accumulated and is relevant to the issues.

Perhaps by listening carefully and understanding the various ethical arguments, and having a reasonably comprehensive knowledge of the animals themselves, will we be able to make considered judgements; putting together results from empirical study of their behaviour, practical knowledge of caring for and training the animals themselves, and the ethical arguments. Such an holistic approach would no doubt benefit the welfare of the animals as well as assist the advancement of biological science into the post-Newtonian age!

We must therefore summarise briefly the arguments that people have made for and against circuses. Inevitably this will seem superficial, but the reader is referred to the bibliography should he or she wish to go further with this. It is also inevitable that, despite my efforts not to, I will have misquoted or misunderstood certain arguments. I can assure you that this is not my intention, although I am not above taking the odd dig, as I am sure others will do of this work.

As a result of considering these questions (more to avoid any hypocrisy in one's own mind and life, than to argue for a strongly held view), one comes to some sort of conclusion: a *modus vivendi*. Not all the problems are solved; compromises have to be made. It is a question of **where** the lines are drawn, and **why** they are drawn in one place or another.

While I would never go so far as to say that they are 'true and right' and all others are just wrong, I believe that these are rational conclusions genuinely supported by the relevant information and that the lines have been drawn as well as they can be in the light of present knowledge and understanding.

At the end of the day, however, my only truly strongly held view is that I believe in debate and that our worst enemy is anyone holding unthinking, unquestioning, narrow minded, bigotted views - be she or he politician, scientist, religious fanatic, animal liberationist or zoo or circus fan.

Chapter 2

About Circuses

Circuses come and go overnight in city parks, town market places and village greens. The circus is not only a moving theatre which provides its own building, sets, seats, lights, generators, actors (some of whom are of different species), but also living accommodation, kitchens and food for all the different species. By contrast, professional human theatres often find it difficult to even build the sets and operate the lights, never mind constructing the building, and moving it around!

This is not the place for a sociological study of the people in circuses, but some background to how the human community and the circus as a whole works is essential in order to understand the importance, role and treatment of the other species within it.

Anyone in the circus will help with any job that needs doing within their capacity, and there are jobs for toddlers and grannies. There are of course squabbles within the circus community, as in families, but the unity and cooperation towards a common goal of the people in the circus is something that is not often seen elsewhere. Children grow up learning their chosen skills, of which there are many on offer: from horse trainer, to trapeze artiste or clown, electrician or mechanic, public relations officer, public speaker, or lion presenter. At the same time, they have the discipline of having to muck in and help wherever they can and are needed.

The tented circus is essentially a nomadic multi-species community. The life of all involved can be divided up into different phases:

- the residential tented phase;
- the performance;
- the 'pull down', transport and 'build-up' phase;
- and the 'winter quarters' when the circus is out of season for a period of often less than three months and retires to static quarters to rehabilitate, paint, brush up and collect and practise new acts.

We will describe briefly how the humans and animals live in each phase.

The tented circus on tour

Fig. 1. Not all circuses are large. A small circus encampment touring the village greens, with a llama, a couple of ponies and dogs, a clown and trapeze artistes. The people and the animals have a variety of acts and chores.

The residential tented environment consists of the Big Top, surrounded usually in a circle by the caravans and trailers in which the humans and some of the animals reside - i.e. pet dogs, and some young animals that are being hand-reared e.g. jaguars or lion cubs, or young primates (Figure 2). The stable tents in which the the larger performing animals are kept are usually near the artists' entrance to the Big Top and inside the trailer ring. In the relatively small British circuses there may be one large tent with elephants, and a variety of ungulates, and perhaps another with horses and ponies and other species. The carnivores - the big cats, bears etc. - live and are transported in custom-built trailers, known as 'beast wagons' (Figure 3). These wagons are also within the outspan and near by. The cats have a netted runway into the ring so that they can run directly into the ring from their wagons. Netted runways afford safe and easy ways of making or allowing the big cats to move from one place to another. The exercise cages for the big cats are usually adjacent to their wagons so that they can leap down into them or run through a short netted runway.

Fig. 2. A young jaguar and lion who are being hand reared in the rearer's caravan.

Fig. 3. A typical beast wagon. .

The service vehicles (trailers for props, the Big Top etc.) will be parked in the surrounding ring, or within it, and other necessities such as the generator, toilets, washing facilities, any canteen etc., will also be strategically placed within the circle

Services such as electricity and water and sometimes drainage are usually available, in Britain, by plugging into the mains on site. This is not always the case, however, and the circus has to be self-sufficient in such arrangements. Connections to each caravan and the stable tents, as well as the Big Top, are made quickly on arrival. A skip is hired or provided by the site-owner, and rubbish including animal manure is deposited in it. Not all the circuses provide proper clean toilet and washing facilities for either their own community or the public. This is an area which could and should be improved.

There is considerable competition between the circuses for sites, and areas around which they will each travel that year. The Association of Circus Proprietors was apparently first set up to avoid squabbles and clashes and to establish a fair distribution of sites to each member. This has, it seems, worked to a degree among the members, but non-members are not controlled by the same good sense, and often 'gazump' by rushing into a good site before the scheduled circus arrives. This happens to a degree because the site-owners charge considerable sums for hire of the site and it can be attractive to let it as frequently as possible.

Inevitably, holes are made in the ground for tent poles and so on, and the elephants are prone to dig. If it is wet and the site has no hard standing, it can be churned up to a muddy mess. Not only do all the trucks with the circus paraphernalia, animals etc. have to come on to the ground, but often parking for the audience's cars is also provided.

Some councils have, under pressure from anti-circus groups, banned circuses with performing animals from their grounds. The results of this have sometimes been that the circus has found a private ground which may not have the same services. I visited two or three sites of this type which with inclement weather had turned into muddy swamps, good for neither human nor beast.

Mud is something circuses have learnt to live with over the years, and they have in general efficient strategies for cleaning the tents, animals etc. and keeping them clean, putting down hard standings, and pathways, and coping as well as possible. However, the weather in Britain frequently gets the better of them, particularly in the autumn and early spring. The circus proprietors are, in general, acutely aware of the need to keep the encampment clean and tidy in order to make a good impression on the public to whom they are on view 24 hours a day. Bad weather and the enormous amount of extra work it entails can be depressing for all involved.

Disasters do strike, for example floods throughout the circus encampment happen from time to time; but the most frequent disasters are winds blowing down and ripping the Big Top. The threat of a real gale will be almost the only occasion on which a performance will be cancelled, and the Big Top taken down.

We will now consider how and where each group of animals live in the tented circus.

FIGURE 4 CARNIVORES and PRIMATES
Keeping conditions in British circuses.

SPECIES	TOTAL	perform-ance	solitary	group house	beast wagon	exercise yard	individual handling
		No	No	No	No	No	No
Lions	43	40	0		43	30	22
Tigers	58	57	1	57	58	35	10
Leopards	8	8	3	5	8	5	5
Snow leopards	5	1		5	5	5	4
Puma	5	3	2	3	5	4	3
Jaguar	2	1	0	2	2	2	0
Lynx	2	tr	1	0	1	0	0
Hyena	2	tr		2	2	0	0
Wolves	2	tr		2	2	0	0
Dogs	43	43		43	43	25	43
Bears (black)	7	4	3	4	7	5	4
Primates Rhesus Monkey	1	1	1(H)				
TOTAL-	177	157	11	123	177	111	91
MEAN %		88	6	69	100	62	51

KEY H = kept with humans, tr = training

The carnivores

The carnivores are usually kept and transported in 'beast wagons'. These are cages on wheels which can be sub-divided into sections from the outside. In this way, the cages can be cleaned and the animals can be manoeuvred from cage to ring without the handlers going into the cages. Three sides are solid metal and the fourth long side is barred, over which a metal canopy can be secured at night or during travel. The animals may be kept in adjacent sub-divisions of the beast wagons, or in one group. The number of cubic metres per individual varies between 0.17 and 4.5 for an adult lion, tiger or leopard.

They are usually fed six days a week - on heads of cattle or sheep which are easy to come by and cheap. They are given a mineral supplement as well, and watered two or three times a day. They were given between 0.5 and 3 kg per animal per day.

At the start of this study, there were many carnivores that were not out of these wagons except for the 10 minutes or so of the performances per day. This meant they were severely restricted behaviourally. However, since November 1987, the circuses in the Association of Circus Proprietors themselves have brought in inspection procedures and necessary provisions for animal welfare in the circuses (see Appendix 1). One of the provisions is that no animal should be confined to the beast wagons all the time, but must have exercise yards or rings provided. This self-imposed regulation is subject to spot checks by the circus veterinarian, or other appointed personnel.

Nevertherless, there are times when the animals do not have exercise areas available, and some animals, particularly those out of public view at winter training grounds, have access to these very little, if at all. Confining the animals to small beast wagons for all their working lives is not ethologically or ethically sound (see Chapter 9), even if they do not show high levels of distress (see Chapter 6) and it is imperative that proper exercise yards and rings are provided for ALL the carnivores at least during the hours of daylight. Some argue that if the animals are allowed into large areas to play and exercise for long periods, then they are less willing to work energetically in training or at the performance. If this is the case, and the animals will not work satisfactorily when provided with these minimal facilities, then they should not be kept.

In addition to the provision of exercise areas, much could be done with the beast wagons themselves in order to enrich the environment for the animals. For example,

Fig. 5. Exercise runs can be attached directly to the beast wagon so that the carnivores can go in or out at will.

shelves could be provided which would allow the animals to use the third dimension, and also to climb and lie high up which leopards in particular seem to prefer. Branches, tyres, ropes, hammocks and so on could be provided in the wagons, and 'toys' could be provided more liberally in the exercise enclosures which could be easily and quickly constructed around the wagon.

Both zoos and circuses can have problems with their animals not taking enough exercise. In circuses, this can be overcome in the training and performing sessions, but if for some reason this is not possible, then certain strategies to encourage exercise, such as chasing moving objects, or searching for food, could be initiated.

Bears are also kept in beast wagons although they are often handled more and taken for walks and so on. One bear keeper had constructed a swimming pool inside the beast wagon for the bears, which they used in hot weather. However, proper exercise yards/enclosures should always be provided.

The domestic dogs are often kept inside trailers, either in groups or in individual cages and only taken out for walks twice a day and for the performance. This is an unnecessary restriction. The dogs should have proper exercise yards, possibly attached to their trailers which they can use at will. Alternatively, they can be tethered around the campsite or in one area. If they bark continuously, the solution should *not* be to shut them up more so that they cannot be heard, but rather to look at the cause of this persistent disquiet (often related to frustration of the dog in one way or another), and try to accommodate it. If this cannot be done and the animals cannot be trained not to bark at inappropriate times, then once again the environment is not ethologically sound and they should not be kept. Ideally, domestic dogs should be so trained and obedient that they can be left to run around the campsite without causing a problem of any sort; this is by no means impossible to achieve.

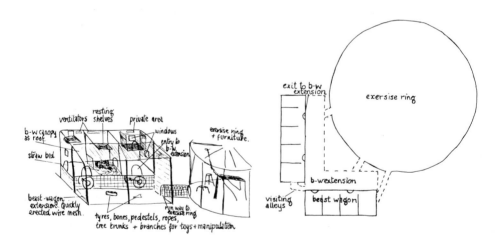

Fig. 6. Proposed improved living accommodation for the carnivores.
The beast wagon has an extension that is quick and easy to erect and to which the animals should have access to, at least all day. This can open into the exercise yard or ring and to the circus ring by netted runways. The wagons/sleeping areas should have appropriate furniture for the species. For example, leopards should have private boxes they can retire to at will, shelves for sleeping on, ropes and branches to climb and use and so on.

FIGURE 7 PAENUNGULATA and UNGULATES
Keeping conditions in British circuses

SPECIE	TOTAL	perform-ance No.	soli-tary No.	group house No.	tied No.	loose yard No.	occasionally free No.
Paenungulata							
Indian Elephants	31	31	3	28	31	15	14
African Elephants	5	5	1	4	5	5	5
Ungulates, Artiodactyls							
Pygmy Hippopotamus	1	0	1	0	0	1	0
Pig (domestic)	8	8	3	5	0	8	0
Reindeer	5	5	1	4	2	4	0
Eland	1	1	1	&Co	1	0	0
Bison	1	1	1	&Co	1	0	0
Water Buffalo	1	1	1	&Co	1	0	0
Zebu Cattle (Bos indicus)	1	1	1	&Co	1	1	0
Ankole Cattle (B.indicus)	2	2	0	2	2	2	1
Highland Cattle (B.taurus)	3	3	1	2	3	3	2
Goat (domestic)	2	2	2	&Co	2	2	1
Camel (Bactrian)	19	19	4	15	19	10	0
Llama	16	16	4	12	16	12	2
Guanaco	3	3		3	3	3	3
Alpaca	1	1	1	&Co	1	1	0
Perissodactyls							
Zebra (Grevys)	1	1	1	&Co	1	0	0
Zebra (Hartmanns)	15	15	4	11	15	4	0
Mule	3	3	1	2	3	1	2
Donkey	1	1	1	&Co	1	1	1
Pony	49	49	2	47	24	22 LB	7
Horse	75	75	20	52	30	45	4
Marsupials							
Wallaby	1	1	1	&Co	1	1	0
TOTAL	245	244	55	190	163	141	42
MEAN %		99	22	77	66	57	17

KEY &Co = with other species, LB = loose box

The elephants

In the tented circuses, the elephants are traditionally kept shackled. They are shackled by a front and a hind leg by covered chains. They stand on boards 4 metres by 3 metres. They can lie down, with difficulty, and they can move about 1 metre forwards and backwards. Each elephant has its own place. When the study began, some of the elephants were kept shackled for 24 hours, except when they were taken off for performance. This is not an ethologically acceptable way of keeping elephants since it restricts their behaviour greatly. However the Association of Circus Proprietors (ACP) brought in an edict that the elephants must be unshackled for a considerable amount of time each day, other than for performance. One of the problems is how to leave elephants outside, loose, in safe, easily erected enclosures. I suggested that it might be possible to use electric-wired enclosures, provided the elephants had some training to the electric fence, and then keep them at least for the majority of the daytime loose in groups. This was tried out by one circus in the summer of 1988 and found to be very successful; so was quickly adopted by several others.

Fig. 8. Young Indian elephants in a European circus shackled on boards.

Fig. 9. African elephants in an electric-wired enclosure within the circus encampment. A normal electric fence used for farm stock can be used.

The elephants are also sometimes tethered and given objects to manipulate, or taken for walks or allowed to play about free in open ground, on the beaches, in rivers or wherever it is permitted by the local landlords and councils. One aspect of the efforts of organisations trying to ban circuses has been that they have been prevented from going down to the beach, or going for walks in certain areas (e.g. Blackpool). This has **not** improved their welfare.

Fig. 10. Indian elephants out for a graze and walk with their trainer (on the bench).

There is no doubt that shackling elephants for prolonged periods is ethically and ethologically unacceptable. There are other ways in which the elephants can be kept for much of the time in circuses, and these must be insisted on for the majority of daylight hours at least. They are highly manipulative, curious and intellectually able animals which must be provided with sufficiently stimulating and interesting environments. This is not impossible to achieve in circuses, although husbandry systems must continue to change.

Elephants are social animals and should be kept, as a rule, in social matriarchal groups. Certain adult individuals which have been kept alone all their lives are not able necessarily to integrate well into elephant society, and this must be considered in recommending changes. Provided the animal has a strong emotional bond with its handler/trainer, this may be best for the animal, although the next generation should be brought up in social elephant groups.

Wild elephants feed for over 16 hours a day. Thus, when captive, elephants should have access to high-fibre food almost continuously to enable them to do this. They also often like to manipulate and strip leaves off branches, or the bark, or even make tools for scratching themselves out of pieces of stick. They are often given fruit, vegetables and bread by local greengrocers and bakers which adds variety to their diet.

Figure 11. Shackled elephants in their tent have eaten all the leaves off the branches they have been given. One has broken the stick to a convenient size and is using it to scratch: an elementary form of tool use.

Bull elephants have a reputation for being unpredictable and difficult to handle. However in Sri Lanka they are tamed, trained and worked alongside cows; although when in musth they must be confined [26].

There was only one bull elephant travelling with the circuses in Britain, and another in a safari park. The problem of bull elephants must be faced by circuses. In the wild, bull elephants are not necessarily always with the group [74; 27; 28].But circuses should concentrate on allowing their elephants to breed and live in family groups.

The ungulates (hoofed animals)

There was often only one member of a social species kept in the circuses we visited. This is not advisable (see Chapter 9). When there were more than one of each species, the artiodactyls (cloven-hoofed animals) were often kept in groups, in enclosures, within the stable tent. They are loose and in social groups. Although the social group

Fig. 12. Proposed stable tent and enclosures for the hoofed stock.
The tent has enclosures within it where the animals can be tied for individual attention, ration feeding and so on, but they are free to wander in and out of the tent by using electric wired enclosures. This is quite possible for the elephants and other species, traditionally wild or domestic. They should live in the type of groups structure that they have evolved to live in (e.g. pigs in family groups, elephants in matriarchal groups, horses in batchelor groups or mares and their family groups).

may not be always appropriate for their species, they are able to perform much of the behaviour in their repertoire. They are all usually handled and can be led and taken out of the tent for walks, training and performance. However, they are not often taken out of their indoor enclosures for long periods each day. They also could have electric-fenced outdoor enclosures where they could run in groups.

Figure 13. Stalls or loose boxes with high sides isolating the animal and cutting him off from the outside world are not appropriate.

Figure 14. A tethered eland, not ideal, because he is still restrained and is a social mammal, but better than being confined to stalls or loose boxes in the tent all the time.

Some of the animals are kept tied in stalls. It is even more important that these animals are taken out for several hours a day, and allowed to run free if possible.

The major group among the perissodactyls (single-toed animals) is the equines; although there was a white rhinoceros in one circus I visited. The ponies are sometimes loose in or out of enclosures, and sometimes tied in stalls with little divisions. The horses were either tied in stalls, or in looseboxes (Figures 16, 17). Sometimes these looseboxes had the effect of isolating the animals more from their environments and their neighbours and it appeared from the analysis of the behavioural results that there were more behavioural problems and abnormalities in those horses compared to those in what one would think are the more restricted stalls.. No horses were kept in loose yards which is ethologically and ethically the most acceptable way of keeping them.

Figure 15. Ponies loose in the circus encampment.

Figure 16. Stalled horses divided by bars only.

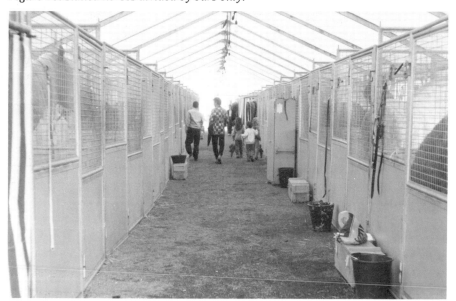

Figure 17. 'Upmarket' loose boxes for some circus horses.
The animals are isolated from each other and the outside by wire mesh. For long periods of the day, there is little going on, and they may only be taken out for training and performance, about half an hour a day. In addition, they may be fed restricted fibre diets (as these were), thus having nothing to eat for long periods. This type of stabling is very widespread among horse owners. There was more evidence of distress as a result of such stabling than in the stalls.

Since the majority of the horses in the circuses are stallions, it is concluded they cannot be run together; yet feral horses do have bachelor groups, and the practice is quite possible with high-quality domestic horses [29]. One circus proprietor is interested in trying such a system out.

The zebras were kept tied in stalls and handled much like the horses. When it is seen how these animals easily adapt and respond to this husbandry, it does seem absurd that zebras in zoos have to suffer darting and drugging before even their feet can be trimmed!

FIGURE 18 BIRDS and SNAKES Keeping conditions in British circuses.

SPECIES	perform-ance	solitary	group house	beast wagon	exercise yard	individual handling
	No	No	No	No	No	No
Birds						
Emu	1	1				1
Canary	20*	0	20			All
Macaw	40*	0	40			All
Pigeon	30*	0	30			All
Snakes						
Indian Python	1	1	Box			1
African Python	1	1	Box			1
TOTAL						

* approximate numbers

The birds

The birds were kept in trailers where they had cages and sometimes free-flying aviaries. One colony of macaws was allowed to fly freely wherever the circus was camped, and the trainer said she had never lost one! The pigeons all flew freely in the acts. The emu, however, was confined to a loosebox and did not appear to be taken out regularly at all. It should be implicit that the flying birds have facilities to fly wherever they are kept; the same, of course, applies to zoo birds.

The snakes

These were kept in boxes and taken out several times a day for performances and training. They were handled a considerable amount, and did not appear to find this distressing. They were fed dead, not live, prey. We need much more information concerning snakes and details of their behaviour before we are in a position to make judgements about them.

The primates

The only primate in the circuses I visited was a young rhesus monkey which lived in a trailer with his trainer. The monkey's environment was stimulating and he had an opportunity for forming strong emotional bonds with humans - although not with other rhesus monkeys. He was young, and may possibly not integrate well with other monkeys later in life as a result. However, he had few behavioural restrictions.

Build up, pull down and transport

Build up is the construction of the camp or temporary township. Usually the circus will pull down the previous encampment after the last night performance (9-10 p.m.), pack everything up and move to the next site before dawn. They may begin to build up immediately on arrival, or they may sleep until dawn or into the morning and build up later in the morning.

Sometimes they have an evening performance on the same day, but usually there is no performance on the first day which is often Sunday or Monday. If they stay in small towns for only half a week (which they often do), then they will usually have performances six days in the week.

There is an enormous amount of co-ordinated work to be done requiring skill and efficiency in erecting the Big Top and the whole circus encampment. In Europe the Czechoslovaks were renowned particularly for their 'tent crews' who used to be hired for the season by the bigger circuses. Because of travel restrictions, this role has been taken over to some extent by Moroccans; while Poles, in Europe, are often hired as stable hands. They may have two or three people whose main jobs are the tent and mechanics. Actually, everyone is expected to help and those that have no other job will also be 'ring boys' - helping with the props, cleaning and changing the ring surface, erecting and taking down the big cat cages, leading on the animals, cleaning the Big Top, driving and so on.

The pull down and build up of the encampment and the speed and efficiency with which it can be done is a matter of pride within each circus. There is no denying how hard circus people work, nor their long hours. It is often said that good grooms are difficult to come by because so few people want to work the hours. Nevertheless, there are considerable possibilities within the circus world for those who start at the bottom of the circus hierarchy as ring boys or grooms to work their way up within a few years to be artistes, performers, animal trainers or business people within the circus. The financial rewards are not great in Britain, except possibly for a few proprietors, but there is a constant stream of people entering the circus world and remaining within it for reasons other than financial gain. The most important of these seems to be the close-knit community that the circus offers - a 'way of life' (see Chapter 8). The great majority of those that have been born and raised in the circus stay within it, moving perhaps from circus to circus and country to country.

Transport

The welfare of animals in transport between, for example, farm and slaughter house is the subject of much concern, and it is evident that the frequent transport of circus animals should be investigated carefully.

There is a major point of difference between the transporting of unhandled naive animals from the farm and the transport of circus animals: the circus animals (similar to some competitive horses) become very familiar with being transported. Unlike the naive animals, where the whole experience appears to be distressing and the animals show physiological signs of stress (including increase in heart rate), the animal familiar with the transport and in a transporter which is relatively comfortable does not appear to find it a distressing experience

We need to do further work in this regard: monitoring heart rates would be relatively easy with the new technology. However, we monitored loading and unloading, and some animals in transport, taking pulse rates at random and found little behavioural evidence of distress.

One measure of whether animals have found particular experiences distressing is that they show unwillingness to enter the area again. Refusing to load is one of

Figure 19. Elephants in their transporter. Note the pedestal to front left which they had climbed on to enter.

Figure 20. Loading zero-handled elephants at a zoo. A circus crew had been hired, and the elephants had to be chained to a tractor with the chain running through the transporter. It took four hours to load these animals.

the most common behavioural problems in horses. To our surprise we found no sign of any of the circus animals not walking in willingly to the transporters. The only exceptions were inexperienced, newly acquired animals. The elephants sometimes had to climb on to pedestals in order to get into the box, and stood quietly inside with the doors open (Fig. 19). This was contrasted with the extraordinary problems we witnessed at a zoo (Fig. 20) where they were trying to load their 'zero handled', unfamiliar elephants. Here the elephant had to be shackled to a tractor with the chain running through the transporter in order to help pull them in! This was a dangerous operation for both the elephants and the handlers. It was interesting to see that despite the generally derogatory attitude of zoos to circuses [9], they had had to hire circus people to help with the loading.

The circus transporters varied from luxurious custom-built boxes to adapted lorries. The animals had their own familiar places in the transporter. Some travelled with padded partitions; others such as the elephants and some of the cloven-hoofed animals, without. The ungulates were usually tied individually and travelled across rather than head to the engine. Although the most common way of transporting horses, head to the engine has been shown to be inappropriate [32]. The big cats and carnivores were usually confined to individual pens in the beast wagon for transportation.

It has been suggested that the animals might get cold during transport. The transporters, although ventilated, were enclosed and during the summer when the animals were usually transported around, it is over-heating rather than the cold that has to be considered carefully, particularly when the vehicles are still. Improved adjustable ventilators and windows which would allow some light in and allow animals to see out are necessary improvements.

For all the carnivores and some of the ungulates, the transporter was also used as the animals' sleeping quarters which of course increased familiarity with it.

Travelling on minor bendy roads tends to be more tiring for the animals than on motorways where horses, for example, will rest one leg and eat and drink as they travel, once they are experienced. Although we were unable to travel with the circus animals, on arrival they were found to have eaten and there was no evidence that they had been traumatised (e.g. dried sweat, injuries etc.).

Pull down (of the circus camp) usually takes place after the evening performance. The animals are then boxed up and moved on to the next site. Before they are released from the transporters, the stable tent has to be erected - a job for the grooms. As a result, the animals may be confined to the transporter until the following midday, a period of 10 or 12 hours. They usually have access to food, and are given water on arrival at the new site, but the main objection to the transportation of circus animals on welfare grounds is that they are often confined for long periods. Recently, with the introduction of the electric pens for the elephants, the time in the transporter has been reduced for these animals. The construction on arrival of pens for the other hoofed stock would be an improvement. Similarly, the exercise yards for the carnivores should be constructed **immediately** on arrival in order to reduce the period in confinement.

There was no evidence to suggest that the transporting of circus animals is necessarily, or even usually, distressing or traumatic for the animals - although it is for naive farm livestock.

Performance

The performance involved the animals being exposed to bright flashing lights, noise, people, flapping tents, explosions and all other manner of sudden and what one might consider frightening stimuli. Going into the ring for a naive animal is indeed a frightening experience, as it is for a naive human being. Of necessity, the animals have to be conditioned, or trained to be able to cope with such environments. The accustoming of the animals to the ring and performances takes months and sometimes years. First, the animals are brought into the Big Top when no one is there and walked round the ring. After some weeks, when they are accustomed to this, they will begin their training. During training, they may well be brought into the ring during actual performances, and introduced to loud noises, applauding humans, flapping tents, music and clowning.

One measure of whether or not the animals found the performances distressing was if there was any resistance to entering the ring. This was not the case with almost any of the hoofed stock and elephants, some of which were apparently keen to get into the ring for performance. However, some of the big cats did have to be encouraged to leave their trailers and enter the runway to the ring by poking a broom handle into their wagon. This was more often the case for the younger, less experienced cats; approximately 40% of the animals had to be encouraged in this way.

In some cases - for example, dogs, mules, chimpanzees, some elephants and horses - there is evidence that the more experienced animals were responding to the audience appreciation. This took the form of repeating actions that had caused applause

Figure 21. A troupe of young African elephants walking without coercion into the ring.

Figure 22. A group of zebras running to the ring for performance, apparently without coercion.

or audience response, even in the case of a group of llamas and guanacos inventing actions, such as rolling and leaping over the ring wall and back (see Chapter 6).

Circus animals have become familiar with many things that inexperienced animals would find distressing because of their past experience, lifestyle and training. The relative naivety of even animals that have been trained to be used to noises was illustrated on one occasion when some mounted police officers on experienced police horses rode past the circus encampment in a London park. There were camels, ponies, Friesian stallions and llamas tethered around the tents which were flapping, and the band was playing in the Big Top. The police horses tensed up as they approached and when they saw the animals they leaped about and took off. It took half an hour for the police officers to encourage the horses to come back past the encampment, while the tethered circus animals were eating in a relaxed way. This shows that although the police horses had been well accustomed to certain types of noise and sudden visual stimuli, their experiences had been relatively limited when compared to those of the circus animals. Therefore the police horses found the circus a frightening experience.

There is little evidence that most of the experienced circus animals find the performances distressing. Training or 'educating' them to enter the ring willingly is all important here.

The winter quarters and static training grounds

Almost all the circuses have a farm or smallholding where they keep the stock not presently travelling with the circus, and where they go for the short winter period. In addition, two British circus businesses do not travel, but are professional sedentary training establishments. They supply animals for travelling circuses, galas, television, advertising, films and so on.

The same criticisms of the keeping conditions for the animals can be made of the winter quarters and sedentary circuses. Perhaps because these areas are not on show to the public, they may not be run very efficiently. Also, since they are where all the tent and truck maintenance is done, they can be very messy places.

The animals are not on public view and proprietors may be lax about ensuring that the animals have their exercise yards and cages and that they are well handled.

The winter quarters should be the annual holiday for the humans **and the performing animals**, when they can move freely, breed, relax, rest and perform some of the behaviours that may have been restricted during the season. They can also continue to learn new acts, meet new individuals who are to join the travelling show for the next season and generally recuperate.

There is usually sufficient land to be able to run many of the animals out in larger paddocks, or enclosures. However, good use of the land is **not** usually made, and often the animals are confined in buildings, which may be of very low quality, for the entire time. Some training is carried out in a structured way when the animals are in their winter quarters, but this is not true in all circuses.

Improvements in land, buildings, land use and running of many of the winter quarters are necessary, and the same criteria of animal husbandry should be applied as in the tented shows.

The circus people are not, nor do they pretend to be, land managers or farmers; but they could and should draw on available expertise for the proper management of their winter quarters and static training areas. They often argue that the animals must continue to be housed all the time because:

a) the weather is bad and they must not get cold, wet, dirty etc.;

b) the animals need to be confined in order to be trained.

The first part of this argument is often invalid. Even species which originated in the tropics can often adapt well to low temperatures, as we see in many zoos. With careful design and available housing which they can go into at will, the proper management for such animals is possible and is certainly desirable.

Secondly, if the animals have to be confined in order to be trained, then the training must be seriously questioned - and maybe either the trainer or the training should be changed. It is not difficult to train animals to come in from the field when called, and after all the circus trainers should be able to train their animals to do things that will be useful to management as well as to do tricks for performance!

During the off-season, when the circus retired to its winter quarters, the humans often depart for their holidays, prepare to join other circuses, or even turn to other businesses. One of the interesting features is that although there is frequently a house at the winter quarters, rarely does even the proprietor move into it. The house is usually used for storage and the people continue to live in their trailers which are, of course, their homes.

Chapter 3

Are Circuses and Zoos cruel in practice?

How can this question be answered? Almost everyone who has anything to do with animals (and almost everyone who does not!) will have an opinion on what is 'cruel' for what animal. On what are these opinions based, and how valid are they? Also, most important of all, is there any concensus in our judgements? Over the last decade and a half how to assess 'cruelty' has received a considerable amount of attention from three groups in particular.

The first are the animal welfare organisations of which there is an ever-growing number, reflecting the public at large's increasing concern with this matter. The members of these groups (although not necessarily their committees which may use any arguments to back up their position in order to achieve legislative change) usually make judgements primarily on emotional grounds: 'I don't like it, there is something wrong, and therefore it is cruel.' Such grounds must by no means be dismissed, but it is of little help if we cannot agree between us on how we feel about a certain case, and in particular why we feel it to be wrong and cruel. There are, of course, cases where we will all agree - such as where animals are starved or grossly physically abused as a result of human interference. But there are many more difficult aspects of the debate where we cannot all agree using our emotional judgements. These are often cases where we feel that the animals are suffering psychologically but there are no obvious physical signs - the animals grow, eat and drink and even reproduce well.

To try to help here, the applied ethologists have been active, thinking, discussing and writing about how to assess, in particular, animal suffering using behavioural indicators [e.g. 3; 4; 5; 8; 33; 31]. The emphasis of this work has been on science, and empirical measurement of behaviour of animals in different situations. There is probably less agreement among such scientists, however, on the question of what is cruel than there is among those making emotional judgements!

The third, and probably the most influential, group of people who have been thinking about this issue are some philosophers who are interested in ethics [e.g.

20; 21; 22; 23; 24; 25; 34]. Philosophy has been described as 'critical thinking', so they have tried to back up whatever position they take with rational arguments and examples. In this way, they attempt to answer the question about what is Right and what is Wrong, what is Cruel and what is Not.

It is by using the techniques, information and ideas produced by all three of these groups, that I shall try to answer the question: 'Are zoos and circuses cruel?'

There are two ways in which the question can be answered, and I think it is very important to understand the difference. The first one is 'Are zoos and circuses cruel **in practice?**' The answer to this question requires a thorough scientific examination of the way the animals are kept and treated with, wherever possible, empirical data concerning how much physical and psychological suffering there is in zoos and circuses.

The second way in which the question can be approached is theoretically: 'Are zoos and circuses fundamentally **by their nature** cruel?' Some people, including various welfare organisations (e.g. Zoo Check) [35] argue that this is the case and therefore such institutions should not exist even though there may be **no** evidence of either physical or psychological cruelty.

In this chapter we examine the way in which cruelty can be measured in practice, and the results we collected from our study of circuses and zoos.

First we have to decide what we mean by 'cruelty'. There are many possible definitions of this; the *Oxford English Dictionary* defines it as being: 'indifferent to, delighting in, another's pain or distress'. Ethologists have concentrated largely on trying to measure 'suffering', particularly prolonged suffering. They have argued that if an animal is suffering, then the environment can be considered inadequate; the animal's welfare is poor: in other words, the husbandry is cruel. But this begs the question.

'What for goodness sake **is** suffering and how can it be measured?' The first approach to this was to use what has been defined as 'stress'. If it is possible to demonstrate that the animal is 'stressed' - which is based on certain physiological measurements (e.g. level of certain steroids in the blood) - then it can be argued that the environment is inadequate. But as Selye [6], the originator of these ideas on stress, pointed out: a certain degree of stress is a good thing for the animal or human. Indeed, he went so far as to call this set of responses 'the general adaptive syndrome' (GAS) because it helped the organism to adapt to difficult situations. It is only if the GAS continues for a long time that this group of physiological responses begins to be destructive to the body. We do then have some ways in which we can measure physiological suffering (although taking these measures may often be very difficult to do in practice).

It is easier to assess physical suffering in practice, up to a point. For example, we can assess the animal's general physical condition, any wounds or signs of ill-health, malnutrition or neglect causing physical damage. This is what is done when assessing cruelty cases in law. Illness which is the result of occupational disease (e.g. wounds or damaged limbs as the result of training or performing) is another measure of ill-health. We should also look at the length of life of the animal and consider whether this is more or less than in the wild or other types of husbandry. This is particularly relevant to zoos and circuses where animals are not being reared for slaughter.

Is this enough? Is this all there is to it? If the animals are not displaying signs of physical ill-health, can we conclude that they are not suffering and that the system is not cruel? Animals can suffer psychological disease [e.g. 1; 3; 4; 40]. There is also the question of the interaction of mind and body: Can some physical disease be the result of psychological problems, and vice versa? [41]

Although we see no direct signs of physical or psychological suffering in the animal we are immediately concerned with, this may be because it has suffered treatments to reduce or eliminate such signs. For example, it may have been treated with drugs (immobilisers, tranquillisers or sedatives, or prophylactic antibiotics). Perhaps one index of possible suffering or inadequate environments for the animals might be the degree to which such drugs are used.

Surgery may be used for various reasons other than for immediate life-saving; for example, for cosmetic reasons; or to stop an animal performing an undesirable behaviour. Castration of males and hysterectomy of females (other than for strict medical reasons) are cases in point. This leads to a consideration of the sex ratios and the amount of castration that is usual in circuses and zoos, and any other use of surgery other than for immediate clinical reasons.

Is the use of drugs and surgery for behavioural reasons necessarily 'cruel', and therefore unacceptable? Such practices are not normally acceptable for human

FIGURE 23 CARNIVORES and PRIMATES

The numbers, origins, sexes, ages and how many individuals have reproduced themselves in British circuses.

SPECIES	1 No.	% of mammals	2 ORIGIN C	Z	W	3 AGE range	mean	4 SEX M	F	Cas	No. bred
Carnivores											
Lions	43	10.2	27	16	0	0-15yr	4yr	14	20	9	10
Tiger	58	18.7	32	6	0	0-15yr	5yr	41	17	0	15
Leopards	8	1.9	5	3	0	Ad	?	3	5	0	4
Snow Leopards	5	1.1	4	1	?	0-Ad	?	0	1+y	0	2
Puma	5	1.1	3	2	0	0-Ad	?	2	3	0	2
Jaguar	2	0.5	2	0	0	Ad	?	1	1	0	2
Lynx	1	0.2	0	1	0	Ad	?	1	0	0	At
Hyena	2	0.5	?	?	?	Ad	2yr?	2?	0	0	0
Wolves	2	0.5	0	2	0	4m	4m	2?	0	0	0
Dogs	43	10.2	43	0	0	0-12yr	6yr	5	3 0	8	10
Bears (black)	7	1.6	4	3	0	?	?	5	2	0	3
Primates											
Rhesus Monkey	1	0.2	0	1	0	6m	6m	1	0	0	0
TOTAL	177	41.9	77	35	0			77	79	17	48
% of carnivores	-	-	54.3	40	0	mean %		43.5	44.6	9.6	28

KEY C = circus Z = zoo W = wild caught Cas = castrated yr = year m = month Ad = adult y = young At = attempting

beings (although this does not always apply for the mentally ill). However, perhaps we should give the animals (particularly in zoos and circuses) the benefit of the doubt and assume that such practices are **not desirable**, although they may not immediately demonstrate 'cruelty'.

In this chapter we look at the results of these different possible measures of 'cruelty', 'suffering', or 'distress' in circuses and, in some cases, zoos.

The physical condition of circus animals

The easiest assessment of possible ill-health and distress is to look at the physical condition of the animals, to look for wounds, or any evidence of malnutrition or neglect of certain essential husbandry procedures. The majority of the circus animals were considered to be in good physical condition. Twelve individuals of different species, and ten horses, were in medium condition - usually slightly too thin and not showing a high gloss to the coat. Several of the horses and two of the cats also had coughs. (Figure 24).

Three of the Indian elephants, two old lions, one camel, four ponies and three horses (2%) were assessed as being in 'poor' condition. All of these were too thin, and in addition the camel, which was moulting, appeared to have a bad infection of lice.

However, the percentage of the animals in the winter quarters that were in peak condition was much lower: 30%, compared to 90% on tour. It is inevitable that the winter quarters would show a higher percentage of animals in poorer condition since they are used to house the animals that are not considered well enough to travel, for whatever reason. Nevertheless, this percentage of animals not in peak condition is too high.

The figure of 10% of the animals on tour not in **peak** condition is relatively low. Farms, stables, kennels and other animal-keeping enterprises often have much higher percentages than that. It would be interesting to have comparable figures for zoos. They always remove animals from the public eye if they are not looking as well as possible and place them in their 'not on public view' section.

The question remains, however, of what percentage of the animals should we expect not to be in peak condition at any one time? Indeed what percentage of human populations not in excellent health is acceptable? Inevitably there will always be some animals or humans who are sick or not in very good shape, but above what percentage do we consider that this indicates real problems with where and how they live?

Longevity

Figures 23, 25 and 26 give the age range of the animals in British circuses, and the average age. The animals were, as a general rule, trained as young adults, and would then work in the circus until either they die or become too senile. Old animals that were not sufficiently physically impressive to remain in the act, although they might be able to perform well, were usually retired rather than slaughtered. Circus trainers respond to a long association with an individual animal and, just as many other people who have worked with individuals for long periods (dogs, horses or elephants), they find it difficult to slaughter them when the animals get old. The result is that there were some old animals in the circuses and the average age of the animals is relatively high, when compared, for example, to the usual ages of horses in a riding-teaching establishment (9-10), or racing stables (2-8). The horse's lifespan in reasonable domestic situations is around 20-30 years, yet relatively few of them are permitted to live this long. Competing horses are considered 'old' at 15 and insurance premiums go up. If they had not been subjected to increasing chances of occupational diseases, they should be in their prime at this age.

Lifetime expectancy of dairy cows has declined radically in the last few decades, from an average of around 10 lactations (a lifetime of around 13 years) to just over 3 (a lifetime of 5-6 years). This has happened because of the increasing chances of occupational diseases such as lameness, mastitis, calving problems, infertility and as a result of the modern 'high input, high output' management. Organic farmers who manage their cows differently ensure that they have longer lives which in the end are more productive [128].

It would be interesting to compare the longevity of circus and zoo animals, and economic incentives for zoos to keep older animals alive. The zoos one would expect would have less incentive to keep old animals passed reproductive age alive since their self-confessed *raison d'etre* is to breed animals.

Apart from the emotional reasons for keeping animals longer in the circus, the economic reasons for keeping older trained animals as long as possible are obvious. It takes considerable time and expense to train circus animals, and therefore the longer they live and are fit and healthy to present to the public and perform their acts, the better from the economic point of view. The animal and its transport, the trainer/presenter and his or her trailer can represent the entire capital of an individual or family whose income may rely on this one animal.

FIGURE 24 SPECIES, THEIR PHYSICAL CONDITION & USE OF DRUGS & SURGERY IN CIRCUSES

SPECIES	CONDITION G	M	P	Vacc-ina-tions	Illness	Dea-th	Anti-biot-ics	Anae-sthe-tics	Anal-ges-ics	SURGERY Cast, Hyst,	Oth	Rest-raint
Lions	49	1		C W	2	2	+	0	0	9	0	0
Tigers	*			C W	1 HB	1	+	0	0	3	0	0
Leopards	*			C W	0	0	+	0	0	0	0	0
Snow leopards	*			C W			+	0	0	0	0	0
Puma		2		C W	0	0	0	0	0	0	0	0
Jaguar	*			C W			+	0	0	0	0	0
Lynx		*		C W	0	0	0	0	0	1	0	0
Hyena		*		W			+	0	0	0	0	0
Wolves		*		A W	0	0	0	0	0	0	0	0
Dogs	*			A W	0	0	0	0	0	0	0	0
Bears (black)	*			F T W	0	0	0	0	0	0	0	
Indian Elephants	20		3	W	2 Col	0	0	0	0	0	0	0
African Elephants	4			W	0	0	0	0	0	0	0	0
Pygmy Hippopotamus	*			0	0	0	0	0	0	0	0	0
Pig (domestic)	*			W	1 Sic	0	+	0	0	0	0	0
Reindeer	*				1 Col	0	0	0	0	0	0	0
Eland	*			W	0	0	0	0	0	*	0	0
Bisonl		*			0	0	0	0	0	0	0	0
Water Buffalo	*				0	0	0	0	0	0	0	0
Cattle	*			W	0	0	0	0	0	*	0	0
Goat (domestic)	1	1		W	0	0	0	0	0	0	0	0
Camel (Bactrian)	17	1		D W	2M 1L	0	0	0	0	0	0	0
Llama	24			W	1 W	1	+	0	0	1	0	0
Zebra	16	1		W	0	0	+	0	0	2	0	0
Mule	1	2		W	0	0	0	0	0	0	0	0
Donkey		*			0							0
Pony	28	17	4	W	4 Cou 1 col	0	0	0	0	0	0	0
Horse	52	10	3	W	10Cou 1 col	0	0	0	0	0	0	0
Rhesus monkey		*			0	0	0	0	0	0	0	0
Emu	*				0	0	0	0	0	0	0	0
Macaw	*				0							*
Pigeon	*			W	0	0	0	0	0	0	0	*
TOTAL	458	43	11					0	0	0	0	0
%	89	8	2									

54

ANAESTHETICS column refers only to there use for routine maintenance.
ANALGESICS column refers only to their use to allow the animal to work.
SURGERY - CAST./HYST = castration/ hysterectomy. OTHER = other behavioural surgery.
RESTRAINT = use of physical or chemical restraint to allow handling.
VACCINATIONS - C = cat flu, F = flu, T = tetanus, W = wormer, = trivac, D = deloused.
ILLNESS Col = colic, HB = hair ball, Sic = sick, M = mud fever, Cou = cough, L = lice, W = worms
ANTIBIOTICS - + = used for severe infection
DEATHS - 5 reported 1986 - 1988 = 0.97%

Occupational disease

One argument used against animals in circuses is that the animals may be physically injured in training and/or while performing acts dangerous to themselves. A proper investigation of this topic must involve records for many years. These were unfortunately not available.

The information in Figure 24, columns 5-7 indicate that analgesics, antibiotics and anaesthetics, and even deaths, are very infrequent in circuses. There were 11 cases where the animals had minor injuries.

Comparative figures are not available for zoos. They are likely to be considerably higher as they certainly have to use physical and chemical restraint frequently. Also, they use surgery widely for breeding as well as for medical reasons [9].

Occupational disease is much higher in competing horses than in the circus horses (33% in racing stables, 32% in teaching yards, 2% in circuses - see Figure 27).

The question is how low should it be? In human sport, the only way not to have injuries is to have no sport; should this apply to animals too, and particularly animals in circuses? Or would a certain level of occupational disease be acceptable if the animal showed no other evidence of prolonged distress, indeed apparently enjoyed the activity, as many horses apparently enjoy galloping and racing?

FIGURE 25 PAENUNGULATA and UNGULATES

The numbers, origins, sexes, ages and how many individuals have reproduced themselves in British circuses

SPECIES	1 No.	% of mammals	C	Z	W	range	mean	M	F	Cas	No. bred
			2 ORIGIN			3 AGE		4 SEX			
Paenungulata											
Indian Elephants	31	7.3	2	0	29	10m-35yr		2	29	0	2
African Elephants	5	1.1	0	0	5	5-15yr		1	4	0	0
Ungulates, Artiodactyls											
Pygmy Hippopotamus	1	0.2	?	?		20yr	20yr	1	0	0	0
Pig (domestic)	8	1.8	F			6m-2yr	1.8yr	4	4	0	0
Reindeer	5	1.1	F	2	0	1-5yr	4yr	5	0	0	0
Eland	1	0.2	1	0	0	2yr	2yr	1	0	0	0
Bison	1	0.2	1	0	0			0	1	0	0
Water Buffalo	1	0.2	1	0	0	1.5yr	1,yr	0	1	0	0
Zebu Cattle (B.indicus)	1	0.2	1	0	0	3yr	3yr				
Ankole Catt (B.indicus)	2	0.4	2	0	0	2yr	2yr	2	0	0	0
Highland Cattl(B.taurus)	3	0.7	3	0	0	1-21 ,yr	2yr	1	0	2	0
Goat (domestic)	2	0.4	F	0	0	9m	9m	0	2	0	0
Camel (Bactrian)	19	4.5	15	0	0	3m-24yr	12yr	13	6	0	5
Llama	16	3.7	13	3	0	1wk-12yr	7yr	11	4	1	10
Guanaco	3	0.7	3	0	0	1-6yr	4yr	1	2	0	2
Alpaca	1	0.2	?	0	0	?	?	1	0	0	0
Perissodactyls											
Zebra (Grevys)	1	0.2	0	1	0	1yr	1yr	0	0	1	
Zebra (Hartmanns)	15	3.5	5	10	0	6m-10yr	5yr	10	4	0	
Mule	3	0.7	?	?	?	10-20yr	18yr	1	2	0	0
Donkey	1	0.2	?	?	?	14yr	14yr				
Pony	49	11.6	21F	28	0	1-20yr	12yr	27	12	10	10
Horse	75	17.7	42S			2-28yr	15yr	39	30	6	4
Marsupials											
Wallaby	1	0.2	?	?	?	1yr	1yr				
TOTAL	245	58	68	14	34			120	101	18	33
MEAN %	71.5	-	27	5.7	13.8			48.9	41.2	7.3	13.4

KEY C = circus, Z = zoo, W = wild caught, F = farms, S = sales, yr = year, m = month.

FIGURE 26 BIRDS and SNAKES

Table of the numbers, origins, sexes, ages and how many individuals have reproduced themselves in British circuses.

1		2			3		4
		ORIGIN			AGE		
SPECIES	No.	C	Z	W	range	mean	BREEDING
Birds							
Emu	1	?	?	?	Ad		O
Canary	20	20			all		+
Macaw	40	40			all		+
Pigeon	30	30			all		+
Snakes							
Indian Python	1	0	1	0	Ad male		-
African Python	1	0	0	1	Ad male		-
TOTAL	91	90	1	1			
MEAN %		98	1	1			

KEY C = circus, Z = zoo, W = wild caught, Ad = adult.

Drugs

Drugs are very widely used, not only to cure or control disease, which may itself be the result of the system, but also to prevent a common disease of the system occurring (e.g. infeed antibiotics for calves and pigs to control or prevent outbreaks of bacterial diseases and to act as a growth promoter). They can also be used to reduce physical pain as a result of the system (e.g. Butezanodole to eliminate lameness in horses - Figure 27). Drugs are also used to control or eliminate undesirable behaviour within a system, such as tranquillisers and sedatives to reduce or control flight and aggression. They can also be used to increase desirable behaviours, such as artificially produced pheromones (chemical messengers); for example, the active components of boars' saliva is sometimes used to encourage sows to stand for artificial insemination. Steroids are widely used in many animal breeding systems to encourage libido in the male, or ovulation in the female, or to synchronise oestrus and even parturition (e.g. oestrogens, testosterone and progesterone). Steroid implants are also used to encourage growth or production in some farm animals.

Other drugs are used simply to stop the animal behaving at all, such as immobilisers and anaesthetics. Immobilisers are particularly widely used for zoo animals in order to allow many of them to be handled and treated even for routine medication, such as worming in some species, or feet trimming in zebras, for example.

The morality of all these types of drug use must be seriously considered.

FIGURE 27 THE USE OF ANALGESIC DRUGS, SURGERY (DENERVATION) AND THE OCCURANCE OF BEHAVIOURAL PROBLEMS IN A SAMPLE OF STABLED HORSES

	RACING STABLES		TEACHING STABLES *	
No. of establishments	5		12	
No. of horses	76		150	
	number	%	number	%
No. on Butezanodole	5	6.5	43	28
Denervated	20	26.5	6	4
TOTAL	25	33	49	32
Wood chewing	70	92	50	33
Crib biting or wind sucking	6	7.8	9	6
Weaving or stable walking	12	15.7	10	6.6
Head throwing or tossing	10	13.1	20	13.3
Stable kicking	8	10.7	15	10
High aggression levels	30	39.4	35	23.3
Stable neurosis	26	34	47	31.3
TOTAL	162	212.7	186	123.5

* = BHS approved

Surgery

This can be used in the same sort of way: for example, to overcome physical illness, the result of innappropriate management or neglect (e.g. worm-induced colic in horses), the result of insufficient worming, and/or inappropriate feeding [42]. It can also be necessary as a result of inappropriate breeding - for example, hip surgery for German shepherd dogs, nasal surgery for bulldogs and boxers or eye surgery for pekinese. Caesarian sections for Belgian Blue cattle are standard procedures.

Surgery can also be practised for cosmetic reasons; for example, ear and tail clipping of certain breeds of dog, vibrissae cutting for show horses, or denervation of the tail of Morgan horses.

Surgery is also used to prevent behaviour that is undesirable but which may be normal; for example, castration of males, hysterectomy of females, declawing of cats, debarking of dogs. It may also be used to prevent behaviour that is abnormal and the result of the system, for example the cutting of the neck muscles in crib-biting and wind-sucking horses, the docking of the tail or clipping of the ears on tail- and ear-biting pigs, or beak cutting of intensively housed chickens to prevent them defeathering and even killing and eating each other.

Surgery may also be used to overcome occupational disease; for example, denervation of the lower leg of some lame horses who have damaged legs as the result of excessive or prolonged over-exertion. Such drug and surgery use reflect on the inadequacy of the system. It effectively indicates that the husbandry system is outside the normal range of adaption of the animal and is therefore unacceptable; in fact, the use of drugs in this way is an indication of environmental inadequacy and animal distress. In these cases, the drugs are being used to suppress or eliminate other signs of distress and therefore are unacceptable. Both drugs and surgery were little used in circuses for these reasons.

Because surgical sterilisation is very widespread in all husbandry systems, we should look in a little more detail at the sex ratios of the animals in circuses.

The sex of circus animals

On farms where the animals are bred, the ratio of females to males is as a rule artificially high. Males not selected for breeding are usually castrated and then slaughtered as young adults for meat. Among companion animals, the ratio of males to females is more equal but in order to control populations, welfare organisations in particular are very active in encouraging castration of males and hysterectomy of females. In Britain (although not everywhere else in the world where horses are kept as companion animals, for recreation and work), the vast majority of males are castrated for behavioural reasons; entire males have a reputation for being more difficult to manage, train and ride.

Zoos which exist, they argue, mainly for breeding endangered species of animals, prefer as a rule to have a predominance of females. Having said this, one of the problems of breeding endangered species is keeping a rich genetic pool. Animals that breed easily (e.g. lions) - which are not endangered and for which there is little market within the zoo world, or outside it (such as circuses) - are frequently castrated or hysterectomised. Zoos do, however, often produce more males than they require, or can house. What do they do with them? Many of these animals are slaughtered. Some are sold to circuses who because they are not primarily concerned with animal breeding prefer spectacular animals, and invest a lot of time in training individuals. It is particularly important to start with good looking and/or spectacular animals.

As a result, they are one of the few animal husbandry systems who have a **higher** percentage of entire males to females in many species (zebras, horses, camels, llamas - see Figure 25). Entire males of any species do have the secondary sexual characteristics of that species, which include: horns or antlers, manes, larger size, spectacular colours or more exaggerated postures and movements; males sometimes 'show themselves off' better than females.

Circuses can and do provide a life for some males of some species which would otherwise have been slaughtered and they do not, as a rule, have animals castrated or hysterectomised.

The debate concerning the ethics of castration and hysterectomy must involve an assessment of the cost and benefits to the individual; however, this does **not** mean that animals not predominantly kept for breeding should be castrated or hysterectomised as a matter of course, any more than this would be acceptable for human beings who have a worldwide problem of population control. Less intrusive surgical practices which do not change the behaviour and personality might often be more appropriate, such as vasectomy or the cutting of fallopian tubes; techniques that are used to sterilise human beings. Why are they not more widely used for animals?

Physical restraint and force

Another possible measure for assessing the humaneness of an animal husbandry system can be the degree to which severe physical restraint is required:

- muzzles, twitches, hobbles, yokes, crushes, cradles, nose pinchers, and special use of ropes and other gadgets often outlined in veterinary books [e.g. 44];

- or to overcome 'vices' [e.g. 45] in order to allow handling or routine veterinary care;

- or in breeding (e.g. hobbling and twitch of mares for covering by stallions, standard practice in thoroughbred studs [46]);

- or transporting (e.g. use of chains and tractors to pull elephants into transporters).

Such physical restraint causes some form of distress (otherwise it would not be necessary) and often causes injury, trauma and even death of an individual. Its use must therefore indicate the inadequacy of the environment in one way or another, although again a cost benefit analysis for the individual must be assessed. The use of such restraining techniques can be almost totally eliminated by appropriate handling and training. We see this to be the case in the circus animals where they were **not** used.

Conclusions

To summarise, there is little evidence of physical maltreatment and cruelty in the husbandry, training or performing of circus animals. The great majority of animals were in excellent or good condition, and there was little evidence for frequent diseases or high mortality. In fact, the longevity of circus animals is greater and the occurrence of occupational disease less than for other animal husbandry systems, such as competitive and teaching horses, and possibly for some zoos.

Other indices of physical suffering of animals may be assessed by the use of surgery for cosmetic or behavioural reasons; by the need for antibiotics, analgesics and anaesthetics; and by the use of severe physical restraint. On all of these assessments, the circus scored very low indeed. Although the detailed figures are not available for comparison with many other husbandry systems, where there is information the circus appears to use all these techniques less than many other husbandry systems, in particular zoos. We must conclude therefore that circus animals show no more evidence for physical cruelty or maltreatment than many other animal husbandry systems, and in some cases less. There are not many figures available for zoos, but certain practices - such as intrusive surgery, sterilisation and chemical and physical restraint, which can be considered in relation to physical maltreatment - are relatively high for animals in the zoo environment.

Chapter 4

Psychological ill-health: Distress

So far we have considered how 'cruelty' (prolonged or acute suffering to animals) can be assessed in terms of physical indices, and disease.

In this chapter we are concerned with psychological suffering, and how we might be able to measure this in animals. To do this we have to assess the animal's behaviour - what it does, or sometimes what it does not do, perhaps because it cannot due to the limits of its environment. First then we will consider the degree of behavioural restriction which is the result of the environment. This might help us with this thorny problem.

Behavioural restriction

Over the centuries 'behavioural restriction' has been, and still is, one of the most important intuitive indicators of 'cruelty'. Why do we feel that chaining a dog up for 24 hours a day is 'cruel'? Probably because this restricts what the dog can do, where it can go, who it meets and so on. Why do we send people to prison as a punishment? The answer in part is because it restricts their individual freedoms.

The first ethologist to suggest this as an important indicator of assessing animal welfare (and thus cruelty or its absences) was Thorpe [13]. He suggested that an animal should be able to carry out its 'normal behaviour', but he left it at that. Hediger [48] used this idea in his consideration of animals in zoos and circuses. Recently this idea has been the subject of controversy within ethology [12]. Some argue that we don't know what 'animal needs' are anyway, and that knowledge concerning them cannot be assessed from our evolutionary knowledge and observation of what the species does when allowed to do anything it likes, but must be tested by giving the animal a choice of environments and seeing which one it chooses [e.g. 51] or how much 'work' it will do in order to obtain an environment with better facilities [e.g. 52]. These discussions give rise to many theoretical problems concerning motivation, what it is or is not, and how it works.

Although these discussions are very interesting and may in the long run add to our total sum of knowledge, they are not I believe directly relevant to the present debate. I suggest that we already have knowledge on what a particular species of animal does and therefore what it is likely to need or want to do. We have this knowledge from our studies of the animal in a wild or feral state where the animal has few behavioural restrictions, and our understanding of evolution which tells us that the way the animal behaves in such circumstances is the way it has evolved to behave and therefore the optimum for that species. In order to avoid possible **suffering** that it might undergo if it is deprived of being able to do any of its evolved behaviours, we should provide the animal, when under our jurisdiction, with an environment in which it can perform **all the behaviour in its repertoire, provided that does not cause prolonged suffering to others.**

FIGURE 28 **ELEPHANTS Behavioural restrictions**

	wild	s.park	zoo	circus	tied
move freely whole body	O	O	+	+	++
never unenclosed	O	+	++	O	++
scratch, lie, get up etc.,	O	O	+	+	++
manipulate objects freely	O	O	+	+ +	++
choose social partners	O	+	+	++	++
mixed sex groups	O	+	+	+	++
sexual behaviour	O	+	++	++	++
maternal behaviour	O	O	+	+	+
monotonous environments	O	+	++	+	++
all gaits exercise	O	O	+	+	++
food, water and shelter always	+	O	O	O	+
possible change of environment	O	+	+	O	++
learning & occupational therapy	+	+	++	O	++
close relationship to humans	++	++	+	O	+
TOTAL Restriction quotient	4	9	17	12	25

KEY: 0 = no restriction   + = some   ++ = severe restriction

This means, in effect, that the animal, when under the jurisdiction of human beings, should be either in the type of social and physical environment in which it has evolved, or a good substitute. The animal should be given the opportunity to exercise all its behaviour, social and physical. Thus, for example, pigs should root about, beavers should build dams [53], mammals should raise their own young and all should be able to associate together in appropriate groups, be able to court and mate. Lions, dogs and other predators should be allowed to 'hunt'. However, since hunting and killing will cause suffering to others who have a right to no prolonged or severe suffering, live prey should be substituted in one way or another. For example, at San Diego Wildlife Park, cheetahs hunt a mechanical antelope; and greyhounds race after a mechanical rabbit; pet dogs hunt and chase sticks and balls, domestic cats play with balls of wool.

The 'wild' or feral (gone wild) environment may not be free of all behavioural restrictions. For example, the animals do not always have sufficient to eat or drink; they may be too hot or too cold; they contract diseases perhaps more readily than when they can be inoculated against them or treated for them, and they can be caught and eaten by predators, if they are preyed on. All of these things can cause severe prolonged suffering and indeed death, and they are behavioural restrictions that may be more severe in the wild than when under human jurisdiction - 'domestic' or 'captive'. They must therefore with caution be taken into account in our assessment of behavioural restriction, animal suffering and 'cruelty'.

FIGURE 29 **BIG CATS Behavioural restrictions**

	wild	s.park	zoo	circus	E.Y.	B.W.
move freely whole body	O	O	O	O	O	+
never unenclosed	O	+	+*	+	+*	+*
scratch, lie, get up etc.,	O	O	O	O	O	O
manipulate objects freely	O	O	+	+	+	++
choose social partners	O	+	++	++	++	++
appropriate social structure	O	O	+	+	+	+
sexual behaviour	O	+	+	+	+	+
maternal behaviour	O	O	O	O	O	O
monotonous environments	O	+	++	+	+	++
chasing, hunting & killing	O	+	+	+	+	++
climbing, leaping etc	O	O	O	O	O	+
food, water and shelter always	+	O	O	O	O	+
possible change of environment	O	+	+	O	O	O
learning & occupational therapy	+	+	+	O	O	O
close relationship to humans	+	+	+	O	O	O
TOTALS Restriction quotient	3	8	12	8	8	14

E.Y. = exercise yard. B.W. = beast wagon
KEY: O = no restriction + = some restriction ++ = strong restriction +* = impossible to provide

FIGURE 30 **BEHAVIOURAL RESTRICTIONS IN DOGS
UNDER DIFFERENT HUSBANDRY CONDITIONS**

	1 Feral	2 Urban Feral	3 Rural Pet	4 Urban Pet	5 Working	6 Breeding	7 Show	8 Experim.	9 Circus
Movement	O	O	O	O	O	+	++	++	++
Gait	O	O	+	+	+	++	++	++	++
Grooming-unrestricted	O	O	O	O	O	O	+	+	O
Social contact	O	+	+	++	++	++	++	++	+
Sexual behaviour	O	O	+	++	++	++	++	++	+
Maternal behaviour	O	O	O	O	O	O	O	+	O
Social hunting	O	O	+	++	+	++	++	++	++
Environmental stimulation	O	O	O	+	O	++	++	++	+
Total	0	1	4	8	6	11	13	14	9
Food & water always available	++	+	O	O	O	O	O	O	O
Shelter from temp. extremes	++	++	O	O	O	O	O	O	O
Possible important social relationships with humans	++	++	O	O	O	O	O	+	O
Possible intellectual stimulii through training	+	+	O	O	O	+	+	+	O
OVERALL TOTAL Restriction quotient	7	7	4	8	6	12	14	16	9

CONDITIONS   Breeding = Dogs in breeding kennels
Show = Dogs kept in kennels predominantly for show
Experim = Experimental dogs kept in laboratory conditions
O = none, or very rare restriction
+ = occasional restriction
++ = usual restriction for majority of the day
Total is only intended as a gross guide. No attempt is made to assess the
relative importance of these various activities to the dog.

Figures 28 to 31 give an assessment of the behavioural restriction in some of the
species found in the circus, in zoos and/or in domestic situations. The behavioural
categories I have taken are designed to cover the full range of behaviour. However, no
attempt has been made to assess their relative importance to the animal. For example,

FIGURE 31 BEHAVIOURAL RESTRICTIONS IN HOOFED ANIMALS UNDER DIFFERING HUSBANDRY

	Wild/ feral	Exten-sive pastures	Enclo-sures	Small enclo-sures/ yards	Loose boxes		Stalls	
					mobile	static	mobile	static
Unrestricted movement	O	O	+	+	++	++	++	++
All gaits	O	O	O	O	++	++	++	++
Unrestricted grooming	O	O	O	O	O	O	+	+
Unrestricted social contact	O	O	+	+	++	++	++	++
Choice of social partners	O	O	+	+	++	++	++	++
Sexual behaviour	O	O	++	++	++	++	++	++
Maternal behaviour	O	O	+	+	+	+	+	++
Unrestricted feeding	O	O	+	+	++	++	++	++
Environmental stimulation and change	O	O	+	+	+	++	+	++
TOTAL	0	0	8	8	14	15	15	17
Adequate food & water always available	+	+	O	O	O	O	O	O
Shelter & protection from temperature extremes	+	+	O	O	O	O	O	O
Possible important social relationships with humans	++	+	+	+	O	O	O	O
Possible intellectual stimulation through training	++	++	++	Z C ++ O	O	+	O	+
Restriction quotient	6	5	11	Z C 10 8	14	16	15	18

Z = Zoo   C = Circus

being able to move unrestricted for short periods each day may be more or less important to the individual than being in an enclosed yard all day, or shackled part of the day, or having sex or giving birth. The possibility of being able to have positive emotional relationships (i.e. become fond of others), even if this is between species one of which is a human being, may be far more important to certain species and individuals than many obvious physical restrictions. The appalling story of the quasi-scientific mismanagement of the elephant Pole Pole in London Zoo [54] whose policy of minimal handling and ignorance (or ignoring) the animal's emotional needs ended in her death, illustrates this.

We do not know all the answers, but I think nevertheless it is time that we tried to draw some serious comparisons between the degree of behavioural restriction in different husbandry systems rather than relying on personal, intuitive assessment every time. For the benefit of the numerically minded, we can add up all the restrictions and give each husbandry system a 'behavioural restriction quotient' (the final total in each column in Figures 28 to 31). If we do this, we find there are some surprising results. For example, it is not clear that circus animals are much more restricted in their behaviour than zoo animals (see Figures 28 and 29). In fact, there are indications that the opposite is sometimes the case. It is obvious that when animals are tied or shackled they are more behaviourally restricted than when loose in yards. What is not commonsense is that even if they are shackled or tied some of the time and completely unenclosed at other times, they may be less behaviourally restricted than those who are always in enclosures and/or isolated (columns 3, 4, 5 and 6 Figure 31).

How much behavioural restriction is acceptable? In the best of all possible worlds there would be none - and yet would there? Can animals or humans live lives with **no** behavioural restrictions? Also, even if this were possible, is it best on balance for the community or the individual? The debate rests on how much behavioural restriction is acceptable. Where should the line be drawn? I consider that we should draw it in much the same place as we do for human beings: that the animal should be able to perform all the behaviour in its repertoire, at least for some part of each day, provided it does not cause prolonged suffering to others, and that while under our jurisdiction the animals should not suffer other avoidable behavioural restrictions, such as from thirst or hunger or controllable disease.

It is clear that almost all our husbandry systems leave much room for improvement in this regard. Ideally surely, the majority of animals should be loose and unenclosed all the time, and remain with us because they choose to, not because they have to, like many of our pet dogs and cats. Is this so impossible? I don't think so, but it will involve much thought and some training to obtain it.

It is, of course, very important to conserve animals in the wild where they can live with minimal interference from humans and other animals - but there is no evidence that this is the **only way** in which the animals can live without behavioural restrictions or prolonged suffering - any more than this would be considered the case for human beings.

Behavioural distress

Suffering can and must also be measured in terms of behavioural indices [cf. 4; 5; 51]. In this context it is preferable to use the term 'distress' [5]. The term 'distress' refers in particular to behaviour that the animal does which indicates (although this has not always been tested to date) that there are possible physiological parameters of stress.

Empirical information on the degree of 'distress' exhibited by the circus animals was accumulated as described in the methods section (Appendix 2). This was work recorded in the field with no possibility of setting up controlled experimental situations. As a result, there were many variables which may well affect the results. Nevertheless, it gives some indication of the amount of 'distress' exhibited by the circus animals and

FIGURE 32 ELEPHANTS :
Behavioural changes with environment

BEHAVIOUR		INDIAN	AFRICAN	CIRCUS	ZOO	LOOSE	TIED	AVERACE	24hr
standing	min/hr	54.64	56.25	54.76	53.33	47.83**	57.3**	53.36	49.88
eating	min/hr	27.1**	40.28**	27.52	22.22	25.66**	27.47**	27.67	23.47
moving	min/hr	4.36	5.42	4.06	7.78	7.55**	3.0**	5.1	3.61
lying	min/hr	1.66	0.34	1.8	0	5.94**	0.4**	2.89	6.69
sleeping	min/hr	0.24	0	0.26	0	0	0.37	0.23	0.78
drink	occ/hr	3.62**	1.69**	3.93**	0.06**	0.19**	4.39**	2.43	3.13
defaecate	occ/hr	0.3	0.69	0.27	0.56	0.43	0.27	0.4	0.28
urinate	occ/hr	0.23	0	0.24	0.06	0.17	0.26	0.22	0.27
human contact	min/hr	6.37	2.64	6.15	8.89	5.85	5.3	5.86	N.R
No. of hours		226	36	208	18	53	150		366
No. of individuals		36	6	26	6	17	21		8

KEY: min/hr = minute per hour observed   occ/hr = occurances per hour observed
N.R. = not recorded   ** = $p < 0.01$ sign test

compares this with other forms of husbandry, such as zoos and commercial horse stables.

For some of these indices of distress to be assessed in the circus animals it is necessary for us to have more detailed recordings on the wild or feral conspecifics (members of the same species) than have been made to date. Wherever possible, comparisons have been made.

An important area of discussion here is related to whether or not all suffering, or even all pain, is bad and must be avoided. It is clear that some pain is necessary and often life preserving; for example, that related to having a tooth extracted or some types of life-preserving surgery. Equally, athletes will often suffer considerable pain voluntarily in getting themselves fit, and even keep-fit classes can cause pain, but the beneficial results are considered worth the pain. Thus all pain is not necessarily to be avoided; **it is only pain and suffering where the benefits do not outweigh the costs for the individual and sometimes others** that must be considered so. It is probably true to say that rarely, if ever, is prolonged severe pain in this category [23; 25]. The same argument, it would seem, is relevant to psychological pain or 'distress'. A certain degree of 'distress' may well be acceptable because the benefit outweighs the distress caused. Thus, for example, signs of possible frustration such as head shaking or pawing when a horse is confused in a training session one might argue is permissible, just as in a child fiddling around when not able to solve a problem in arithmetic. What, however, is a sign of inadequacy is if the head shaking or pawing continues for prolonged periods, and perhaps becomes stereotyped. Life does involve both pain and pleasure, distress and joy. To some extent pleasure and joy are perceived as a result of having pain and distress, and there is no way that life can be so constructed for humans and other animals so that it consists **entirely** of pleasure and joy; and even if this were possible, it is arguable if it is desirable. Thus, inevitably, there will be some pain and distress in the circus as in every other place where sentient beings are. The argument concerning the rightness or wrongness of animal management systems revolves at present around what are the acceptable levels. How can we measure where these might be?

Apart from using behavioural restrictions which we have already discussed, there are, I suggest (and many other ethologists agree at least in part with me) [e.g. 3; 31; 40; 51; 57] other behavioural indicators we could and do sometimes use to help us.

These often involve making a comparison between the behaviour of a feral or wild animal and that of the captive, confined animal. It simplifies the problem to divide this behaviour into the following six categories. This is not to say that if the animal shows a change in any one of these categories that it is necessarily suffering and the environment is necessarily unsuitable, but if several of these categories are shown to be significantly different, then we could consider that the animal may well be distressed.

1) Behavioural abnormalities

Evidence of unacceptable levels of distress come, in part, from an assessment of the frequency of obvious behavioural abnormalities. Not all behaviour that does not occur in the wild is necessarily going to cause animals, or humans, to suffer. In fact, some behaviour that is 'abnormal' in that it does not occur in the wild may well be beneficial for the animals' emotional, physical or intellectual wellbeing; for example, reading and writing is not 'natural' for humans but literacy is considered to be beneficial as the individual will then be able to have a fuller life. This is an important point and one that needs more consideration and thought. A large number of people consider that anything that the animal does in the wild is 'natural and therefore good' and anything that he or she may do in captivity which is not in the wild repertoire is necessarily bad and wrong. This precludes the animal working in any way for humans, and humans working for animals. We discuss this in more detail later. At this point suffice it to say that this is both a moral and ethological question which is definitely highly disputable.

Our task here and now is to define what abnormal behaviour may be the **result** of prolonged distress and suffering and therefore be an indicator of it. We know little about this, but there are some abnormal behaviours which are often frequently repeated and which can occur in both animals and humans in captive or institutional environments [59; 60] and which apparently fall into the latter category... or might do. These behaviours are not fixed in all details, but they are repeated; such as running at the bars, repeated playing with a chain or pacing back and forth in caged or stabled animals.

2) Stereotypies

Another particular class of abnormal behaviour which can be relatively easily identified and which is therefore particularly useful in assessing distress or unsuitable animal environments are known as **stereotypies**. These are behaviours that are **'fixed in all**

details, apparently purposeless and repeated' *(Oxford English Dictionary)*. They include behaviours such as constant chewing, or crib-biting on particular objects in the environment, weaving, certain head circling, nodding or rocking movements. Recent research on stereotypies has indicated that when the animal is performing a stereotypy, there is an increase in the secretion of natural opiates from the brain [61]. In other words, it seems that the performing of the stereotypy functions to divert attention away from the external environment on to self-stimulation which in turn produces drugs to further dull the effects of the unacceptable external world.

Fig. 33. Crib-biting horse. They grip an object, often the stable door, and suck in and swallow air, contracting the muscles of the neck near the head at the same time.

Stereotypies, however, are often of high 'habit strength': addictive - the more they are performed the more they are likely to be performed as they are self-rewarding. This means that changing the environment will not necessarily stop them, once they are well established. So their performance may not always reflect the inadequacy of their **present** environment [e.g. 1; 29]. Thus it is necessary to consider the individual's past history. I believe now that we do have enough knowledge on the cause and development of stereotypies as well as some other behavioural abnormalities in most birds and mammals so we should be able to design environments so that they will **not** develop in the young animals. We do not, however, have sufficient knowledge to be able to cure established generalised stereotypies.

We must, though, make allowances for the present generation (e.g. stereotypic performing polar bears [63], lions or horses whose past experience was conducive to their development). The next generation **can and should be raised without any, or very few, of these behaviours developing, if the prerequisites of environmental design outlined in Chapter 9 are adhered to.**

3) A substantial increase in aggression

Another possible indicator of environmental inadequacy and psychological distress is the amount of aggression that the animal performs relative to that which it would normally perform in an unrestricted wild or feral state. Aggression tends to increase in some psychologically stressed and disturbed animals and humans. Social living animals tend not to be particularly aggressive to members of their social group, if they are, then the group tends to split up.

Disturbed, neurotic animals in pain and distress will tend to be more aggressive both to their social partners and to other species. To collect detailed information in order to make this comparison, we may have to spend many hours watching the animals. On the other hand, as is the case with some dogs, horses and lions, individuals are known to be particularly aggressive and that aggression often increases with pain [64], fear [65], frustration [66] and conflict [67]. Isolating, confining and restricting animals is also used as a technique to increase aggression by comparative psychologists [68]! Aggression is one of the behaviours which can be linked to psychological responses to stress. Thus, if we have animals which are more aggressive than their wild or feral cousins, whether the aggression is directed towards other members of their own species or to other species, this is likely to be because they are distressed. The elephant Pole Pole in London Zoo illustrated this well [54].

It is quite wrong to assume that 'animals as a general rule are **by their nature** serously aggressive and unreliable'. Studies of animals considered very ferocious in the wild, such as wild dogs [69], wolves [70], lions [71], tigers [72], elephants [27; 74; 75] and other species, indicate that the reverse is often the case. If the management of any animal husbandry system finds this to be the case - whether they are dealing with mice, men, bulls, elephants, lions or any other animals - they must reassess their management: they have got it wrong. The animals have been made aggressive by the environment. As Daphne Sheldrick, who has much experience of raising many species of wild animal, points out when considering the plight of the mismanaged young elephant Pole Pole: '...If she is difficult, aggressive and vicious, then there is a good reason for it, for elephants under normal circumstances are not naturally so...'[76].

4) Time budgets

Here we are assessing how circus and zoo animals distribute their time between behaviours and differences in this from the wild or feral animal. One of the problems for zoo and circus animals in particular, but also for stabled horses and many farm livestock, is, since they are provided with food, the animals often do not have to search for it. Also, their food may be of such a high nutritive level that they spend much less time eating it than they would the lower quality foods in the wild. They may be in restricted environments and less able to spend time in purposeful movement, and the environment may be sterile and lack stimulation of any sort. As a result, the animals may have a lot of 'spare time'. In some cases the animals, or humans in similar environments, will either sleep or rest much more than normal, or they may invent ways of self-stimulation such as performing stereotypies. Thus, assessing the time budgets of the animals in different environments can give us indication of the suitability of the environment for that animal's behavioural needs. (Figure 34).

5) Increase in amount of behaviour related to frustration or conflict

Behaviour that can be related to frustration and conflicts, involving, in particular, whether an object is approached or avoided, is very varied. However, there is now some evidence that at such times, when the animal would like to perform something that it is unable to do, it will perform something else. The something else is often related to behaviours that are not normally of top priority, for example scratching (the result of skin irritation). Quite commonly we find that humans and other animals in such situations will scratch themselves, wag their tails, shake their heads, and so on [77; 78]. The individual might suddenly look the other way, or engage in some other behaviour that appears to be irrelevant to the situation, such as eating. Such behaviours are sometimes called 'displacement behaviour' as the behaviour appears to be out of context. These behaviours may often develop their own particular characteristics: they may be incomplete, or performed in an offhand sort of way, or they may become what is termed 'ritualised': rather fixed in their form [79]. Any behaviour that may be self-directed (e.g. scratching, licking, head shaking or tossing and so on) or directed against objects (e.g. chewing or licking things) may be the result of frustration and conflict in anyone's life, but by measuring how frequently these sorts of behaviours occur in animals in different environments we may obtain some idea of how much frustration or conflict they suffer, and whether this is much greater than normal.

6) Increase in the amount of behaviour related to fear

Behaviour related to fear is relatively easy to measure. It includes continued avoidance of things or routines, persistent running away, shivering, sweating, and sometimes over-reacting to slight environmental changes. It may involve 'defensive threat'; that is, aggression, or 'freezing' immobile. There are often physiological changes, such as an increase in heart and respiration rates, defaecation and urination [84].

7) 'Ontogenic' (individual developmental) behavioural changes

This means, effectively, that the animal is not performing the normal behaviour for its species at that age or stage of development. For example, the veal calves that I studied [5] walked when released from their crates at 16 weeks as if they were only a day or so old. Other behavioural changes, such as delayed social behaviour or prolonged infantile behaviour, would come into this category.

These then are the ways in which we may be able to assess behavioural distress in animals. They are summarised:

POSSIBLE INDICATORS OF DISTRESS IN ANIMALS

- **Evidence of physical ill-health (including poor nutrition, wounds etc.)**
- **Evidence of frequent occupational diseases**
- **Need for the use of drugs and/or surgery to maintain the system of husbandry**
- **Behavioural changes:**
  a) performance of abnormal behaviours (that are not normally in the animals' repertoire, and which appear to be of little benefit to the animal: e.g. running at bars, pacing)
  b) stereotypies i.e. the performance of repeated behaviour fixed in all details and apparently purposeless (e.g. crib-biting, wind-sucking, weaving, head twisting)
  c) substantial increase in inter- or intra-specific aggression compared to the wild or feral state
  d) large differences in time budgets from the wild or feral animal
  e) substantial increases in behaviour related to frustration or conflict (e.g. often behaviour relating to locomotion and/or cutaneous stimulation)
  f) substantial ontogenic behavioural changes (animals performing behaviour characteristics of a very different time in their development e.g. calves of 16 weeks walking as if they were a day or so old)
- **Behavioural restrictions - this is the inability to perform all the behaviour in the animals' natural repertoire which does not cause severe or prolonged suffering to others.**

The results from measuring these indices in zoos, circuses, and some other animal husbandry systems are given in the tables we have discussed in Chapter 3. The detailed behaviour changes are now discussed.

ELEPHANTS

1. Abnormal behaviour

Figure 35 gives the frequency of occurrence of abnormal behaviours for Indian and African elephants, in zoos and circuses, loose and tied. Abnormal behaviour consisted of bar-biting and playing with the shackle chain.

ELEPHANTS . Time Budgets.

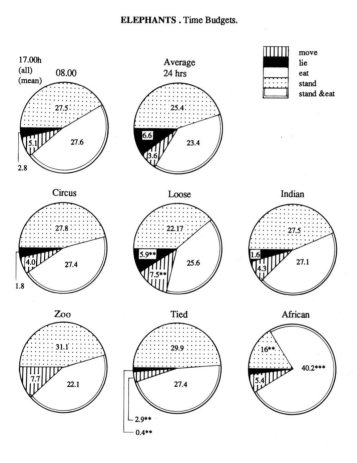

Fig. 34. Elephants. Time budgets.

There was no evidence for neuroses and behavioural pathologies in the individual elephants. Individuals reacted differently to different stimuli, and some showed particular skills or weaknesses.

Several elephants also banged their trunks on the ground when excited and when requiring further individual attention particularly from the handler. Whether wild elephants perform this behaviour has not been reported. The differences in the amount these behaviours were performed in the different environments were not significant.

2. Stereotypies

All the elephants in both zoos and circuses performed stereotypies. These took the form of weaving or swaying backwards and forwards on the spot, and/or head nodding, often accompanied by trunk swinging. The stereotypies were performed from 6 to 15 minutes per hour observed. Most of this behaviour was recorded in the shackled/tied elephants, and least in the young Africans. There was no significant difference in the amount these behaviours were performed in the different environments, although the total numbers of hours recorded were small for the zoo elephants.

3. Increase in aggression

Two of the elephants were described as slightly unreliable and possibly aggressive towards human beings. However, this was not apparent in their behaviour to other elephants. Here the remarkable thing is the **low** levels of aggression between the elephants even in confined conditions where it might be expected to be relatively high - only one aggressive encounter recorded.

4. Time budget changes

Figure 34 gives the time budgets that we recorded and the significant differences. The loose elephants stood and ate for less of the time, moved around more and lay down more than the shackled elephants. There were no significant differences between the circus and zoo elephants in these behaviours, and the only significant difference between the African and Indian elephants was that the Africans ate for much more of the time (40.28 min/hour compared to 27.1).

Detailed comparable figures are not yet available for the wild elephants recorded.

5. Frustration and conflict

Head shaking, hitting the wall with the trunk and tail wagging were included. There were no significant differences in these behaviours for the different environments. There was a significant difference, however, between the Indian and African elephants - the Indian elephants performing more of these behaviours.

6. Fear

Panicking (fleeing), shivering, and very frequent high-pitched long and loud vocalisations are some possible indices of fear in elephants. There was no evidence of this behaviour while the animals were being recorded in their living quarters; only two instances were recorded from the elephants at other times.

7. Ontogenic change

There was no evidence of this during the period of study. The young African elephants did show behaviour that may be a precursor of stereotypic behaviour - trunk swinging. Stereotypies were established in the majority of the adult elephants in both circuses and zoos.

Summary of distress displayed in elephants

The most obvious and frequent indicator of possible distress, and therefore an inadequate environment for elephants, is the occurrence of stereotypies which involved, in particular, head nodding and weaving. Bar biting, an abnormal but not stereotypic behaviour (since it was not constant in form), also occurred where there were bars.

These behaviours occurred up to 22% of every observed hour in the zoo and circus elephants. It must, however, be borne in mind that these stereotypies may have become established earlier in the individual's lives. Also, conditions may have improved but the generalised and established stereotypy did not disappear, although the amount they are performed could well be cut down; for example, the elephants performed most when they were shackled and had no food. Being sure that the elephants always had food and other objects to manipulate on offer, even when shackled, cut down the performance of these stereotypies.

The circus elephants were not observed weaving and head nodding when out for walks, performing, during training, or when being handled by their handlers. Increasing the interest of the environment, possibly the mental challenge of training, problem-solving and the possibilities for manipulation might well reduce these further.

The occurrence of these behaviours in loose enclosures in zoos, with many things to manipulate, suggests that there are more factors involved in its etiology in elephants, than simply behavioural restriction.

The young African elephants performed little weaving or head nodding, but they did perform trunk swinging which might well develop into weaving as they grow up unless serious consideration is given to their husbandry and mental stimulation.

FIGURE 35. THE AMOUNT OF DISTRESS IN ELEPHANTS
compared in the different species and environments.

	Indian	African	Circus	Zoo	Loose	Tied	Average	24hr
Number of hours	226	36	208	18	63	150		366
No. of individuals	36	6	26	6	17	21		36
Abnormal occ./hr.	1.84	1.11	1.65	3.38	4.27	0.69	2.15	3.82
Frustration occ./hr.	0.83*	0.59*	0.5	0.83	0.73	0.72	0.7	3.51
Stereotypies min./hr.	13.63	6.12	13.73	12.3	7.74	15.9	11.05	12.95

* - sign test - $p < 0.05$

THE BIG CATS
1. Abnormal behaviour
There were no obvious signs of neurosis or pathology in the circus or zoo big cats. Pacing was the most common abnormal behaviour. It is not a stereotypy because it is not constant in form, and also possibly does have a purpose in exercising the animal. It was performed on average in these different species and environments for nearly 5 minutes in every hour, about 8% of the daytime.

Figure 37 row 7 gives the amount of pacing for the big cats in the different environments. There was insufficient data on the lions in zoos, but it is notable that there was no pacing shown during the recorded observations in the zoo tigers and there was no significant relationship here; in fact, for the lions and the tigers the trend was the other way:

lions - 2 min/hr beast wagon and 3.3 min/hr exercise yard

tigers - 8.4 min/hr beast wagon and 7.5 min/hr exercise yard.

There is no clear pattern. Nevertheless, the performance of pacing indicates environmental inadequacy.

2. Stereotypies

Although some big cats do develop head twisting or bar biting stereotypies, none of these were recorded in these animals in any of the environments.

3. Increase in aggression

One lion, a tiger and a leopard in the circuses were described as rather aggressive by their trainers. Such observations are not generally made on the zoo animals as no serious effort is made to have individual relationships with them or understand their individual personalities.

The leopards showed a trend towards more inter-specific aggression than the other cats, although only in the exercise yard, surprisingly. This was slightly higher than the inter-specific affiliative behaviour.

Until we have detailed information from the wild, it is not possible to assess whether these figures are very abnormal for the big cats.

4. Time budget changes

It is widely believed that the big cats, particularly lions, spend the majority of their time lying about resting [71] which it has been argued [84] makes them relatively easy animals to keep in captivity. Our records show that the amount of time spent lying varied from 27 minutes/hour to 50, with an average of 40.6 minutes/hour, 67% of the observed day.

The lions and tigers did not vary their lying time in the different environments nor between the zoos and circuses; but the leopards did. They spent only 27 minutes/hour (45%) lying in the exercise yard, while 50 minutes/hour (83%) of the daytime was spent lying down by leopards in the zoos.

The tigers and lions seem to indicate no gross changes in lying time from the wild. However, we will have to await results from wild studies before we know how significant the figures for leopards are. The lower resting time in the circuses may reflect that they have become more diurnal in this enironment since they have fewer behavioural options at night when they are enclosed in the beast wagon. This is backed up by the significantly greater sleeping time in the daytime in the zoos, and less time moving (rows 2 and 6 of Figure 36) when they are not shut up at night.

FIGURE 36 BIG CATS. Maintenance behaviour in different environments
(mins/hour/animal observed)

	LIONS		TIGERS				LEOPARDS			MEAN	%
	BW	EY	C	Z	BW	EY	C	Z	EY		
Observed hours	161	6	250	10	232	14	37	6	39		
Number of individuals	32	6	47	5	42	7	19	3	8		
1) Lying	48.8	45.0	39.2	43	40.1	40.7	33.7 **	50 **	27.2 **	40.6	67
2) Sleeping	6.5	?	1.5	4.5	1.6	3.2	5.5	3.2 **	1.4 **	4.2	7
3) Standing	4.2	6.7	3.7	2.5	3.8	2.1	3.1	0.8 *	3.7 *	3.4	5.6
4) Eating	2.5	0	5.6	0	6.0	0	1.6	0	1.9	2	3.2
5) Sitting	0.4	2.5	0.9	0.5	0.7	1.9	3.2	7.5	6.2	2.6	4.4
6) Moving	3.9	1.7	6.6	12.0	6.8	12.0	11.3 *	2.5 *	16.9	3.2	13.6
7) Touch other (affiliative)	5.7	0	7.4 **	1.0	7.2	1.4 **	2.6	13.3	4.2	4.6	7.7
8) Human contact	0.4 **	4.7 **	0.2	0	0.2	0	1.1	0	0	0.7	1.2

KEY BW - Beast wagon. EY - Exercise yard, C - Circus (all data). Z - Zoo (all data). Tabulated figures are in minutes/cat/hour observed. Significant effects of the keeping conditions on behaviour are shown: * = p<0.05, ** = p<0.01 (Mann Witney test). Tattersall (129) recorded the time budgets of 4 captive zoo leopards at Marwell Zoo. The % lying time is lower for her leopards (28-40% of daytime) than the zoo leopards we watched.

Number of times/ observed hour the named behavioural categories occured

	LIONS		TIGERS				LEOPARDS			MEAN	%
	BW	EY	C	Z	BW	EY	C	Z	EY		
Observed hours	161	6	250	10	232	14	87	6	39		
Number of Individuals	32	6	47	5	42	7	19	3	8		
1) Frustration	0.5	0.3	0.1	1.5	0	1.1	0.5	1.8	0.5	0.7	1.1
2) Social a) affiliative	4.6	8.8	5.7	4.2	4.9	3.1	4.6	?	6.2	5.3	8.7
b) aggressive	0.3 **	0 **	0.8	0	0.8	0	3.7	?	6.9	1.6	2.6
c) all vocalising	1.7	5.7	3.9 *	0.9 *	4.1	1.1	5.9 *	?	11.3 *	4.3	7.2
3) Object directed	2.8	2.4	0.7	4.9 *	0.6	3. 7	2.4	1.7	2.6	2.4	4.0
4) Self directed	5.0 *	0.5 *	4.0	5.6	4.0	4.9	5.4	?	2.3	4.0	6.5
5) Locomotion	0.5 **	10.0 **	0.9	2.2	1.0	1.0	1.5 **	1.2	1.0 **	3.3	5.5

KEY - BW - Beast wagon   EY - Exercise yard   C - circus   Z - zoo
* - p<0.05   ** - p<0.01 sign test

5. Frustration and conflict

The big cats and other canivores can develop self-licking behaviours which may even develop into self-consuming behaviour [82]. The lions in the beast wagons did show significantly more self-directed behaviour than those in exercise yards; and the leopards had a high score (5.4 times/animal hour) in the beast wagons too.

6. Fear

Typical responses to fear in the big cats include fleeing, and defensive threat including ear flattening and hissing. There were few incidences of this in any of the cats.

7. Ontogenic changes

There was no evidence of gross ontogenic changes in the big cats, although there is little information in this area.

Summary of distress displayed in the big cats

Possible evidence for distress in circus and zoo lions, tigers and leopards might be particularly related to pacing, which should not occur at all if the environment was completely adequate. There were, however, some other behavioural differences particularly between the lions in the beast wagon and exercise yards; for example, in the beast wagon they performed significantly more self-directed activities (scratching, rubbing, grooming, sniffing themselves - Figure 37, row 5) and less other locomotion, such as leaping and rushing around (row 6). The leopards, by contrast, showed significantly **more** locomotion in the circus recordings, including the beast wagon, than in the exercise yards only!

One might expect in confined and behaviourally restricted environments that the few behaviours that can be performed would be performed more than normal. Another interesting difference is that the circus tigers vocalised much more than the zoo ones - much of these were purrs directed at humans, particularly their handlers and trainers. The leopards vocalised more in the exercise yards than in the beast wagon.

The conclusions from this are that apparently the big cats differ in how their behaviour changes in relation to their captive environment, and apart from the occurrence of pacing, there are no other **clear** indications of environmental inadequacy, and therefore possible behavioural distress, although the leopards' more dirunal habit and relatively higher level of frustration may point towards this.

FIGURE 38 BEARS Maintenance behaviour.
Number of minutes/bear hour observed.

	BEARS
Observed hours	65
Number of individuals	9
1) Lying	18.0
2) Sleeping	3.8
3) Standing	7.9
4) Eating	3.7
5) Sitting	6.2
6) Moving	10.1
7) Drink	1.2
8) Hind leg (stand)	0.2
9) Defecate and urinate	0.1
10) Abnormal (stereotypes)	0.5
11) Touch other	4.0
12) Human contact	16.8
13) Pacing	18.3

FIGURE 39 BEARS Other behaviour
Occassions/observed bear hours the named behavioural categories occurred.

	BEARS
Observed hours	65
Number of individuals	9
1) Abnormal	2.3
2) Frustration	2.4
3) Social a) affiliative	11.4
b) aggressive	0
c) vocalise	0.7
4) Object directed	6.0
5) Self directed	7.2
6) Locomotion a) run	0.03
b) climb	0.38

85

THE BEARS

1. Abnormal behaviour

The bears displayed no obvious signs of neurotic or pathological behaviour (Figures 38 and 39). Pacing occurred for 18.3 minutes per hour (30%). This is very high. The bears were not studied in zoos so we have no comparable figures. Other studies (e.g. 63) suggest that this figure may well be in line with the normal figure for zoo bears.

2. Stereotypies

Bears are particularly prone to developing stereotypies, particularly in zoos. One circus bear had a stereotypic head twist. This occurred for 0.52 minutes/observed bear hour. No other stereotypies were observed, although the sample was small.

3. Increase in aggression

The bears showed no aggression either to humans or to other bears during the observational periods.

4. Time budget changes

The bears were active during the observational periods, spending over 10 minutes in every hour moving around in their small beast wagons. They lay for 18 minutes/animal hour, but only 3.8 minutes were spent sleeping. They also sat, stood on their hind legs, spent time touching each other (4 minutes/animal hour) and much time in human contact (16.8 minutes/animal hour). We have no comparable figures from the wild or zoo animals at present.

5. Frustration and conflict

Behaviour that might be associated with frustration or conflict, such as head shaking, head nodding, running at bars, self-scratching, vocalising, was relatively common: 2.4 times/bear hour - relatively high compared to some of the other species.

6. Fear

There was no evidence of fear (fleeing, freezing) recorded in the bears.

7. Ontogenic change

We have no information here.

Summary of distress displayed in bears

Bears did show some evidence of distress; some stereotypic performance, abnormal pacing and bar biting, relatively high levels of behaviour possibly associated with frustration. They were active, perhaps abnormally so, but remarkably unaggressive.

FIGURE 40 CAMELS Maintenance Behaviour
Number of minutes/observed hour the named behavioural categories occured.

	CAMEL	LLAMA	CATTLE	BUFFALO	REINDEER	PIGEONS
Observed hours	52	56	24	4	1	1	50
Number of Individuals	16	14		2	3	1	50
1)Lying	13.9	25.4	27.7	21.3			6.8
2)Sleeping	0.1	?	?	?			
3)Standing	43.9	27.0	27.1	30.0	48.3	60.0	14.0
4)Eating	19.9	14.0	13.0	11.3	11.7	45.0	9.
5)Moving	2.3	4.3	3.4	5.0	13.	05.0	7.4
6)Stereotype		1.4	0.9				
7)Touch Other (affiliative)	10.9	2.8	2.8	?			4.4
8)Human Contact	16.8	1.1	2.2	8.8			1.1
9)Cudding	13.8	3.4	3.5	3.8			9.3

THE CAMELIDS

The behaviour of these animals was only recorded in the circuses; therefore no comparisons with the zoo animals are possible.

1. Abnormal behaviour

One camel salivated greatly when in training and in the ring, and two other young camels salivated when being trained. This seemed to indicate a degree of anxiety, but could hardly be classified as neurotic or pathological behaviour.

The camels occasionally bit the bars (Figure 41 row 5) and two of the llamas chewed wood.

FIGURE 41 CAMELS Other Behaviour
Number of times/observed hour the named behavioural categories occured.

	CAMEL	LLAMA	CATTLE	BUFFALO	REINDEER	PIGEON
Observed hours	52	56	24	4	1	50
Number of Individuals	16	14	2	3	1	50
1) Pleasure	3.9	0.1	0.1			0.4
2) Drink	1.6	0.5	0.3	0.5		0.04
3) Defecate & urinate	0.7	0.2	0.1			0.1
4) Cough		0.2	0.2			0.06
5) Abnormal	0.4	0.1	0.1			
6) Frustration	4.22	0.9	0.8			0.67
7) Social a) affiliative	0.7	0.7	1.0			1.1
b) aggressive	0.5	1.0	1.4			0.73
c) vocalise	0.1	0.1	0.1			7.4
8) Object directed	0.4	0.9	0.7	0.7		0.72
9) Self directed	2.4	3.3	2.9	1.3	1.0	3.4
10) Locomotion						1.67

24Hr - Observed over 2 whole 24 hour periods.

2. Stereotypies

Camels and members of the llamadae in zoos quite frequently develop stereotypies, usually involving elaborate head movements. We did not, however, see any of these in the circus animals.

3. Increase in aggression

High levels of aggression were displayed. One camel occasionally bit, two spat, and two llamas bit and spat quite frequently in contact with humans. On the other hand, several camels could be tethered among the public and showed no sign of aggression, even when being touched by over 200 people per hour! Inter-group aggression was relatively high in the llamas (1/llama hour observed, compared to 0.5 for camels, and 0.3-0.4 for horses).

4. Time budget changes

We have no detailed information on the time budgets of feral or wild camelids, so it is not possible to assess the changes in time budgets. Nevertheless, it is interesting that camels spend more time standing, and llamas spend more time lying down. In addition, the llamas spend less time ruminating than, for example, cattle (5% of the time compared to around 20% for cattle) [55; 73].

5. Frustration and conflict

Both the camels and the llamas performed behaviours that are often indicative of frustration relatively frequently. These are tail wagging, head shaking, pawing and foot stamping (occurring in camels 4.2 and 0.9 llamas/animal hour). It may be that these displays are common in any case in the camelids - we do not have any data from wild or feral animals with which to compare.

6. Fear

Spitting appears often to be related to defensive threat and did occur occasionally in training and during handling of the camels and llama. Ear flattening and biting can also be related to defensive threat, and did occur (see 3).

7. Ontogenic change

We have no information here.

Summary of distress displayed in camelids

There do not appear to be obvious signs of distress in the camelids, although some periodic signs of anxiety and possible discomfort are seen.

THE EQUIDS

1. Abnormal behaviour

Neurotic and pathological behaviour is relatively common in individually stabled domestic horses (Figure 27, page 58). In the circus horses and ponies, three individuals (1.6%) could be described as neurotic.

Behaviour not normally in the animal's repertoire, such as playing with the tether chain, chewing and biting objects, and door kicking, occurred in the majority of circus horses, but not in the zebras and mules. The mules' sample was, however, very small.

FIGURE 42 HORSES, PONIES, ZEBRA & MULES -
Other Behaviour
Number of times/observed hour the named behavioural categories occured.

	HORSES			PONIES	ZEBRA	MULES	MEAN	FERAL PASTURE *
	TIED	LB	24hr					
Observed hours	160	155	329	80	26	14		
Number of Individuals	64	49	14	35	10	2		
1) Abnormal	0.8	0.6	1.1	2.0	0.1		0.8	
2) Frustration	2.4	1.8	2.3	1.2	9.3		3.4	
3) Social a) affiliative	0.6	NP	0.6	1.6	0.6		0.7 **	0.2 **
b) aggressive	0.4	NP	0.3	0.4	0.3		0.3 **	0.09 **
c) vocalise	0.5	0.7	0.5	0.8	0	1.1	0.6 **	
4) Object directed	0.7	0.3	1.5	0.3	1.8	0.1	0.8	
5) Self directed	0.7	0.85	0.4	0.7	1.0		0.5	
6) Locomotion	0.8	1.7	0.8	2.7	7.6			
7) Cough	0.3	0.1	0.8	0.2			0.4	
8) Defecate & urinate	0.2	0.4	0.2	0.2	0.2	0.2		

TIED = tied in stalls   LB = loose box   NP = not possible   24hr = 24 hour observations
* = from Goldsmidt - Rothschild 1976, and K-Worthington 1987.   ** = p<0.01 Mann Witney.

2. Stereotypies

Domestic stabled horses often perform stereotypies (crib-biting, weaving, wind-sucking etc. - see Figure 27). Six animals (3.3%) in the British circuses performed a stereotypy. In the Swiss circus, where all the animals were housed in individual looseboxes, fed unrestricted diets and with practically no contact between them or to the outside, 60% of the animals performed a stereotypy of one sort of another. This is nearer the normal level for racing, competitive and teaching stable yards (36.6% racing stables, 25.9% teaching stables).

3. Increase in aggression

Aggressive animals were not common in the circuses: 5 (2.8%) were aggressive towards human beings. The inter-specific aggression was low 0.3-0.4/animal hour, although

FIGURE 43 HORSES, PONIES, ZEBRA & MULES - Maintenance Behaviour
Minutes/observed animal hour

| | HORSES | | | PONIES | ZEBRA | MULES | | | | | STABLED % | |
| | TIED | LB | 24hr | | | | MEAN | % | FERAL % | YARD % | GROUP | ISOL |
	1	2	3	4	5	6	7	8	9	10	11	12
Observed hours	160	155	329	80	26	14			2000	288	216	288
No. of Individuals	64	49	14	35	10	2			13	3	6	
a) Lying	3.8	1.0	6.0	0.5	4.2	10.7	4.4	7.2	10	10	10	15
b) Sleeping (doze)	1.1	2.3	1.5	1.8	1.5	1.4	1.6	2.7				
c) Standing (all)	43.5	58.5	46.1	53.1	53.3	47.5	50.5	84.1	80	80	87	80
d) Eating	20.9	35.6	22.1	29.3	29.6	31.1	28.1	46.8	60	57	47	15
e) Moving	0.8	1.7	0.9	2.7	7.7	1.4	2.5	42	10	10	5	0
f) Standing only	22.6	22.9	24	23.8	23.7	16.4	22.4	37	20	23	40	65
g) Stereotypes	0.08	0	0.04	0.9	0.1	?	0.2	0.4	0	0	10	50
h) Touch other	0.3	0	0.22	1.4	0.4	?	0.4	0.73				0
i) Human contact	9.7	11.8	7.6	2.6	4.1	?	7.16	11.9			2.4	2.1

a) to e) are not mutually exclusive. More than one activity can be performed at once.
f) Standing only = standing doing nothing else.

slightly higher than in pastured animals (Figure 43). Aggressive interactions were lower than affiliative behaviour, as is the case in pastured animals [30].

4. Time budget changes

The time budgets for the horses, ponies, zebras and mules in the different environments are given in Figure 44. There are no significant differences from the way time is spent in the feral or yarded horses (see columns 8, 9, 10). This is different from the time budgets of single-stabled, quality horses fed restricted fibre in Britain which spend much more time standing doing nothing (65% compared to 37%) and less time eating (15% compared to 46.8%) [29]. One particularly important factor here is that the circus horses, as a general rule, had access to hay and/or straw to eat at all times.

5. Frustration and conflict

Behaviour often associated with frustration, such as tail wagging, head shaking, pawing, body shaking etc., was relatively common particularly in the zebras who performed such behaviour 9.3 times/hour observed.

6. Fear

Fear responses include fleeing, freezing, shivering and sweating, and defensive threat involving ear flattening and biting frequently. No avoidance of humans was recorded in the circus animals, although there was some aggression (see above). Evidence for shivering and sweating in fear was absent.

7. Ontogenic changes

There was no evidence for these in the circus horses. However, many of them were not ever allowed free social access to other horses. It may well be that their social development was not normal. This is very frequently the case of isolated and stable-restricted domestic horses.

Summary of distress displayed in equids

The degree of distress shown by the circus horses might be considered lower than that for the competitive racing and teaching stabled horses. There was some evidence of distress, and the keeping conditions could certainly be improved. The answer may rest in keeping the horses in groups in yards, rather than changing them from stalls to looseboxes which does **not** apparently reduce possible evidence of distress (Figure 42). The zebras did not show any greater evidence of distress than the horses; in fact, in some respects less, although they did perform more behaviours that could be related to frustration.

Conclusions

In summary, we can have some idea when an animal is distressed from looking at various aspects of his management, the degree of behavioural restriction as a result of this environment and management, and certain indices in his behaviour. These are summarised on page 76. **It is true to say that there was evidence of**

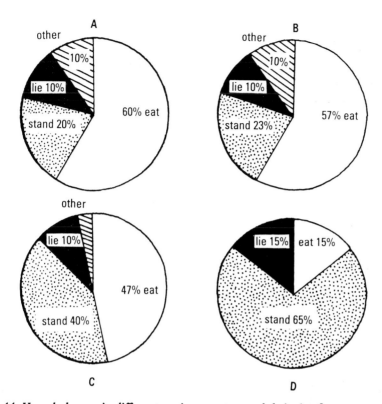

Fig. 44. How do horses in different environments spend their time?

A: *The average time budgets for Camargue horses throughout the year. (After Duncan 1980).*

B: *Time budgets for a group of eight horses in a yard with* ad libitum *hay and straw.*

C: *The time budgets for three horses in individual stables fed ad libitum hay and straw and able to see and touch each other.*

D: *Time budgets for horses in stables where they cannot touch each other and only see each other over stable doors; they were fed restricted fibre (about 3kg/day, horses of 15.2-16hh).*

prolonged distress and abnormal behaviour found in both zoos and circuses, but it is equally true to say this is the case with almost any animal husbandry system today. There was not significantly **more** distress shown in the circus animals than in the same species in zoos or domestic systems.

We must conclude therefore that there is no evidence to back the case that circuses **necessarily** cause suffering any more than zoos or other animal systems do. What it does say is that circuses are no better and no worse than other husbandry in this respect. There should be no evidence for prolonged distress in **any** animal or human husbandry system.

It also argues for improvement in husbandry of all the animal keeping systems. There should be no, or very little, signs of suffering displayed in any appropriate animals' husbandry. It would seem that more thought about the environment's design and the treatment of the animal within it is needed here. This applies not only to animals that are traditionally 'wild' but to traditionally domestic animals too.

Chapter 5

Do animals in circuses and zoos feel pleasure?

To date there has been some discussion concerning the measurement of distress in animals in different types of husbandry, but little or no concern with possible behavioural measures of pleasure. That mammals at least feel something like pleasure or joy cannot be denied by any person who is prepared to admit that animals feel pain [23; 25]. The commonest example is of course the domestic dog which shows its pleasure at a mistress's arrival or the possibility of a walk, often in no uncertain terms; the dog leaps about, wags its tail, sometimes barks, may rush backwards and forwards to the mistress, and may pant.

Whether or not the circus and zoo animals are feeling something like pleasure or joy at any time during their life that we observed, is crucial to reaching a decision concerning the ethical acceptability of zoos and circuses.

One question which is constantly asked is whether or not the animals like to perform in front of audiences. Do they derive pleasure or joy from this, in the same way as an actor might, although it might also be somewhat nerve wracking; or alternatively, do they show dislike of going into the ring and performing. How is this to be assessed in the different species?

One way of identifying pleasure on behalf of the animal is by the performance of behaviour which can, as a general rule, be associated with excitement [83; 88]. This is defined as: **an increase in activity and often the speed of moving around, and the performance of more activities more often.** In our dog example, he leaps around, rushes backwards and forwards, tail wags, may bark, or bite playfully at objects, pick up and carry objects around, show a higher postural tonus (head and tail up) and so on. Most of the other canids show similar behaviour although the threshold at which they respond may be different.

Hoofed mammals tend to do similar types of things. They will move around more and often faster, sometimes leaping around. They will sometimes shake their heads or toss them. Their postural tonus may go up and they may snort, blow or vocalise. Llamas and the other smaller members of the camel family will tend to gallop around, then stop and stare around with a high postural tonus, leap and cavort. The problem is that, like other behaviour, if situations conducive to excitement continue too long, or are too severe, then the animal may become distressed rather than apparently feel pleasure. For example, what might start off as a run with a high postural tonus, snorting and staring, as a result of one animal perceiving a strange object, may turn into flight - accompanied by behavioural signs of fear: sweating, shivering etc. The other problem which at present we have no answer to is that even though the animal may not be showing any behavioural signs of either distress or pleasure, there is no guarantee that it is not feeling them.

Fig. 45. Tigers' social play in an exercise area.

Fig. 46. Loose young elephants playing with their handler.

Social or object play may also be used as an indicator of good health and pleasure. Other self-caring activities, such as self-grooming, stretching, care about lying places, nest building and breeding at appropriate times, while not necessarily indicating joy and pleasure are often used by farmers, zoo-keepers and other animal managers as indices of good health [84].

The list below shows the behaviours of the different species we are concerned with primarily, which might be identified with pleasure or joy. We have no physiological measure of this any more than we do for distress. However we do have 'commonsense' evidence... the evidence of our own eyes and ears as human beings [see e.g. 14; 20; 84 for discussion of commonsense evidence].

Relaxed animals, if not positively exhibiting pleasure, may be exhibiting **lack** of distress and fear. So animals that are relaxed in their home areas, or in company with human beings and in training sessions might be described as **not distressed**. This is particularly obvious in circuses where animals in all conditions, if they are under the jurisdiction of a good animal trainer, will be relaxed. It is often stated that a 'good horseman' is one who has relaxed horses. It is possible therefore, using such criteria, to assess the attitude of the animals, and the humans to the animals by walking into any stable or farmyard. It is equally easy to see the opposite: fearful behaviour from both human stockperson and animal (lack of pleasure, and possible distress) when humans approach the animals in some circuses, zoos, stables, kennels and farms, particularly those who have policies of 'zero or minimal handling'.

BEHAVIOUR WHICH ARE POSSIBLE INDICES OF 'PLEASURE'

elephants	large cats	camelids	equids	bears
blow	blow	elevated paces------------------		climb
bang trunk	chase	leap/chase---		
cough	mutual groom	--		
play--				
rumble	purr	groan/grunt	nicker	grunt
stretch---				
ear flap	leap about---			
rush about---				
touch other---				
squeal	play bite---			
trumpet	smell/lick other---			
roll about---				

------ = *occurs in each species*

FIGURE 47
The frequency of performance of behaviour possibly related to
"pleasure" in the circuses

SPECIES	Play 1.	"Pleasure" 1.	Affil- iative 1.	Total	Touch other 2.	Human contact 2.
African elephants	1.8	3.6	4.7	8.3	21.1	2.6
Indian elephants	1.5	5.9	3.7	9.6	7.9	6.4
Lions	0.9	3.4	6.7	11.1	5.7	2.6
Tigers	0.79	2.5	5.7	8.2	7.4	0.2
Leopards	0.81	3.2	4.6	7.8	2.6	1.1
Bears	6.5	7.4	11.4	18.8	4.0	10.8
Camels	3.9	3.9	0.7	4.6	10.9	16.8
Llamas	0	0.1	0.7	0.8	2.8	1.5
Horses	0.9	0.3	0.6	0.9	0.2	10.8
Ponies	0.3	0.1	1.6	1.7	1.4	2.6
Zebras	0.2	0.2	0.6	0.8	0.4	4.1

1. Number of times/ animal hour (pleasure, affiliative and play.)
2. Minutes/animal hour (touch and human contact.)

Evidence for pleasure in the living quarters

Any quantitative evidence for pleasure that we recorded in the one-hour recording periods is given in Figure 47. This quantitative behaviour only relates to the animals in their living quarters; any observational evidence for pleasure exhibited in the animals during training or handling is discussed in Chapter 6.

How pleasure was assessed quantititively is outlined for each species. It is stressed that this is a first effort at doing this, and it requires much more detailed knowledge on the quantitative differences between species - the species 'telos' or differences - than we at present have.

Other indices of possible pleasure may be the amount of affiliation that is shown between individuals (Figure 47 column 3), how much time they spent touching each other (column 6). There will be species differences in this - some species are more social and contact loving than others. Nevertheless, affiliative behaviour will give some pleasure, whatever its immediate cause.

Finally, the amount of voluntary contact between animal and human must give some indication of pleasure in each other's company. The humans would not spend time with the animals and the animals would make no voluntary contact with the humans if the experience was not pleasurable for both. Measuring how often and how much time animals choose to be with humans when allowed a choice may prove to be very important in our further understanding and development of inter-species communication.

The elephants

Pleasure in elephants was summated from: blowing, bang trunk, cough, play, reach to human, rumbling, squeaking, trumpeting. We recognise that these behaviours are also used at other times and are not necessarily only indicative of pleasure; however, this is a first attempt.

Moss [27] says of greeting in African elephants that it is to her demonstrative of pleasure and involves these activities. I agree with this assessment from our own observations. However, this greeting in circus Indian and African elephants is often directed to the human handler/companion.

Figure 47 gives the summation of the amount of these behaviours exhibited by the elephants. Zoos have a particularly high score because the zoo elephants were more vocal (more blowing, squeaking and rumbling). Whether this was because they were somewhat frustrated because they were constantly trying to greet people, or this was pleasure remains obscure. Even when the elephants were shackled, they showed some behaviour which might be associated with pleasure, in particular their vocalisations, and touching each other with the trunk which occurred relatively often. It may be that touching one another frequently with the trunk is indicative of insecurity. Some of the elephants showed evidence of excitement and pleasure when greeting their trainer: trumpeting and ear flapping. Once released from the shackles, they approached the trainer and stood very near him, often feeling him with their trunks. They also vocalised and ear flapped on anticipating feed or water. They manipulated any objects within their reach with their trunks, including throwing the hay around and over their heads, manipulating bolts and shackles, or hitting the side of the tent with the trunk. These behaviours are not exclusive indicators of pleasure, but it may be involved.

Touching each other was very common (21 min/hr) for the young African elephants. Unfortunately, we do not have any figures from the wild to compare with. It may be that this might also indicate insecurity in these young animals isolated from older animals. They also had less contact with people. However these differences were not significant.

The large cats

The cats were mostly in social groups (some of them mixed species) for at least part of the day. They had plenty of opportunity for social interaction and play. The amount of playing in the big cats is shown in Figure 47. This involved normal cat-like play, stalking, lying watching, pouncing, wrestling, leaping, chasing and nose-to-nose touching and greeting. Mutual licking was also fairly frequent.

Rubbing themselves on each other and on the bars and purring were other activities probably denoting pleasure.

Lions and, to a lesser extent, the tigers are social cats [71; 72]. Leopards, by contrast, tend to be less social, and in this respect are more like the domestic cat [85]. There is little detailed published information concerning their behaviour.

There is more evidence for 'pleasure' in the exercise yards and zoos (Figure 37) although these figures are only significant for the lions.

The bears

The bears in their home cages were very active and also showed much evidence of affiliation, human contact and 'pleasure' as scored by playing, wrestling, play biting and climbing (Figure 47). We have no information about wild bears with which to compare these figures.

Horses, zebras, mules and donkeys

Indices of possible pleasure in horses, ponies and zebras were: moving around rapidly, a high postural tonus, leaping, rearing and bucking around, chasing, galloping as a group and social playing. Nose-to-nose touching in greeting may also be used as indicative of possible pleasure.

The equids in the tents often had little chance to move rapidly or have free social interactions since they were either in individual looseboxes or tied in stalls. Some ponies were loose in the general circus area and would dart about between the tents (Figure 15). Others were from time to time tethered out of the tents.

Social interaction was significantly more frequent in the confined horses (see Figure 44) than in pastured horses. They also have the highest score for human contact. This may indicate a form of insecurity or compensation for the restriction of other behaviours.

Most of the equids would nicker and neigh at the approach of their handlers and or the food or hay, indicating greeting and anticipated pleasure. This might, in part, be because of their confined conditions.

The camelids

The large camels were relatively lethargic and showed no particular evidence of pleasure by leaping around. They were without exception easy to handle and non-aggressive, and appeared to show some pleasure at the presence of their handlers and food. They did, however, engage in much play-biting which accounts for the high score of 'pleasure' (Figure 47).

The llamas, alpacas and guanacos appeared to be more reactive and were often kept loose in yards where they were able to interact and have some social play. They also could move around relatively freely. However, they show very low levels of 'pleasure' on these scores.

Other hoofed stock

The other hoofed stock were mostly tied and tended not to be particularly reactive. They showed evidence of anticipation of pleasurable experiences in terms of looking for and calling for food around food time and greeting known human handlers. They showed no evidence on the whole of displeasure in being handled and led around.

Dogs

The domestic dogs, as usual, showed much 'pleasure' when their handler (or practically any other person) was paying them attention. Some of the dogs were in pens and could be visited by the public but most of them were shut away in the wagons and were not studied in depth.

Wolves, hyenas etc. were in groups (if there were more than one) in beast wagons, and certainly reacted strongly to food and its anticipation. They were not studied in detail.

Performance

One of the main criticisms of circuses is that the animals may well dislike or even detest having to perform in front of audiences of human beings twice a day. The performances were studied, therefore, with this in mind and we walked round behind the scenes and assessed the behaviour of the animals before, during and after the performances.

One of the first criteria to consider is the behaviour in anticipation of the performance. The lights go on and the music starts, the people can usually be heard coming into the tent, and there can be little doubt that a performance is approaching. This appeared to make little difference to most of the animals. Even when they were being prepared by having their harnesses fitted (if any), or extra grooming and handling which was normal before a performance for most of the animals, they remained generally calm. We saw no reluctance to enter the ring, through the flapping tent sides, often in high winds, and usually past the very loud band in any but the least experienced animals.

Some of the big cats, particularly the younger ones, were not keen on leaping out of the cage and down the tunnel to the ring. Some of the larger cats also wanted to leave the ring at the end of the performance. However, during the performances, most of the cats performed apparently with willingness although not always with great enthusiasm.

Animals that persistently show a dislike of entering the ring and do not act up to the audience's applause, or cannot get used to the noise, lights and so on, are culled. This is expensive, so as a result the trainer will often put some thought into **why** an individual is reluctant to go into the ring or do certain things in the ring. The act will often be changed to accommodate the individual's skills and likes.

There were only three performing bears seen in British circuses when we were visiting them. They showed no evidence or reluctance to go to the ring or to perform. Since bears have relatively inexpressive faces and bodies, it is more difficult to understand their emotional state.

Reaction to audiences

Many of the more experienced performing animals appeared to react positively to large and enthusiastic audiences. The act would be performed with more energy and the animals appeared to be reacting to the audience's emotional responses to the various acts. By contrast, small audiences or unenthusiastic audiences tended to discourage the human and animal performers from making their best efforts or bothering very much at all. Whether this effect on the animals was a response directly to the audience, or to the motivation of their presenter we don't know.

Some animals had learnt that there was much audience response from doing the wrong thing, provided the audience knew it was wrong, such as the llama rolling around or jumping out of the ring, the bucking donkey bucking off its rider, or the dog knocking over its clown master. These animals apparently found the audience response reinforcing and developed the acts themselves up to a point.

However, where the audience did not really know what was meant to happen (and made no response when an act went wrong) - such as a messy presentation of a liberty horse act (which when the horses do not keep properly to place can look chaotic) - or there was no audience response: nothing changed. Horses (as most animals) respond very well to praise and similarly to disapproval. It would be interesting to see how they would have responded if the audience had shown some disapproval when things went wrong!

Transportation

This has already been discussed (see Chapter 2). There was no particular evidence of pleasure but none of distress or displeasure either in loading, travelling or unloading.

Winter quarters

There was evidence of distress in the behaviour of animals at winter quarters, and some of pleasure too, but the winter quarters have many of the disadvantages of restricted and monotonous environments which the zoos have to confront all the time for their animals. There is much that could be done to make these environments more acceptable to the animals and consequently for them to show more pleasure and less distress.

Summary

There are inevitably threshold differences, and differences in how 'pleasure' may be displayed in the different species. The inter-species comparisons are therefore meaningless at this stage. It is interesting to see that these animals do show some possible evidence of 'pleasure' in circuses, and this does not appear to always be less than in other types of husbandry.

This is a tentative effort at trying to assess 'pleasure' quantitatively in the different species in their living quarters and inevitably it has many snags. However, it may prove a fruitful area for research to help assess the relative acceptability of different environments to different animals, and therefore their 'happiness'.

Chapter 6

Handling and training, is it cruel?

The first version of this chapter was published in Animal Training *(UFAW. 1990).*

There is much ignorance and controversy concerning both the handling and training of zoo and circus animals; **if** it should be done at all, and if it is, **how** it should be done.

Handling

Before circus animals can be 'trained' they need to be 'handled', or at least become familiar with human beings. Although handling is a type of training, and involves learning, there is a distinction. Training normally implies that the animal will learn **to do something**, whereas handling implies that the animal may well have to learn **to do nothing** (Figure 48). Handling animals is an area that has received very little attention to date. Serious consideration as to how even domestic animals are handled is rarely given, even though the beginnings of many types of behavioural problems for animals can often be related to inappropriate handling. Even very little handling can have considerable effects later; for example, only 5 minutes a day of handling for one week reduced problems of pigs loading and moving through new environments [87].

The first question is: Should wild animals be handled at all? (Although since there are poor grounds for making distinctions between domestic and wild animals in their treatment - see pages 154-160, this should encompass all animals.) Some have argued that wild animals in captivity should not be handled on grounds that this influences their behaviour and thus they are no longer 'natural'. This is examined more fully later (see page 132). Some zoos take this line and are proud of their 'zero handling facilities'. It seems extraordinary that such people appear to be unaware of the basic fallacy in their argument. If they take this view, how can they possibly justify having animals in captivity at all? After all, it is definitely going to affect their behaviour in one way or another; for example, the animals will become accustomed to humans looking at them when they are on view and learn not to run away, thus they are not behaving 'naturally' (as they would in the wild).

If we argue that (given certain provisos) having and keeping domestic and wild animals in captivity is not **of its nature** wrong (see Chapters 8 and 9), what are the advantages of handling the animals?

First, what is handling? It is defined here as humans interacting with animals by touching, talking to, and being close to them over a period of time. The object of handling is fundamentally to reduce the fear that the animals may have of such close contact with humans and subsequently other unfamiliar objects. Once the animal can be handled easily and shows no sign of fear, as a rule both he and the human handler have begun to establish an emotional relationship, which if it progresses appropriately can develop into affection and pleasure in each other's company. In addition, mutual levels of confidence with each other can build up to a point where the animal has confidence in his handler and will therefore go places and do things with her that he would otherwise be frightened to do.

Fig. 48. A young African elephant being handled in order to groom her.

Fig. 49. A handler/trainer and a lioness. Positive (pleasant) emotional relationships between the species must grow if training is to continue to be successful and a pleasant experience for both.

Fig. 50. Animals that have been correctly handled may thereafter seek contact with humans. Here a zebra contacts a member of the public.

Good handlers can achieve much with animals. They can often achieve a great deal more with a previously badly handled animal than the animal's more familiar owner or keeper. It is not therefore only familiarity with the individual that is important, although this helps.

Good handling remains almost in the realms of the occult where horse handling, for example, was firmly placed by the secret society of horsemen and Whisperers in the eighteenth century. It was said that certain individuals could go quietly into the stable with a 'killing' stallion and walk out with him quiet and gentle in half an hour.

How could this be without the intervention of strange potions, or spirits? Even today people marvel, and often with good cause, at others who are more able to handle horses and can achieve what, to the uninitiated, are often astounding results (e.g. Teddington-Jones, masseur for the US Long-distance Equestrian team, who gave a demonstration at Equitana Exhibition, Essen, Germany in 1988; Monty Roberts' demonstrations, Stoneleigh 1983).

Handling involves understanding the animal's body language, but also being able to control one's own so that it does not portray certain emotions that one might be feeling, for example, fear. Good handling must leave the animal with a pleasurable experience, otherwise the animal will quickly learn not to be handled. It is not difficult to teach most interested humans the first steps in good handling of animals, but how this develops with experience in that human depends on their interest, sensitivity and skills.

A key feature of good handling is that the animals and humans must have **mutual respect**. Insufficient respect for the animal and insufficient sensitivity of the human may result in the animal becoming more frightened of humans, and sometimes attack in defensive threat. Insufficient respect of the human by the animal will result in the human being completely manipulated by the animal and, as a result, the animal may become aggressive when it does not get its way, or simply bad mannered, pushing, pulling, barging, and generally ignoring the human's desires [88]. Bad handling may cause individuals to become more frightened of humans, aggressive or simply to ignore humans.

As a general rule, most good trainers are also good handlers, although the reverse does not necessarily hold.

The first, and most obvious advantage is that animals have to be moved around from time to time. If the animal can be handled and has learnt to be led or moved without panic and trauma, this will be easier for the human managers. It will also be easier on the animal since he will not have to suffer the traumas of being drugged by immobilisers and its accompanying risks and the fear of new sudden and unexpected closeness to humans, being manipulated by them, and all the other unfamiliar and potentially frightening things that might happen at such times. It will also cut down the risk of injury to the animal that might be inflicted on him by the drug use, or that he might inflict on himself by panicking.

The next advantage in having an animal easy to handle is that routine veterinary care can be done without drugging, panicking the animal under physical restraint and so on, whether this is the injection of cat flu vaccine, examination and treatment of wounds or administration of normal prophylactic medicines. Captive wild animals in zoos can often only be treated by being first darted with immoblisers, or by being physically restrained with ropes, and so on (see page 61 and Figure 20).

Fig. 51. A young tiger who has been hand reared out for a walk with her rearer and emotional companion.

109

Everyday management of the animals is easier if good relaxed relationships between the human stockpeople and the animals are the result of good handling. Elephants can have their feet cut in the circus compound while the everyday routine goes on around them; a young tiger can be taken for walks to become accustomed to moving around new and different objects (Figure 51). The animals can be moved about and there is a noted lack of tension in the air. By contrast, a zoo trying to transport elephants which are unfamiliar to being handled has to chain the elephants to a tractor with the chain running through the transporter in order to restrain them and get them to load. In addition several people, often all somewhat frightened and excited, must be around to lift and pull objects, and the operation may take hours to complete.

It is, I suggest, unacceptable that animals in zoos must be injected with immobiliser in order to have routine treatments, e.g. a zebra having its feet trimmed, an operation which thousands of horses and ponies, and zebras in circuses have done regularly with no drug treatment.

Handling also has positive attributes in terms of the education of human beings. By being allowed to touch and handle animals, as they often can in the circuses (Figure 50), humans who may never have had an opportunity of being so close to a large animal before are able to experience their feel, touch, warmth and relate to them as other **sentient and intelligent individuals**. Most people who are interested enough in animals to go to a zoo or circus, will want to get very close, to touch and to interact with the animals. This is why zoos have such a problem with people feeding their animals, and why they often introduce petting corners where there are a few domestic animals that can be touched.

In the circus, the animals have come to a normally human dominated area: the town - not the people to the animals as in the zoo. In addition, there is a certain informality about the tented encampment and trailers, people and animals wandering round about. These factors encourage the public to approach and watch the routine husbandry of the animals and indeed to touch and handle them where permitted. A camel was tethered and I counted that 200 people in one hour came up to her, not just to pass by as is often the case in the zoo, but to touch her and look into her eyes, and have her respond to them. When I told the circus proprietor that I had done this count, her immediate response was: 'Poor camel, we must stop this!' However, it is clear that the animal herself can also have some say in how much is enough. If the animal finds so much attention excessive, she can always show it, by for example nipping or threatening, as many ponies do in similar circumstances. In which case, the animal will no longer be tethered where the public can touch it!

Handling, then, can allow individual humans to relate **individually** to animals, become more familiar with them and learn to respect them more, as well as being imperative for reducing traumas, discomfort, pain and fear and the need for using surgery, drugs or restraint for management. One could say that, ideally at least, all capture bred animals which are **not** going to be repatriated to the wild in urban zoos and circuses **must** be handled by their keepers and trainers. If keepers and trainers cannot do this, then perhaps they should change their job!

Training

Many are now beginning to accept that the handling of wild animals in captivity is often beneficial to their welfare [e.g. 84]. In addition, it can engender a greater respect in humans for the animals. However many still argue **against** the training of animals. This is an area for debate, and like many other aspects of our treatment of animals, it has been subject to much partial and woolly thinking. Some of the reasons why the training of circus animals particularly comes under attack are:

a)   because they are wild animals which are very unfamiliar and often frightening to human beings, even to those who are very familiar with domestic animals (this argument is considered in Chapter 7);

b)   because they are trained to do elaborate, and sometimes remarkable and astonishing things. The public, again even those experienced with everyday animal training often cannot believe that this is possible without using 'cruel' methods. It is almost a situation where the observer feels they could not do it, so how could anyone else?

Take one simple example. In training the ungulates (hoofed mammals) the first thing that the animals are taught after learning to lead, is to come to the centre of the ring when their name is called. First they are led in, and then they are called by name and led to the centre where they are given both a food and a voice reward. When this has been well learnt, they will then do it at liberty, coming into the centre when their name is called. It is a remarkable sight to see 12 young 2/3-year-old Arab stallions trotting around at liberty, and when the name of one is whispered, that horse **only** swirls into the centre. How many horse owners bother to teach their horse to come when called **always**, not only when he is hungry? Let alone perform at liberty? Such behaviour is 'circus' and frowned on by the majority of the horse establishment; it is almost in the realms of the occult!

Despite the above, the accusations directed at the training of circus animals should be investigated properly. These can be placed into six groups:

1) Circus training inevitably involves 'cruelty'. This can involve physical restraint, goads and whips, and even electric shock and burning. B. F. Skinner (backed by the money, equipment and approval of the scientific establishment) used shock and pain to 'condition' animals. This 'scientific' approach has been enormously influential among behavioural scientists and the lay public; as a result, it is widely believed that the development of Conditioned Responses by Negative Reinforcement is one of the most important ways in which animals learn. Is this really the case in animal training?

2) Training consists of dominating the animal and serves only to enhance the anthropocentric belief in humans' superiority. This results again in humans having less respect for the performing animal, and more for the presenter or trainer.

3) There is a loss of dignity in performing animals.

4) Training is essentially 'unnatural'. Animals should only learn what is 'natural behaviour'.

5) Wild animals should have 'special status'. It may be appropriate to train domestic animals, but not wild ones (Chapter 7).

6) Nothing can be learnt about animals from circuses. They cannot contribute to conservation, research or human or animal education therefore any entertainment value is essentially worthless (Chapter 7 again).

The general husbandry of the circus animals, as we have seen, was sometimes tradition bound and (although improving) would benefit from further updating. This is true of almost every type of animal management system, from farming to kennels, horse racing stables to zoos. However, it is only in circuses that wild animals are trained, and where there is any serious attempt at forming emotional or working relationships with those species not normally in close association with humans.

During my observations on training, it was clear that not all animals found learning all the tricks easy, or all trainers found the training easy. Inevitably, some individuals became somewhat anxious before they were asked to do difficult things, or when they did not understand what was required.

In this brief review, we will first look at evidence for and against the arguments 1 to 4 above.

1–2) Circus training inevitably involves 'cruelty'
Cruelty is defined here as activities that cause unneccessary, severe or prolonged distress and anxiety.

Some of the acts or tricks that circus animals perform are elaborate and apparently difficult for the animals: an elephant balancing on a revolving ball, a bear dancing on his hind legs, a lion jumping through flaming hoops. The average member of the public cannot visualise how the trainer can possibly train the animals to perform such acts without using extreme coercion, including such things as tying animals up with ropes and other forms of physical restraint, or electric shocks, thrashing with whips, and so on.

There are poor and bad trainers, and such things have, no doubt, gone on in some places. But to what extent are such methods used today in British circuses, and in particular are they **essential**? Or is it possible to train animals to do such things without 'cruel' methods, and if so what methods can be or are being employed?

There are various considerations and we must discuss techniques in relation to animal training. These are:
a) physical or chemical restraint
b) word command
c) anxiety or distress exhibited by animals during training
d) the use of negative reinforcement to make the animal act - or the use of 'punishment' **after** the act or lack of it
e) the use of the whip and human dominance

f)   the use of positive reinforcement (reward) and evidence for pleasure in training.

We will look at how each of these is used in circus training.

a) Physical restraint

Physical restraint - such as ropes, lead reins and side reins - were used in the initial training of all the hoofed stock (Figures 52, 54). The carnivores were trained loose, diversionary tactics being used in the case of a dangerous situation (a second person was often in the ring with the young animals). The elephants were also trained loose - an elephant hook was carried, however, by most of the handlers and trainers. The hook used behind the animal's ear can obviously be an unpleasant stimulus, but I saw no evidence that it caused any wound.

No twitches or hobbling of animals, such as is recommended practice in veterinary ethology textbooks for hoofed stock [cf. 44] were used while I was there, and I saw no evidence that they ever were. Also, I found no evidence that any chemical restraint - such as tranquillisers, sedatives etc. - were used either during training or at any time in the circus, although they are often recommended for the management of zoo animals.

Fig. 52. The hoofed stock being led round the ring.

Initially, lead reins and lunge reins were used to lead the hoofed animals around the ring, whip positioning and body postures were used to encourage the animals to stand on the ring edge and on pedestals. Ropes were used to hold a leg up when encouraging a horse to bow, to do the Spanish walk (exaggerated front leg action), to encourage the camels to kneel, and so on. Some animals did fight the restraining ropes and leap about: for example, the camels and some horses when learning to kneel and lie down. In some cases, the use of ropes was unnecessarily rough.

As a general rule, there was more than one human to each animal in the training sessions, and the animals would be walked through the routines by the human helpers. If the animal was particularly uncooperative, such as a young zebu bull which tended to be aggressive, and a zebra stallion which tended to leap about, then two helpers were used to lead the animal (Figure 53), the emphasis being on calming the animal, rather than exciting it with whips.

The next step is for the animals to perform the routine off the lunge. This took weeks, sometimes months of training.

Fig. 53. A young zebra stallion in a training session, getting to know the ring, the lights, staff moving around, scattering sawdust etc. This stallion was led by two people to ensure cooperation.

Fig. 54. Training of a liberty horse act starts with individuals on lunges.

Fig. 55. It gradually develops until the horses respond to the body position and posture and position of the whip of the presenter.

One thing that seems to be important is that the amount of physical restraint used to make animals do things is inversely proportional to the skill and relaxation of the trainer. For example, a young nine-foot Reticulated giraffe was bought in to walk around the ring for the first time when I was watching a training session. This was a large, strong and slightly anxious animal which was led by a head collar and lead rope. At any time the animal could have run off, trampling everything and everyone around. The trainer simply walked calmly in front of him, talking to him and giving him small rewards; in this way, apparently instilling confidence and goodwill to the animal so that he did what was required by choice... walked quietly around the ring, keeping close to his familiar handler.

b) Word of mouth command

In animals that had previously worked in the circus and particularly those that had been trained by the same trainer, word of mouth was used to ask for a different activity; for example, elephants learning a routine involving holding a person in their trunks, were simply told to pick him up and hold (Figure 56). Horses which had performed before were told to go 'a deux' or 'a trois' when and where required, and would obey the word command.

Fig. 56. Two elephants holding their trainer in their trunks as a result of word commands only.

In the normal use and association with humans, very few animals, with the exception of dogs, are taught to respond properly to their names. By contrast in the circus training, the first thing that all the liberty animals (elephants, horses, ponies, zebras, eland, llamas, camels, goats and pigs) were taught after they had become familiar with the ring and being led around it, was to come to the centre when their own name was called.

As the training advanced, so more and more words were understood by the animals, although some species were better at this than others. It was taken for granted that the elephants, for their day-to-day management, understood round about 50 word commands; their name, 'stand still', 'lie down', lift different legs etc. They also understood concepts such as 'left' and 'right'. The animals were also scolded by word of mouth when they did the wrong thing, and if this did not have the required response, it was backed up with a repositioning of the whip, or the animal might even be touched with the whip. They were also praised frequently when they did the right thing, and sometimes rewarded with tit-bits. It was particularly interesting how frequently verbal praise was used by the trainers, and how effective it was.

Once the animal has learnt what 'Yes' and 'No' signify, it is a great deal easier for him to understand what is required thereafter. If a proper training schedule is continued, it is axiomatic that the animal accumulates an understanding of many more word commands. This is rarely done with domestic animals - only a few necessary word commands are taught, after that particularly with the larger animals, physical restraint, pushing or pulling, leading, tying and holding are used instead. The animals are not expected to understand the words and thus they do not learn them.

c) Anxiety or distress exhibited by animals during training

There was no evidence of prolonged or acute distress, or high levels of fear or anxiety during the training of any of the circus animals that I witnessed in the 200 animal hours I watched training. There were occasions when the trainers became short-tempered, but even then their use of the whip and administration of punishment was restrained. It was probable that the trainers were being restrained because of my presence, but allowing for that it is not possible to describe any of the training that I witnessed as very distressing for the animal, as judged by the animals' behaviour.

Some of the young animals were frightened initially of the new experience of coming into the ring; for example, the young cats, and a young giraffe. The former, because they were anxious, were left in the ring daily for hours at a time so that they became used to the ring before any serious training was begun. Behavioural indices of when this had been achieved were used by the trainers. One of these was if the cats were playing together; another if they were relaxed enough to sleep.

Two llamas spat during training sessions, and two camels salivated profusely and leapt around growling - possibly signs of anxiety. Some animals certainly showed behavioural evidence of frustration and approach avoidance conflict from time to time (head shaking and tossing, tail swishing, yawning, lip licking, and staring away) and some refused to perform certain acts, such as the goats climbing up on to a plank over some cattle (figure 59), or one camel refusing to kneel down.

d) The use of negative reinforcement

It is widely believed that animals can only be trained to do the sorts of things they do in circuses by the wide use of negative reinforcement, that is being forced to do the action by having some unpleasant thing done to them if they don't do it. The perennial example given of this approach is: how could bears learn to stand up and 'dance' except by placing them on a heated plate so that their feet burn and they lift them? This suggestion may be appropriate for the Skinnerian scientist in the laboratory, but for the circus trainer, apart from any other considerations, it is rather impractical! This is particularly so if there are easier, simpler and much less risky ways of teaching such a behaviour, which there are of course. The 'burning feet' approach has other disadvantages which the circus trainer who must live and work with the animals thereafter is unlikely to ignore; for example, a hurting bear will be a frightened and/or aggressive bear who may attack in defensive threat. Hurting the bear may also damage relationships between trainer and bear irreparably. This is an important factor as the trainer will find it impossible, or at the least very expensive, to obtain another bear. The trainer looks forward to working with this animal for many years. It is also possible that the trainer does this job because of a strong interest in animals, and in particular the bear. The trainer may also be fond of his bear. This sort of behaviour which is likely to scar the relationship will often make the trainer's job more difficult, because the animal becomes frightened and aggressive. Any knowledge of learning and learning theory points out how inappropriate and self-defeating the approach of training by using severe negative reinforcement may be.

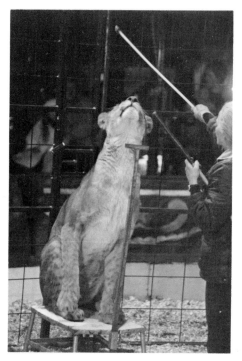

Fig. 57. A young lioness learning to stand up on her hind legs by positive reinforcement: reward of a piece of meat on a stick. She learns to go to the stick, and receives her reward.

Circus animals have to be handled and moved around daily, and although negative reinforcement can be used successfully to train isolated animals in Skinner boxes, or could be used possibly to train small animals which can be easily restrained, it is very inadvisable to use such techniques for large, possibly dangerous animals. The reason is that it is when animals are scared and hurt that they attack in defensive threat, or flee. Thus the use of fear and pain to train large carnivores is selected against. Trainers who use these techniques get eaten! Frightened elephants are also something to be avoided, particularly if they are in collapsible tents!

Frightened animals are dangerous, whether they are bears, bulls, dogs, horses, sheep, cats, elephants, llamas, camels, tigers, leopards, lions or jaguars. Thus one

120

of the first lessons a trainer of large animals learns, if he or she is going to remain alive and retain all their appendages, is not to frighten the animals. The early training of the big cats that I witnessed with three different trainers concentrated initially in simply getting the animals used to being in the ring alone. Over a period of weeks the animals gradually become accustomed to the trainer (in one case this was a six-months' pregnant woman) and perhaps a helper being in the ring cage with them while great care is taken not to frighten the animals. If this happens then the training must go back and repeat the previous learning steps. All the training of the big cats is based primarily on reducing levels of fear and on positive reinforcement: rewards of pieces of meat on sticks (Figures 57; 58). The human's word of mouth command, body position and the position of the two sticks or a whip are the cues for controlling the cats' movements. Similarly, elephants will work for titbits. One of an elephant trainer's greatest worries is sudden loud noises, or visual changes outside their control that might frighten the elephants; for example, dogs chasing them, or helicopters flying a few metres away. The answer to this problem, the trainers have discovered, is **not** to keep the animals away from all such stimuli, but rather to expose them to them so that they become used to them. Inevitably, even with the best trained, most experienced animals there are anxious moments like when the Royal helicopter landed a few feet away from one circus's elephants, and the 'Royal' emerged to smile sweetly at the elephants while the trainer sweated, but the elephants stood stock still!

e) Dominance

It is widely believed that it is not possible to train animals at all without dominating them and showing 'who is boss'. This is something I as a trainer have thought long and hard about. It is easy to accept the hypothesis of 'dominance hierarchies' and apply it as an explanatory concept to all animal societies, but we are gradually realising that in many cases this is an oversimplification, and can lead up the garden path and even into the garden pond! In the first place, no one seems to mean the same thing by 'dominance'. They vary from situation to situation, and sometimes are artefacts of behavioural disturbance [e.g. 1; 29; 96]. In fact, it is a misguided and overused term that is only useful very occasionally.

Fig.58. A young elephant following the trainer's hand with a tit-bit in it, off the pedestal. Having achieved the right position, the elephant is rewarded with the tit bit.

In practice, we often take 'dominance' to mean 'showing who is boss'. In training animals, is this necessary or indeed useful? In my experience this attitude, far from being helpful, is often positively harmful in educating either humans or animals. Suppose we rephrase it to be 'inculcating a basic moral sense, and showing mutual respect to the child/animal'? In other words, teaching the adult, child or animal what type of behaviour is approved of and desirable by the teacher, parent, trainer or society at large, and what type of behaviour is not? This is what good teachers of children do.

Such a change in terminology immediately makes a difference in the attitude of the educator. Instead of the teacher requiring absolute obedience, and submission [cf. Federation d'Equestre International and British Horse Society assessment of Dressage tests] from the student, he or she aims at **cooperation and communication**. The result is that correct behaviour is praised lavishly, and incorrect behaviour is disapproved of. The educator's job is to present the problem, or the action, so that the student **wants** to do it. The problem to the educator is not one of disciplining and dominating, but one of motivating. Such an approach reduces or eliminates the need for punishment, which is difficult to apply correctly, and frequently causes rather than reduces problems. It encourages self-criticism on the part of the trainer/educator, and avoids confrontation of wills, and the concomitant high 'negative/emotional tension' (i.e. temper losing, anger, fear and aggression). It opens up the possibility of using many of the ideas and techniques of educational psychology in animal training.

If one looks closely at good animal training, in the circus or anywhere else, from fleas to human beings to elephants, dominance and submission is a long way from what is actually going on. Interestingly enough it is not what the audience wants either apparently. The most popular acts are often those where the **animal** is apparently in control, such as the bucking donkey, or the trick dog who gets the better of her human partner.

Thus I argue that 'dominance' is not a *sine qua non* of circus training. Although some basic moral education and motivation to learn for both animals and humans is.

As whips feature much in circuses, it is often considered that they are used not only indiscriminately in the training of the animals (it is rare to find people complaining that they are used severely in performance), but that they also serve to demonstrate the dominance of humans over the animals, and thus underline the anthropocentric idea of animals being demonstrably inferior to human beings.

Whether or not these are the reasons for the association of whips with circuses, it is certainly true that whips have a traditional place in circuses. It is also true to say that many circuses in Britain today are bound by tradition. Some are more concerned with history and keeping tradition going than developing a possible art form and educational medium for teaching people about animals. Circus people make whips, talk about whips and pride themselves on their 'whip craft'. However this does not mean that they whip each other or their animals more than other people!

The whip has become one of their props, like the 'macho' image of the lion tamer and his self-displaying garments. It is perhaps unfortunate and detracts from the potentially important attributes that the circus has.

The first questions then are: How is the whip used in the circus? Also, is it necessary for all presenters to carry whips, crack whips and generally play around with whips for the animals to perform?

In answer to the second question first, I asked a trainer and presenter of, among other things, a liberty horse act if he needed the whip? He said not and to prove it he presented the horses at the next performance with no whip and his hands in his pockets. The act was as good as ever, and he received excellent applause from the audience, although nothing had been announced to draw their attention to this. This demonstrates that it is not necessary always to present an act with a whip, either to ensure the animals perform properly, or to obtain the approval of the audience.

Animals in training, or new acts, may need the presenter to have a whip as the animals will be less skilled at picking up the cues. In the early training of any large animal, one of the first things that the animal learns is to go away from the whip. Thus it is the position of the whip relative to the animal that gives the cue. The whip is not there to whip the animals with, it is there rather to emphasise the message, like using flags to emphasise the arms when sending semaphore messages.

Circuses should move away from their traditional association with the whip, and progress as a rule (rather than as an exception) towards teaching animals to respond to the human arm position, or perhaps even the lift of an eyebrow, or a whistle. This would be more impressive, interesting and informative to the public and it would emphasise cooperation between performers and presenters rather than domination over the animals by the presenter.

Nevertheless, the whip is not usually used willfully or excessively in the circus. In fact, there is much more thoughtless and unnecessary whip usage at markets, on farms and in domestic animal training establishments, particularly among amateur trainers. If the whip is one of the reasons for disapproving and trying to ban circuses, current practices in horse training should also be looked at carefully.

The whip, it has been argued, is a symbol of human domination over animals, and this comes to its zenith in the circus. Even if this was once the case, it is again not a *sine qua non*. It does not mean that circuses necessarily have to demonstrate the domination of humans over animals.

The assumption that the most attractive thing about riding a horse, working a dog, or presenting a lion act is the feeling of 'domination' over the animal is often stated. It is an interesting idea and one that must be considered carefully. It is possible that this is the reason why some people train animals, but I would suggest that many more like to work with animals **for their own sake.**

Another approach is to consider **cooperation** as being important. It would seem that the first reason why many people train and work with animals is to achieve this sense of cooperation where the different skills of the disparate species are combined to a mutually beneficial end: the closest we can get, perhaps, to inter-species communication. There is no doubt that some (maybe many) circus people work with animals, train them and present them in acts because it is a rather unusual thing. It will enhance their social status; they will be admired as artists, perhaps become famous and so on. The circus is, after all, like the theatre in many ways. That **dominating** the animals is the main motivation - and this is what the public come to see - may not necessarily be the case.

This is best illustrated by the remarkable success of extremely simple acts where the humans come off worse. One case was quoted to me of where a bucking donkey and his presenter were hired to a large American circus. Their act was to follow the Viennese Riding School. This school is considered the epitome of cultured riding; it is very rigid in approach; there is a right and wrong way for every movement being performed and each horse must be obedient (i.e. dominated) so that it performs the acts exactly as required. The horse has only very narrow confines within such a discipline in which to exercise any of its own initiative or possible creativity and invention. However, what 'brought the house down' was a single donkey doing a humorous bucking act with its trainer. There were some set moves in the act, but no two performances were ever alike - different acts were performed in different orders and with different amounts of enthusiasm; it depended on the audience's response and the 'mood' of the donkey and his trainer as to how things worked out. Here there is an act which demonstrates the lack of dominance of the human and not only allows but encourages the donkey to use his own sense of timing, initiative and perhaps imagination. The reason for the act's popularity may well have been the contrast with the previous act, highly specialised Riding School act - and the blatant **lack** of domination of animal by human. Even 'learnt disobedience' gives the animal considerable scope for initiative!

There are more examples of acts which set out to show that humans do not necessarily dominate the animals. The act itself, although it may have been well planned in a certain way before training started, is nearly always modified and changed as a result of the animals' responses. In fact, the animals in some circuses are often **encouraged** at certain times in the performance to develop their own way of doing various movements or of demonstrating their individuality.

i) A llama act

There were superb props and costumes for this act. Four llamas came into the ring one after the other, to a commentary explaining that they were related to the camels, came from South America and that there were other close relatives such as the guanaco and alpaca. The music then began and the various members of the llama family who were clearly supposed to trot around the props set about investigating the audience on the ring fence, rolled in the sawdust and generally not doing what was required. Eventually in each performance the presenter, a young woman, managed to get them going round the ring and doing some of the routine. Then one llama, when expected to jump over poles, persistently went underneath, even though it had to do a limbo act. On questioning the trainer about this act, it turned out that these behaviours were not trained in the llamas; it had started as a straight liberty act, but the llamas themselves had invented these extra-curricular activities - one sometimes even jumping out of the ring and wandering up and down the aisles between the audience.

The effect was delightful, both amusing and instructive; whatever else was going on it was evident that the presenter was **not** dominating the animals and this, in particular, seemed to be what was appreciated by the audience.

ii) The training of a farm animal act

One of the routines in this act was that two goats were to climb up and walk over the backs of several cows on a wooden plank, and then walk down the other side. The goats had no difficulty climbing up the plank, but when crossing the cows' backs, the cows moved and the plank wobbled. Several times the goats jumped off. Subsequently, they were suspicious and slightly scared of climbing up the planks, and resisted climbing them. Once the problem had been appreciated, a solid bridge over the cows was used so that the plank did not move. The goats were then induced with rewards to climb and cross the plank.

Fig. 59. A farm animal act which was changed by the goats refusing to cross the plank when it was on the cattle's back.

In another part of the act, a pig was meant to go on the see-saw with a bunch of geese on the other side. The pig would always jump enthusiastically on to the see-saw before the geese had fully prepared themselves on the other side. This frightened the geese and they ran off noisily. The act was changed so that the two pigs see-sawed together on one see-saw and the geese on another.

These examples show that, firstly, the presenter is not necessarily dominant; and also that the trainer must be sensitive to the animals' responses to the situation.

The majority of animal acts are to some extent unpredictable - the animals may react differently on different days, in different places and with different audiences - they have 'moods'. The art of the presenter is often to make what has happened look as if it was meant to happen. This does not, of course, only apply to animal acts but to all the acts in the circus.

The most educational and creative circus act might be described as one in which the animals have first of all - like a human artist or ballet dancer - been schooled thoroughly in the relevant techniques; such as various behaviours and movements. This basic training is then used in different ways by different individuals for the development of the act: the animals being encouraged to use their own initiative and possibly 'creativity and imagination' to participate willingly and develop, to some extent, their own act. This can be encouraged by a sensitive trainer or presenter, good relationships between human and animals and cooperation.

We do not talk about good education of humans as demanding only obedience and domination but rather one in which the human is given the basic tools (which may require considerable application and motivation, hard work and obedience, too). Once these have been acquired, the human is encouraged to use them to develop his or her art and particular skills. Some end up great artists and dancers; some are mediocre. What makes a great performer, though, is not blind obedience and the domination of one individual by another, but imagination, sensitivity to each partaking individual and willing cooperation. How much greater our respect for all participants then becomes.

If we have yet to see this with animal acts in circuses, it is not that it **cannot** happen, it is just that it has not yet been thought about and efforts made to try it out.

f) The use of positive reinforcement

If this thesis has some basis we might expect to see some evidence of pleasure in the animals when they get things right; for example, when they are praised, they may even enjoy the process of learning as some humans do, finding the mind-stretching nature of appropriate and well-taught ring work exciting and rewarding in itself. Did we see any evidence of this?

All training sessions used positive reinforcement in the form of food rewards and praise with the voice. The food rewards varied from lumps of sugar, mints, lumps of meat, or a specially made biscuit called 'vitamins'. The first important tenet in training is to find something that an animal will work for. This may simply be the trainer's approval (word praises and scoldings were used persistently to encourage and discourage an animal at all stages of training), or initially some sought after small tit-bit. In some cases, I think we could consider the animals as enjoying their ring work, but we need to have much greater understanding of possible pleasure in animals. Usually, they worked enthusiastically for the rewards.

Another way of training animals (or humans) to perform certain tasks is by **'moulding'**. This is where the animal, or its appendage, is placed in the required position, and then the animal praised and positive reinforcement used. This is best done without force or any unpleasant stimulation. It was used successfully by the Gardiners in their work with teaching Amslan to the chimp Washoe [94].

3) Loss of dignity in performing animals
Another accusation is that animals performing in circuses is 'unnatural' and 'undignified' - the animals are made to look like stupid human beings and lose dignity thereby. The loss of dignity is probably in the eye of the beholder, if an animal finds a particular activity degrading, presumably it will either refuse to do it, or if coerced will show evidence of distress (Chapters 3 and 4). Since this will interfere with the training and performance, the usual thing to do is change the act for that individual. Certainly acts which humans find degrading may tend to decrease the human's respect for the animals themselves. On the other hand, representing animals as slightly handicapped humans elicits on occasion the 'ah' reaction ('Oh, how cute'.') and thus care-giving behaviour from the human audience. Different humans will consider that this is either good or bad in terms of the benefit to the individual.

Let us consider the human judgement in more detail as, even if there is no evidence for loss of dignity by the animal, it does reflect what humans feel. The acts most humans find to be 'degrading and humiliating' for animals are ones where, as a general rule:

a) the animal is made, they feel, to look like a human in one way or another - and in particular an inadequate or stupid human; e.g. the RSPCA's literature against circuses. In this case, the point is doubly made as the lion depicted is wearing a clown's or dunce's cap and a thick nose.

b) the act is highly unnatural to the species.

From the educational point of view, this type of approach does not put across an acceptable or desirable image of animals. It tends to reinforce people in their belief in the homocentric attitudes of superiority. Far better would be to put across the idea of the animal as an intelligent, able and beautiful sentient individual; perhaps more intelligent, able and beautiful than we had previously supposed.

Some will argue that this is what television films do, and that it can **only** be done by displaying the **natural** behaviour of the animals. This is, I suggest, disputable.

First, let us examine if this is what television wildlife films do. The vast majority of television footage shown is not, as a casual viewer might suppose, the animal 'caught in the act' as the camera operator happened to walk by. It is highly structured, often involving elaborate set-ups with sometimes live animals used as decoys or killed in order to make the footage. There are serious ethical arguments involving the use of animals in the television and film industry [113]. This is being changed by legislation so that at least animals do not suffer while they are filming. However, there is another serious disadvantage to assuming that wildlife films offer a sufficient education concerning animals. It is incorrect to assume that the television films are displaying the animals as they are. What is caught on film are the **dramatic highlights of animal life**, just as in human theatre. The result is that the observer may gather a completely incorrect idea of how animals live. The vast majority of the time the animals go about their lives with little melodrama, little obvious sign of the 'tooth and claw of wild nature' that the television camera is so keen on capturing. This is not to say that nothing is going on in their lives, but rather that what is going on in their societies is less obvious and, in fact, may be completely unseen or not understood by those who are not skilled observers. For example, in the four years of living in the bush of Africa studying antelope, I never once witnessed a chase and kill by a predator; although I did accumulate a great deal of information on the relationships between individuals, their ecology and many aspects of their behaviour. I have yet to see any television footage of gnu, gazelles or zebra in the Serengeti, for example, which does not include a hunt and kill by the large predators. Often, the footage is obtained by elaborate set-ups, both the predators and the prey being driven, manipulated and sometimes killed **for** the cameras.

Whether or not this is justified ethically is not my concern at this point. I am simply making the point that film footage does **not** usually display the **normal natural behaviour of the animal**. It shows only the melodramatic moments of it; also, it manipulates it by setting up situations. This is what human theatre and films do too. We should recognise that wildlife films are also theatre; that does not make them useless or invalid, however.

The film footage can never allow the direct experience of the animal and any interchange between the human and the animal. Indeed, it could be argued, that the display of animals in wildlife films often emphasises the **differences** of animals from humans. It might encourage some respect, impart some knowledge, but only in a sense as we would have for Martians as something quite alien and unrelated.

Fig. 60. Elephants don't stand on pedestals with horses running underneath them in the wild. Such an act is certainly 'unnatural' in the sense that it does not occur in the wild, but is it undignified for the animal, or is this some humans' perception of this act?

131

Another possibility is that presenting the animals as 'stupid' human beings shows them in a way that exercises our compassion and responsibility to them - as we must respond to children or handicapped human beings. It is a question of whether we believe that compassion for the underdog, or respect for a highly intelligent and able other being, is most desirable in humans, and of most benefit to animals in the long run. The members of animal welfare organisations are often highly motivated towards the former; the latter would appear much more acceptable but often requires a rather 'new world' view.

Circuses in Britain, in any case, have over the last few years become extremely sensitive to this criticism. I did not see a single act where animals were dressed up like humans.

4) Training is 'unnatural', therefore wrong

We did, however, see acts where the animals were taught to do behaviours that are **not** in their natural behavioural repertoire, although at least one trainer denied that this was the case, and that he had seen elephants in the wild standing up on their hind legs, reaching for things, or balancing on their front legs while drinking, and so on. This is no more absurd than the horse establishment, led by the classical Spanish Riding School, maintaining that all movements taught to horses in Dressage are natural movements and not 'tricks' which is a demeaning term used for what circuses teach their animals.

There are two points that need examining here:

● What are we to consider as 'natural behaviour'? Is this something that the animal does only in the wild, or when not in association with human beings? In which case we must include all dogs walking on leads, horses being ridden or pulling things, cows being milked, and so on since none of these behaviours are in the animals' natural repertoire. If it is maintained that training domestic animals is alright but not wild ones, then good reason for making this distinction must be put forward. These are discussed in Chapter 7.

Or are we to consider 'natural' only the behaviour which is easy to do and requires little training. Complex tasks, such as balancing on things, twisting and turning in involved patterns, or - taking the analogy to humans - reading and writing, are tasks which require long and carefully structured training. In that sense, they are not natural.

● The second point is that even if we can agree on what we mean by 'natural', are any other behaviours that are not apparently in this category necessarily wrong for the animal or human to perform and if so why? An example: elephants do not normally stand and balance on revolving spheres, yet some can be taught to do this and perform this in the circus. This takes a long time, a great deal of patience and a lot of skill on behalf of the **trainer and the elephant** and it is not every elephant that will learn to do this. It is not possible to use negative reinforcement to teach an elephant to do this type of thing since however much it might **want** to do it as a result of coercion and fear, it will **not be able** to do it unless it has practice - it will just fall off. When an animal trainer, or anyone who has even a little understanding of animal education, sees such acts, what they admire is the mutual skills of animal and trainer in achieving it. Such a viewer may become increasingly impressed with the incredible abilities of such a large and apparently cumbersome animal in being able to control her weight and balance to such a sophisticated level, as well as admire the elephant/human mutual trust and understanding that has risen in order for the elephant to do this.

So not only is it debatable what we are going to define as 'natural' but it is also debatable that only 'natural' behaviour should be performed by animals in circuses, if what we are after is increasing humans' respect, understanding and awareness of other animals as other intelligent, sentient, admirable beings.

There is the question of possible injury to the animal while performing some acts, and certainly it would be sensible to ensure that if an animal does fall, or something goes wrong with the act, it is unlikely to be seriously hurt. This is considered for human beings (e.g. by the provision of safety nets for trapeze artists) and should also be considered seriously for the animals.

Thus the dignity of the animal, and the wrongness of performing 'unnatural' acts by both domestic and wild animals in circuses and zoos are difficult concepts to define. The performance of such acts from the animals' point of view may not be such a bad thing.

It is true, however, that many humans find such acts displeasing. Is this not a matter of taste? I find plastic garden gnomes odious but I see no rational reason to ban others from having them, unless the having of them causes further problems (such as using up scarce resources of materials). However, at the same time, the having of them may be an indicator of other attitudes which I might think was undesirable or even harmful. If this were the case one would perhaps, in a reasonable democracy, not **ban** garden gnomes, but rather by example and persuasion try and change people's attitudes so they themselves change the plastic gnome into a beautiful garden scuplture. Changing circus acts in this direction would be possible.

The next question is: Are there any positive sides to the training and performing of circus animals? The RSPCA and others devoted to the total banning of circuses argue that in no way **can** they contribute to conservation, education or research, which are the usual arguments used by zoos to justify their existence. Is this true? Also, can the animals and humans benefit in any way from being trained, training or performing?

I think there are arguments to be made here, some of which are new:

● Training or educating the animal can act as a form of occupational therapy for the animal in captivity. There are strong arguments that some individual animals may benefit from captivity. The strongest is that they are alive instead of dead - 40% of carnivores and 5% of ungulates in the circuses were unwanted zoo animals that would otherwise have been killed.

If some animals are going to be in captivity, then it is the responsible human's duty to ensure a life of some quality for the animal. One aspect of this is to ensure that it is intellectually, as well as socially and physically, in an appropriate environment. Failure to do this for active, intelligent, able beings is at last being recognised by zoos in Britain - it is called 'environmental enrichment' [95; 97]. Appropriate circus training can also act as occupational therapy, but because of inter-species communication it could be of an even more enriching nature perhaps!

● The essence of circus training is that it concentrates on the **individual**. Every animal has a name, and his personality known and is discussed at length. Zoos, by contrast, actively discourage this. There is in many zoos a sort of unspoken belief that recognising and naming individuals, and having emotional relationships with them, is 'unscientific', and therefore to be discouraged. The zoo's self-confessed aim is to have 'exhibits that are good representations of **the species'** [9]. There may be a place for zoos, but there is equally a place for circuses which are doing something rather different.

The recognition of an animal as an individual, to be related to, with the possibility of having the whole gamut of desires, emotions, likes and dislikes is I believe crucial in the development of equal consideration and respect for other sentient beings. The public recognise this intuitively. The first thing many people want to know about an animal is 'what is his name?' (i.e. to identify with the animal as an individual) [see also 98]. The circus can demonstrate this, particularly in the informality of its approach, where many of the animals are tethered round the encampment and some even running free.

They can interact directly with human beings, experience each other, touch, feel, and smell each other in a way which is not usually possible in zoos or any other enterprise where 'wild' species are kept. In one hour in a London park, I counted over 200 adults and children who went up to a tethered camel, looked into her eye, touched, stroked and talked to her. I cannot help feeling that both species benefited from such direct encounters and go away with a little more mutual respect for each other. To be subjective, I know I do, and I have reason to believe that my reaction is species typical.

● The circus (the only place where many species are trained) can increase the quality of life for the animal and the human by allowing for the development of positive emotional relationships (affection, in other words) between species. Unfortunately, the idea that emotional relationships between species cannot be as admirable, rewarding and exciting as those within species has not received the attention it deserves. Ladies who prefer cats to children are described as 'substituting and slightly cranky', and an animal's affection for a human is described as 'mal-imprinting' (science for 'something gone wrong in the wiring'), neither of which is necessarily the case.

One of the most exciting and interesting findings in the circuses was this mutual respect, trust and affection I often found between the animals - big cats, elephants, zebras, horses, dogs, pigs, llamas and so on - and their trainers and handlers.

● Provided the circus is presented in an appropriate way, the audience's respect, interest and delight in all the animals can be enhanced greatly. They can learn a great deal about the surprising abilities and intelligence of the various animals. Did you know, for example, that an elephant can find and pick up with her trunk a diamond a quarter the size of your thumbnail thrown down in the sawdust of the ring?

● This close association between human and animal inevitably leads to greater knowledge of the species and the individual. Studying the animals in the wild may give us a general background of the species' behaviour, but in order to learn as much as we can about individuals, some interaction with the animals becomes the next step, as Jane Goodall found with chimpanzees, and the Adamsons found with lions. Having a close daily association with animals, training and looking after them adds considerably to our knowledge of their world view, how they respond and feel, what they can learn, how fast they learn, and so on. The circus, where the animals have already learnt to cooperate with humans, is an ideal place for several types of behavioural research. For example, I have much information on slight behavioural differences in the big cats - leopards, tigers and lions - that have not been reported before. Information on cognitive behaviour can also be accumulated; and of course it is an ideal place to study training itself. Thus to assume that nothing can be learnt from circuses and that they cannot contribute to research is clearly silly. Why, for example, do zoo managements often have to hire circus people when they have problems handling or transporting their animals?

● There is another and important aspect to the circus: it is 'art'. As cognitive behavioural studies begin to confirm what trainers often take for granted, and many philosophers have argued for: that animals think; certain animals can use symbols, can count, can conceptualise and so on [50; 108], the distinctions made between the psychological abilities of humans and other higher mammals becomes ever more hazy. For a moment, give the animals the benefit of the doubt and consider whether or not animals could have an aesthetic appreciation, could they not also be creative, imaginative, innovative and have some sense of humour? There is plenty of anecdotal evidence for all these abilities, mostly, I think it is significant to point out, from **animal trainers.**

Presenters and trainers

As a rule, the training in circuses is professional; negative reinforcement was used infrequently and there were no indications of cruelty. What the animals were taught lacked innovation and imagination. The main criticism of the training was that there are very few real trainers in Britain (about six). Almost all the wild animal training is in the hands of one family. The other main criticism was that in British circuses at least there was not enough training being practised, and it was not innovative or always appropriate for the species.

Usually, the animals are trained by a trainer and then they are hired out to a circus; this may be anywhere in the world. Sometimes the animals will go with their groom or 'presenter' to the circus; occasionally the circus proprietor will be the trainer and will keep and present the act; but more usually a 'presenter' is hired who will spend a few weeks with the trainer learning how to 'present' the act in front of the audience. The trainer trains the presenter. There must be a period of becoming mutually familiar for the animals and the presenter before they leave with the act. Some presenters were obviously very serious about their animals and took enormous pains and worked very long hours to iron out any problems before they left with the animals; others were slap-dash and were clearly in the business because of the dashing figure they could cut in the ring rather than their fundamental interest in the animals.

The trainers are usually strict about not letting presenters change the act or try to teach their animals other tricks. This is partly out of professional pride in their own act, but also because it is recognised that as a rule presenters do not have the 'know-how' to train the animals properly and everything may go wrong if they try. Often trainers complain bitterly about the presenters when the animals return, usually on the grounds that the animals have got into bad habits which will take time to overcome.

The reason why the training (when it occurred) was so professional was probably that it is an extremely demanding, exacting, time- and patience-consuming job. Its skills are little recognised by the majority of people and it has little glamour attached, except among the small circle of other animal trainers and circus people. Thus anyone who was not seriously interested in the animals for their own sake would find much more glamorous and better paid jobs to do in the circus.

Anyone can become a circus trainer; usually, however, they are born into the circus and begin to learn to train and present animals almost before they can walk. It is possible to start as a groom, the bottom of the circus hierarchy, and gradually work up to be a presenter and then a trainer. Some people who wish to make the circus their life, after a period as a groom and/or presenter, will buy one or two animals, train them, and then try to get hired by a circus for a season.

It seemed that the personality of the trainer, their interest, skill and persistence, were much more important in their success than any 'tricks of the trade'. Thus I found the trainers, in general, happy to talk about their methods and training schedules. However, they are very conscious of how easy it is to learn **how** to train. This does not mean that anyone will be able to do it but often grooms, having witnessed a few training sessions, will try to set themselves up as trainers. This is usually unsuccessful. It takes years of experience and dedication to become a good trainer. As a result, most circus trainers liked to cultivate a slight air of mystery about their job - but they were delighted to engage in hours of discussion about individual animals' personalities.

There was great deal of repetition in what the animals were taught and what the acts consisted of. This may be partly because most trainers have learnt at their father's knee, partly because of shortage of time available for training, partly lack of thought and partly the sometimes stultifying hold of 'tradition'.

The trainer is, to a degree, caught in a double bind. The act must be 'innovative': the animals doing new and different things. At the same time, the circus must be 'traditional'. It is assumed, probably wrongly, that people go to the circus because they know they will see the same sort of things, and the circus itself is proud of its traditions.

The act must also be spectacular. Often this can be achieved by elaborate props and presenters and sometimes animal costumes and harnesses, rather than sophisticated animal training. The difficult acts to train may well be less popular or less spectacular so there is not necessarily a force to progress and improve training, except from the trainers' peers. The reverse is often the case - popular or spectacular acts may often be very easy to train.

Fig. 61. A movement at least ressembling the attack of the tiger. Is this an appropriate act showing the abilities and skill of the tiger, and the mutual trust between presenter and tiger, or does it simply show the trainer's 'courage' and 'machoism'?

The trainer must have the animals do what the audience likes to see. If they like 'attack trained' big cats (where the cats are trained to look as if they are attacking the presenter) they must train them so, even though the trainer may not like this representation of the cats. Audiences vary in what they like from culture to culture; for example, attack-trained cats go down well in the US and Southern Europe, but some Northern European audiences don't like them at all. It would be possible for the circus to change the public's attitude by, for example, presenting exciting acts enhancing the litheness, grace and affection of the cats, instead of their ferocity.

Trainers and tradition

The trainer is near the top of the circus hierarchy: in part because of this, some are not very willing to learn; they are often bound by tradition, and may consider they know it all! The usual way to become a trainer is to be born into a circus proprietor's family, although as mentioned, it is possible to work one's way up. The trainers are still very jealous about their skills. Training in the circus world (as well as outside it) is surrounded with secrets, mystic and magic. Trainers seem almost frightened that their secrets 'will out' and then everyone will want to be a circus trainer once they realise that there are no secrets - it is simply hard work, experience and skill!

This is unfortunate and obviously not the case since very few people would be interested in putting in the time, dedication and patience to learn the skills (often under very difficult conditions) for the proper training of circus animals. One Swiss circus realised this, and has open, genuine training sessions for the public and always attract a group of devotees who sit all morning watching the slow training of the various animals for the next year's acts, and come back the following year to see how they have progressed.

Over 90% of the circus audiences who returned our questionnaire wanted to see the animals being trained (Appendix 3). Open training sessions are vital if circuses are going to dispel the public's suspicion about cruelty, inappropriate training, and fulfil the role in educating the public about the amazing abilities of the animals, and the sophistication possible in inter-species communications. Unfortunately, it does not happen as a matter of daily routine in any British circus (although I have repeatedly suggested to them that they should have open training sessions). The closest that they have come is to have 'rehearsals' of the trained or almost trained animals. They are, I think, unsure about allowing the public to see the training in case things do not always work well, which of course they do not; yet how it is sorted out when things go wrong is one of the most interesting aspects.

The other reason why circuses are loathe to have open training sessions is because there are very few trainers in Britian, and each circus does not have a trainer who is actively training and travelling with them. This is one of the major criticisms of British circuses: **there is not enough training and not enough good trainers**. Some acts remain the same year in year out and the benefits of training which I have mentioned are then certainly not fulfilled.

Conclusion

The field of animal handling and training is one where little serious thought on the ethics and ethological appropriateness of various systems has yet been devoted. This study of animal training in circuses suggests that some of the widely held beliefs concerning training are not necessarily correct; for example, evidence for serious or prolonged cruelty, suffering and distress in the animals during or as a result of the training in circuses was absent in the 200 hours I studied.

It is necessary to understand the importance of avoiding frightening animals in training (because it is then that they may well be dangerous). As a result, it is not surprising to find that positive reinforcement was used in the training of circus animals more widely and more frequently than negative reinforcement.

The other criticisms that animal welfare organisations have for animals trained for circuses are concerned with possible loss of natural dignity, by the performance of 'unnatural behaviour', and the idea that the only thing demonstrated by animal training is the domination of the animals by the humans. These concerns have been discussed briefly. There is no necessity to ensure 'domination'; a more appropriate approach is one of 'cooperation'. The trainer or educator's job is to motivate the student/animal to learn. Positive reinforcement and emotional bonds between animals and human are usually more effective in achieving this. There are positive things that, provided the animals show no evidence of prolonged distress and are kept in ecologically and ethologically sound environments (see Chapter 9), animal training in circuses can contribute to our respect and understanding of other sentient beings. These positive things are:

a) captive animals should be able to be handled safely in order to reduce chances of suffering during normal routine management, including veterinary care;

b) training or educating the animal can act as a form of occupational therapy for animals, and they can apparently enjoy it;

c) the essence of circus training is that it concentrates on the individual, and respect for him or her, and allows direct experience of the individual;

d) the circus is the only place where many species are trained and it can increase the quality of life for both human and animal by allowing emotional bonds to develop;

e) provided the circus is presented appropriately, the audience's respect, interest and delight in all the animals can be enhanced;

f) the close individual association between animal and human inevitably leads to greater mutual knowledge and understanding;

g) circus animal acts, properly presented and appropriate for the species and individual, can enhance the respect, joy and wonder of the human observers. It can be an inter-species 'art' form, demonstrating also the sophistication possible of inter-species communication, and the animals' creativity and innovation.

It is thus concluded that there is no reason why circus training, any more than any other animal training, **of its nature** causes suffering and distress to the animals, or should be considered ethically unacceptable. There are bad circus trainers, just as there are bad teachers and bad parents, but this does not argue for the banning of circuses, any more than for schools or parenthood. However, there should be more appropriate acts trained to allow the animals to show their unique abilities and personalities and enhance human respect and admiration. There is a strong argument to establish a training school for all animal trainers and ensure that there is a well-qualified trainer travelling with each circus, and actively training the animals.

Properly done, the training of circus animals can, on balance, benefit both animals and humans, and lead to greater inter-species knowledge.

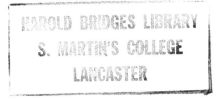

Chapter 7

The arguments against zoos and circuses

Over the last few years, the arguments for equal consideration of animal rights have supported movements against various forms of animal husbandry. Factory farming, which by definition cannot give equal consideration to animals, has come under attack, and has rightly received the main thrust of the offensive [12; 13; 99; 100] and, consequently, of investigative research [11]. This has culminated in the development of codes of practice for farm animal husbandry. Animal experimentation has also been thought about and in many countries ethical committees have been established to examine the acceptability of individual experimental proceedures. In intensive farms and laboratories billions of animals are raised and kept in conditions which prevent them performing much of their behavioural repertoire and where they show obvious signs of distress. With thought and determination, conditions on farms and in laboratories can be improved greatly in these respects for animals, without a lot of extra expense.

Animal welfare movements have been important in motivating public opinion and encouraging legislation and research to make these improvements, but there remains much to be done. Farms can run economically and effectively, and laboratories use some animals for important research where there is no alternative while allowing animals to live in environments where they show little or no signs of distress and which are ecologically, ethologically and ethically acceptable [101]. Old-style zoos, where animals were kept as moving museum specimens, and circuses where animals were kept constantly confined and used as vehicles for derision have rightly come under attack.

However, it is maintained by various groups that both circuses and zoos **by their nature** are unable to give equal consideration to animals, and the animals will suffer in such husbandry systems, therefore they are wrong and must be stopped [35-37].

We have examined so far whether animals in zoos and circuses show signs of distress, and suffer, and we have compared this to other animal-keeping enterprises, such as racing and teaching stables and kennels. There is evidence of distress in all these animal husbandry systems, but is this not because of their bad design or management, rather than because they are unable **by their nature** to exist without causing severe and prolonged suffering to animals? Zoos and circuses can and must change in order to reduce or eliminate any evidence of animal distress, and also to fulfil ecological, other ethological and ethical considerations (see Chapter 9), but there is no reasons why they, like all other animal-keeping enterprises, should not be able to achieve these aims.

The consequences of arguing that animals should not be used or associated with humans leads to what can effectively be called an 'animal apartheid' - in the original sense of 'separate living and development'.

There is a widely held belief that we should give wild animals different treatment - from domestic ones. Therefore circuses and zoos are **by their nature** wrong. That an animal such as a lion that is traditionally wild, even if it has been born and brought up in captivity, must not live in close association with humans or be trained or work for or with people; whereas it is acceptable to catch and train a horse, cat or dog which has been born and brought up in the wild because they are considered 'domestic' animals. In this capter we examine where there is any behavioural evidence for making this distinction, and try to clarify what the important criteria are for species and individuals.

Equal consideration for animals?

This debate has been around longer than that over original sin, but in semi-modern times it was taken up by Salt [102] and then again by Singer [21]. There are those who argue that all sentient life should have equal consideration, even if not equal treatment [21; 24]. Some consider that although this should be the case, where there is a conflict of interests, a hierarchy of interests can be used [14; 22; 23].

One aspect of this debate, on which there is some recent scientific work which is very relevant, is that concerning the similarity or difference between human beings and other animals.

Physical similarities and differences

Even most empirically trained scientists are prepared to admit physical similarities between humans and non-human animals - after all the backbone of modern biological teaching is evolution which teaches that the phylogenetic development of all living species is governed by the same rules. Indeed they argue strongly for the use of mammals in experimentation for medical research on the grounds of physical similarity [104].

Of course not every vertebrate is the same, each species is different and each individual horse or human is also different. There are general similarities but specific differences. This has not and is not always recognised. **Good** science does not use rabbits' eyes to test for irritants to human eyes unless it is certain that the response to the irritants will be the same. Since rabbits' eyes are different from human eyes, this is very unlikely to be the case. However, the rabbit remains more physically similar to a human being than a Honda.

Emotional similarities and differences

Do animals feel emotions, and if so are they like human ones? The ideas of Decartes [89] have had a tremendous influence on this question. He argues that animals, because they have no souls, also have no conscious experience of pain or pleasure: they are only machines. This idea was used almost without question by the behavioural scientists for almost four decades, and is still a major influence in the research and teaching of many behavioural scientists.

When I was a graduate student some 20 years ago, it was heresy to consider that non-human animals might have conscious experiences. One risked expulsion for suggesting it! The change in public opinion, largely as a result of semi-popular books by philosophers questioning such a view, has at last sparked off some self-questioning of this belief by behavioural scientists themselves. Consciousness, cognition and subjective emotional experiences are now exciting 'growth areas' in the research on animal behaviour (90; 91; 106; 108; 109).

In general, few people would deny that animals feel. To my mind a more sensible approach to this issue is to assume that animals **do** feel emotions similar to yours and mine, rather than to assume that the animal is a *tabla rasa* (an empty slate) or a machine. The reason for this approach is commonsense; we see dogs and cats, mice and monkeys responding similarly to humans when frightened or in pain. What are they doing if they are not feeling similar emotions to those you and I would experience in similar conditions?

To say that animals feel pain, but conceptualise it differently [105] is begging the question, as Sapontzis [25] points out, any way you look at it 'pain hurts' and we are in danger of loosing sight of this!

We don't only see animals suffering and in pain, we also see animals apparently feeling happiness or joy, as you or I might: the dog jumping for joy and covering you in embraces on your return, the horse leaping and cavorting around a spring field.

Evolutionarily speaking, it would seem unlikely that emotionality does not enhance survival and therefore even more unlikely that it would have arisen only once: in human beings. It would seem much more likely that other higher vertebrates at least feel, too. A rational approach to the question of what animals feel, which is the approach I favour, is that **until proved otherwise** I must assume that they feel similar emotions to me, just like you do. This means that they not only feel pain, but also pleasure, joy, sorrow, shame, embarrassment and so on. If they do not, why not, and what evidence is there to support this case? The evidence for my case is that I too am an animal, and I feel these things.

Similarities and differences in minds

The sceptic will reply that even if we are prepared to concede that a higher vertebrate at least has basic physical and emotional similarities to us humans, nevertheless the area where animals and humans are profoundly different is in their minds.

What evidence have we for that? It is widely believed that the majority of animal actions are 'instinctive', that they are all prewired before birth.

There are two important objections to this. The first is that as Griffin [106] points out this would require an immense wiring system which it would be difficult, if not impossible, to house in the size of brain that exists. Also, such a system would escalate complexity, something that evolutionary development and biological systems do not usually go in for.

The second objection is that the more we learn about the behaviour of mammals and fish, the more we find how adaptable their behaviour is; in other words, although there are instinctive tendencies to behave in different ways, these can change as a result of lifetime experiences (i.e. learning). Curiously enough, the vast majority of research on learning and how it works has been done, not on humans, but on animals, particularly rats and mice! - a facile recognition of their learning abilities surely!

Even if they learn, the sceptic continues, animals cannot think. True or false? First, what is thinking? If it is putting information together in some sort of pattern and using this knowledge in solving problems or other forms of behaviour, then it becomes difficult to assume that animals don't since they learn and remember. In fact, as Vickie Hearne [107] points out, it is 'commonsense' knowledge that animals think and this is used every day by animal trainers, pet owners and even farmers. If you assume your animal is not thinking, you would not be able to train it... bad trainers and pet owners do, but they soon give up training!

That animals think is now being taken seriously by psychologists. Walker [108], in an extensive review of the subject, concludes that indeed we have to consider **that they do**. To my mind, however, the interesting question is not **if** they think, but **what** they think. This brings one to the field of Cognitive Behaviour. Here the approach is equally two-fold. There are those who put pigeons or rats into boxes and see if they can grasp concepts - such as the concept of a tree, or a hat. Such research has shown that pigeons in particular are able to do this remarkably easily, and they also seem to be able to remember a vast number of individual slides [109].

The other approach is that pioneered by the Gardiners [89] in their exciting research on the chimpanzee Washoe, where the animal became more or less part of the household, and was given a stimulating and complex environment, physically, emotionally and intellectually, and they taught her Amslam - American sign language. Washoe and subsequent young chimps - some raised similarly, some differently - have proved to be able to do relatively complex and original things with language, which was unexpected [50].

All of this adds up to the position that animals are proving to be, even mentally, more similar than different to human beings. If this is the case, then are our current attitudes and legislations for animals adequate, supposing they are a great deal more similar to us than we find convenient to admit? This is a chilling thought because if one continues along this line, it is not just the familiar animal, our pet or that individual or species in whom we are particularly interested whose treatment and use by human beings we must consider, it is all higher animals. This opens the flood gates to doubts about all aspects of our treatment of animals. Should the human bill of rights be applied to animals, and where should it differ?

These doubts have come to me, not as a passing whim but as a serious nightmare. I have to admit that this is not because of my involvement with empirical animal behavioural research for some 20 years, although my interest in this direction prompted this involvement. No, it has come from my involvement in living with animals, in the wild, in captivity and particularly from training or educating animals. To play safe, it would seem ethically obligatory to give equal consideration to the higher vertebrates... birds and mammals at least. But what does this mean, and how can it be managed practically?

There are various positions that have been taken in regard to this:

- Some argue that because of our moral obligations to animals, they should not be used by humans at all [24]. Although there may be some strong arguments for this position, there are serious practical limitations, and it may be that the results are morally less desirable. It is important to examine this position of separate development, 'Animal Apartheid,' which we do in the next section.

- Others will say that it may be acceptable to use domestic animals, within certain limits, because they have been selected over generations to associate with humans, but it is morally indefensible to capture wild animals and force them into contact with humans [36]. Again this is an important argument: does 'wildness' confer special status on animals? If so, why? One of the assumptions for this belief is that species that are traditionally wild behave differently, and therefore have different environmental demands which cannot be fulfilled in captivity. Is this so? We examine this on pages 154-160.

- Others have less well defined positions; for example, some will consider that keeping animals in wildlife parks and zoos is acceptable, but that circuses are **by their nature** morally unacceptable [37]. One thing is clear, and that is that almost all of us who have anything to do with animals are inconsistent in our approach. Some hedge themselves around with rules so that they can shoot some for sport but love others; others distance themselves from animals so that they can then use them for laboratory experimentation or for eating, while treating their own pets with as much consideration as they do people.

- The effects of familiarity on how we treat animals are particularly pertinent to this debate [110; 111]. The more familiar we become with individuals and therefore the greater likelihood of having an emotional relationship with that individual, the more likely we are to give that animal consideration equal to that we give to familiar humans.

- Another approach is to consider that if the animal shows evidence of distress, then the husbandry system is unacceptable. There are problems with measuring distress, but perhaps these are not impossible to overcome (see Chapter 3 and 4).

So the answer to the question of whether animals, at least vertebrates, should have equal consideration is 'yes' because of their similarities to us: physiologically, emotionally and intellectually. But why should this rule out any association between humans and animals; it does not between human and human. Why should it rule out any use of each other provided this is within certain limits. But where are these limits?

Up to this point this book has concentrated on the data that has been collected on the issue of animals in circuses and zoos, and for looking for behavioural indices which may tell us more about what the animal is feeling, at least in terms of distress or pleasure.

The next section examines the above arguments briefly, and attempts to take the debate a step forward by coming to some tenuous conclusions.

This is not the last word of course, nor can there ever be a last word as, unlike Dawkins [15], I cannot have such faith in that puck **truth**!

Animal Apartheid - Animal-human separation

If then we should give equal consideration to other animals - at least other vertebrates - then surely they should all go off and lead their own lives in the wilderness? We humans should have nothing to do with them, use them, or be used by them. This is the position taken by many Animal Rights proponents. Here we consider what the consequences of this would be, who it would benefit, and whether it is necessarily the case that giving equal consideration to animals must result in such 'Animal Apartheid', used in its original meaning : separate development. First, let us look at the consequences for humans.

Human loss and benefit

We will consider if this approach is likely to benefit humans. This, coupled with no killing of animals, means that there would be no killing of animals for meat and little or no use of animal products. This would indeed be a physical hardship to some humans, and a psychological one to others. It would require a very radical restructuring of how society operates, and is unlikely to be implemented. Nevertheless, it could be argued that pain and distress to humans so caused is essentially trivial when balanced against the animals' gains, and therefore in an ideal world this is what we would want to achieve.

I think there are very serious objections to this argument. In the first place, such an approach presents a very anthropocentric world where animals live in Animalistans separated from humans, there is little or no contact between each other, and therefore neither camp has much knowledge concerning the other. This, in fact, is the situation that is gradually being achieved in some urban metropolises, where some individuals and societies are constantly working towards banning animals, including all pets within them. On the occasions that my dog and I have made forays into the cities during this study, we have been made very aware of this. It has indeed resembled the treatment that many coloured human beings encounter in South Africa.

What are the consequences of this? The humans, although they may have access to innumerable beautiful television films, lectures and talks, although they may be taught that animals exist and to respect them and so on, they **never** experience them, or have relationships with them. As a result, the humans grow up increasingly alienated from the natural biological world, from its joys and its traumas. They may have learnt to respect and admire animals as alien beings, perhaps like some of us might respect and admire the Queen, but the vast majority of us will never get to know her as a person, and have an individual relationship with her. Our love of her is restricted to her as a symbol of the Monarchy, Nationhood, Patriotism, or whatever we make it. So with animals - they become symbols of Nature, The Wild, The Biosphere, The Noble Savage etc.

150

Only if we are able ourselves to associate closely with animals can we experience individual relationships with them. Our distant respect can become, through familiarity and emotional involvement, knowledge, respect and responsibility for individuals as members of our family.

One of Oxfam's slogans has been that we should recognise ourselves as the 'family of man'. Could we not benefit by extending this circle to the 'family of sentient beings' perhaps or the 'family of mammals', or 'the family of animals in my immediate surroundings'. The closer we live with the animals, if we want to, the more we may find we have in common, but certainly the more chance we have of loving and respecting animals.

The many areas in which companion animals benefit human beings have hit the limelight recently [112; 113]. There has been some euphoria concerning the importance pets have been found to have in helping handicapped or disturbed human beings. One must be careful, however, that the animals' interests are not carried away on the self-congratulatory wings of human philanthropy.

Thus it is that one must argue that the human losses if we were to have 'Animalistans' are not trivial.

Animal gains and losses

However, do the animal gains from the proposed Animalistans outweigh the human benefits from having contact with animals?

It is widely assumed, given a chance, that animals (here I am talking predominantly about mammals) would gallop off into the wilderness and live happily ever after, and that animals will always, or almost always if they are 'normal', prefer to associate and live with members of their own species. From this it follows that associations with humans, or other species, is forced upon them by humans.

This is blatantly not the case; for example, many dogs given the opportunity do not prefer association with dogs all the time, or indeed the majority of the time. Dogs are a social species, and therefore should surely have free social contact with other dogs at least part of each day, but to suppose that they will always choose the company of other dogs in preference to humans is not the case. It may be that dogs are a special case; cats, however, behave in much the same way, as do many other house pets. There has been little serious study of this question in the larger animals, but elephants, rhino, giraffe, eland, civet cats, duikers, horses, cattle and deer to name a few will frequently choose human company, usually an individual human, in preference to other conspecifics. This, of course, is usually the result of past experience during the lifetime of the individual, but it is not necessary for such animals to have been 'imprinted' on human beings during their infancy as a result of being bottle raised and separated from their mothers.

It is assumed that it is genetically programmed for wild animals to avoid human beings. There are several places where wild animals are not afraid of human beings because they have never met them, or been hunted (e.g. the Galapogos islands), at least until recently. In the Pacific there used to be a group of vegetarian islanders called the Taseday. They lived symbiotically with the wild animals which they did not hunt, abuse or interfere with [115] - so it is possible.

Given a chance then, do all animals that are in contact with humans gallop off into the wilderness and live happily ever after? In other words, do they not only prefer their own species but avoid humans? Again this is the result of past experience; however as a general rule mammals at least tend to have their own home or familiar areas which they will only leave if pursued or seriously frightened in some way. Hill sheep will confine themselves to their own 'hefts' or home areas and rarely if ever move out of them although they could travel often for hundreds of miles. If horses are familiar with having freedom of movement and there is no traffic or other spooks to frighten them, they will not dash off willy-nilly into the sunset. However, if they are frightened they will, but they will make their own way back later.

Field studies have shown that all the non-migratory mammals have home areas of some sort, and even migratory ones will stick to known routes [116]. Provided then that animals have not had bad experiences in the presence of humans, why should they not hang around and have a home area - their own stable and the human habitation?

In the circus, animals such as ponies and horses, dogs, occasionally llamas, and even macaws were sometimes let loose to wander around the tents and trailers or fly where they will, and come back. The elephants in several circuses were also let loose to wander round in the company of their trainer or presenter. This requires a remarkable act of faith as either the animals could be damaged by the public or traffic, who are all around, or the animals could injure the public, or the public's property. That the circus people continue to do this is not I would suggest because they are stupid, but because they know their individual animals well enough to know that they will not want to go away from the camp, attack or injure people or property. The camp may move every few days to a new place, but as with the Bedouins and their horses, camels, sheep and goats, the camp remains the centre of the animals' home area, wherever it is, in the middle of the Sahara or Tottenham Roundabout.

Other examples of cases in which animals choose human-dominated environments in preference to 'the wild' are when wild animals, such as foxes and badgers, move into the suburbs or cities. These areas can act as resource centres, or places where the animals can avoid persecution.

The individual animal's past experience is clearly very important here. What, for example, about the urban dog which has lived in an urban environment all of his life? He may have been for weekends to the country, for bracing country walks, but he is an urban dog. Like his owners, the dog may well be able to get used to the rural environment should he have to, but his familiar life is his flat, the black bitch downstairs, the beastly terriers' mark on the lamppost outside the greengrocers', and so on. It is difficult to argue that such a dog would necessarily be 'better off' and 'happier' in the countryside. The crucial factor in assessing this may well be the degree of behavioural restriction, and his relationship with humans. It is **not** necessarily true that no contact with humans is most important for his happiness.

Even traditionally 'wild' species who have been captive bred and raised often choose to stay around humans. This makes 'reintroduction' programmes difficult [117]. Thus it seems there is no clear evidence that animals that are familiar with humans prefer exclusive association with their own species, or that they will always avoid humans and leave human-infested familiar areas, or that they are necessarily better off, and would have a higher quality of life if they did.

The other argument for 'Animalistans' is that by working for or with humans, entertaining them, or being available to be looked at by them, their personal liberties and dignities are necessarily infringed. In other words, that all animal training by humans is necessarily wrong. This we have examined in the previous chapter. Again, the conclusion is, that provided the animals show no evidence of prolonged distress and are kept in ecologically, ethologically and ethically sound environments (see Chapter 9), there is no reason to assume that this is wrong. In fact, it could benefit the animal and the human and lead to greater inter-species understanding.

Do wild animals have special status?

The behavioural effects of domestication

A distinction is often made between domestic and wild animals in terms of their husbandry and treatment by human beings. Simply put, it is usually considered that a prerequisite for keeping wild animals is that they should be kept in 'natural' conditions, which among other things usually includes having as little contact with human beings as possible. Thus what is appropriate for 'wild' animals is quite different than for domestic animals, and consequently 'wild' animals have special status. For example, camels which have been 'domestic' for some centuries are trained and ridden by human beings, and this is not considered, except by a few, cruel or unethical. However, training and riding a giraffe would more than likely be considered inappropriate and wrong, even though the giraffe may have been born in captivity and been hand-reared whereas the camel may have been born and brought up feral (gone wild). There are usually two reasons that people give for this belief:

i)   that the wild animal is a part of nature, and that only what is natural (whatever this is, see page 00) is appropriate for it;

ii)   that during the course of domestication humans have manipulated domestic animals and controlled their breeding to a point where their behaviour, and consequently their needs and desires, have been genetically changed. We will consider what evidence there is that the fundamental behaviour of domestic animals has been changed genetically.

It is often assumed that because animals' morphology (body shape, size, colours etc.) has changed dramatically as a result of domestication involving artificial selection, that their innately determined behaviour has too. If such is the case, then it would be possible to argue that wild and domestic animals might need to be considered

FIGURE 62 **A COMPARISON OF SOME BEHAVIOUR IN SEVERAL SPECIES OF BOVIDAE INCLUDING DOMESTIC CATTLE ***

SPECIES	Habitat p/f	SocialOrg			Home range	Defend terri-tory	Communication					Food		Source (30)
		A	B	C			1	2	3	4	5	gr	br	
African buffalo	+	+	?+	++	+	-	++	++	+	+	+	++	+	Sinclair 1974
Bison	+	+	+	++	+	-	++	++	+	+	+	++	+	McHugh 1958
Bos Indicus	+	+	++	++	+	-	++	++	+	+	+	++	+	Reinhardt 1980
Auroch (B. taurus)	+	+	?	++	+	-	++	++	+	+	+	?		Cole 1961
B. taurus (feral)	+	+	++	++	+	-	++	++	+	+	+	++	+	Schloeth 1961
B. taurus (domestic + calves)	pasture	+	++	++	?	-	++	++	+	+	+	++	+	Kiley-Worthing-ton & de la Plain 1983
B. taurus (domestic - calves)	housed	+	++	?	?	-	++	++	+	+	+	++	+	Koch1968 Zimmermann M. 1976.Pers.Obs.

* 1st published in 73

KEY
Habitat — plains / forest
Social Organisation — A = small / large herds
B = preference for peers
C = multi-male troupes
Communication — 1 = smell
2 = taste
3 = touch
4 = vision
5 = auditory
Food — gr = grazing
br = browsing

differently. We will examine the notion that animals' innate behaviour has changed dramatically during the course of domestication.

The obvious thing to do first is to look at some populations of domestic animals who have been domesticated for some thousands of years, but who have escaped or been allowed to go wild again (feral populations), or to look at domestic animals which are in close contact with humans, but are able to organise their societies as they wish, and exercise all the behaviour in their repertoires. The behaviour of these populations can then be compared with that of completely wild populations of that species, if there are any (or what we know of them from reconstructions and close relatives) to see the degree to which their innate behaviour has changed. In the last two decades many populations of feral animals - such as cattle, horses, pigs, hens, sheep, goats, dogs and cats - have been studied. Where these comparisons have been made, the evidence is that behaviour such as habitat preferences and social organisation, mother-infant behaviour, courtship, sexual behaviour, and communication has changed very little. In other words, when domestic animals are able to choose how and where they live they behave as if they have never been domesticated in these respects (Figures 62 and 63).

Thus there is no evidence that innate behavioural tendencies **relating to such fundamental behaviours** have changed greatly. It may be argued that there has not been enough evidence collected on this issue; however, there is enough to demonstrate that this is more likely than not to be so, and that, **until proved otherwise,** we must assume this to be the case.

There is another reason why such fundamental behavioural changes are unlikely to have occurred during domestication and this is that there has in general been no rigid selection pressure exerted by humans in the breeding of domestic animals against such behaviours. Humans have been selecting animals during domestication for size, colour, particular body shapes and so on, but such things as how the animals organise their societies have not been of particular consequence and so have not been the subject of selection by humans.

So has the behaviour of domestic animals changed at all during the course of domestication? Have humans selected for appropriate behaviours and what are these? It would seem indeed that they have. For example they have selected for adaptability, so that we find Hereford cattle living in areas with high tropical temperatures (90 degrees C), and also in parts of Canada where the temperatures can be as low as minus 50 degrees C; where the major problem for the cattle is to see as their breathe freezes from their forelock in icicles over their eyes! Adaptability to husbandry conditions is also something we must have selected for, although it is evident from the high level of

FIGURE 63 A COMPARISON OF THE SOCIAL ORGANISATION OF SEVERAL SPECIES OF EQUIDS, INCLUDING FERAL AND DOMESTIC HORSES**

	Source	Family groups	Perm-anent	Bach-elor groups	Soli-tary males	Temp-orary groups	Home range	Solita territ males
Asiatic wild horses	Mohr 1971 Groves 1974	?	5-6	?	?	X	*	X
Plains zebra	Klingel 1974	*	4-7	2-3	?	X	*	X
Mountain zebra	Klingel 1974	*	6-7	4-8	?	X	*	X
New Forest feral/wild	Tyler 1972	*	1-5	?	?	X	*	
Camargue ponies Feral	Duncan 1979 Goldsmidt-Rothschild 1980	*	3-10	?	?	X	*	?
Pryer mountain feral horses	Feist & McCullough 1980	*	5	1-2	*	X	*	X
Grand Canyon feral horses	Berger 1977	?	5	?	*	X	*	X
Domestic horse at pasture	Kiley-Worthington 1987	*	?	*	*	X	*	?
Wild asses	Klingel 1974 Groves 1974	-	NO	NO	-	2-8	*	
Grevys zebra	Klingel 1974	-	NO	NO	-	2-6	*	
Sable Island feral horses	Welsh 1973	?	6	1-2			*	
Shackleford Island feral horses	Rubenstein 1981	*	12	1-4	*	*	*	

** = 1st published in 29   * = occurs   ? = unknown   X = does not occur

physiological stress, disease and behavioural distress (including behavioural problems) and the need for drugs and surgery, that the rate of intensification of housing is outstripping the rate of selection for the ability to survive and thrive in such buildings. It has also been suggested that the onset of physiological measures of 'adaptability' (the point at which stress syndromes are detected) are different in wild and domestic species, as they will be between individuals.

Humans may also have selected, by default rather than consciously. They may have selected in this way for:

- a willingness to cooperate with humans;
- for less timidity towards humans;
- for low levels of aggression;
- for learning to read the methods used by humans to communicate with their animals;

It has been suggested that the threshold of response to a particular stimulus may have changed as a result of domestication. As a general rule, this results in domestic animals often appearing less reactive.

This may be why domestic animals are considered easier to train and handle than wild captive-born animals.

On the other hand it may be:

- our **lack of knowledge** of the behaviour and expessions of wild species that makes them apparently more difficult to train;
- it may be the result of **self-fulfilling** prophecies. This is often very influential on the way an animal behaves. In all contact with animals, the way the human behaves to the animal and her expectations of how the animal is likely to behave is extremely important in determining how the animal actually **does** behave. For example, if the human is told that the dog, cat, lion, elephant, horse (or whatever) is aggressive, unfriendly and dangerous, that human will have certain expectations. This may include apprehension and fear, this will be reflected in body language and conveyed to the animal. The result is that the animal picks up the 'vibes' - fear and apprehension - and himself becomes apprehensive and fearful. This is picked up by the human, who becomes more apprehensive and so it snowballs until eventually the animal runs, or attacks in defensive threat, fulfilling the initial prophecy. If one is told (as one constantly is) that wild animals are 'unreliable, difficult to train, and often dangerous', then these are one's expectations and this is what occurs. This applies to any animal, or human for that matter, as any psychiatrist or trainer knows.
- or **past experience** of the individual animal.

None of these later explanations would require any genetical change to the animals' behaviour. What is clear is that the experiences during an individual's lifetime, grossly affects all these behaviours. For example, rearing individuals away from their mothers affects not only their behaviour towards their own peers, their social organisation and preferred associations but how they behave as mothers themselves [62]. There is a high incidence in zoos of infant rejection and poor mothering usually because the mothers themselves have not been mother reared.

How animals are handled and treated by humans, whether they are domestic or wild, affects how they behave towards humans. Whether they were caught from the wild or are feral; what age they were when this happened, or where they were born also enormously affects their behaviour to humans and how they adapt to new or different environments.

The animal or human is born with certain inherited genetic **tendencies**. These, among other things, are to perform all the behaviour in its repertoire when appropriate. Domestic animals may have an inherited tendency to be adaptable but this does not overrule their species' specific behavioural tendencies. How an animal, wild or domestic, develops these tendencies is up to its lifetime experiences.

These considerations argue that domestic and wild animals must be given similar rather than different status since fundamental behaviour has not apparently been changed genetically. They also argue that it is particularly important to take into account the individual's past experience when considering the ethological soundness and ethical appropriateness of the husbandry: if it is 'cruel'. So giving different consideration to wild, as opposed to domestic, animals must depend more on whether they have been captive bred or wild caught and at what age, and their other individual past experiences, rather than their status as a species of being 'Wild' or 'Domestic'. This effectively means that sometimes horses, cats or dogs could find circus life more inappropriate than lions, leopards or elephants (see Chapter 9), as well as vice versa.

There remains the argument that wild animals (whatever their individual origin) are closely related to nature and must remain so. It is 'unnatural' for lions to be in an exercise cage or the ring, and therefore by definition wrong. This of course depends on how one is to define Nature and Natural. This we have already discussed (page 132) and it would appear to be more difficult than at first sight, and even if we can agree on what is natural, then why should doing other activities necessarily be wrong? Or is it only certain types of other activities that are wrong, and on what grounds are these decisions to be made?

Let me make it clear here that I am **not** arguing that **all** animals should live in close association with human beings. There is an important, perhaps vital, place for truly wild species to live their lives in the wilderness for either human or non-human animals ('Animalistans' sometimes). But this is **not the only environment** in which they can and should live, either for humans or non-human animals. That their experiences must always be restricted to this is at least questionable. Yet there remains the sceptic who, although aware that there does not appear to be any evidence for genetic change in fundamental behaviour as a result of domestication, still considers that a lion with a similar background is likely to respond differently to a human than a domestic cat, and that it is 'more difficult' to cater for a traditionally wild animal's physical and behavioural needs and desires. This seems to be an intuitive idea many people have which may well be cultural. It appears to be in the same camp as the Descartian idea that animals do not have conscious experiences which so many have accepted for so long. At the very least, it needs careful examination and testing.

It would therefore seem that as a rule and **until proved otherwise,** that there is little rationale from which to argue that wild and domestic animals have different status, unless the terms 'wild' and 'domestic' relate to the individual's past experience rather than any other characteristic. There are, of course, certain wild or domestic animals who might have special status, for example an endangered wild species such as the panda, or a very rare domestic breed of rat. However, this status is **not** related to their **wildness** or **domesticity** but in this case to their **rarity** [118].

If we are to give equal status to both wild and domestic species, this means that the same criteria for acceptable management must be applied to both (see Chapter 9). This will mean as many changes to our husbandry of traditionally domestic animals as to the husbandry of traditionally wild animals.

Chapter 8

Arguments for zoos and circuses

The arguments usually given for zoos are:

1) The conservation and breeding of endangered species.

2) The carrying out of research as a result of having animals available.

3) Education of people, in zoology and particularly in environmental issues.

4) Provision of entertainment, and recreational facilities.

The majority of zoos are privately owned and have to survive financially on their own earnings; unlike farms where often the main stated aim is given as:

5) To run an efficient business which makes some money.

Zoos very rarely, if ever, mention this as one of their aims, although it clearly must be, even if only to cover costs.

Circuses have been slower to state their aims and put themselves across to the public as doing a social service. They usually therefore confine their stated aims to (4) and (5), and sometimes (3). However, on questioning, the main reason for the people who actually travel with the circus being there is:

6) A way of life.

There is no particular reason why, in theory at least, they should not try and fulfil (1) and (2) (breeding of endangered species, and research) and in fact one British circus has been more successful in breeding the endangered snow leopard than many zoos.

All of these seem, at face value, worthy aims that few would quarrel with, even if they do consider that animals should have equal consideration to humans and are beings of moral worth. The arguments arise from:

a)   the degree to which these aims are, or can in fact be fulfilled, and

b)   the sacrifice of the individual animal to a low quality of life in order to try and fulfil these aims - whether the end justifies the means.

There are other arguments that can be made for and against zoos and circuses which to my mind have not received the attention that they might.

We will consider each argument in turn, and examine the degree to which the aims can or are being fulfilled

1) The breeding of endangered species

This argument is used often by zoos as their central *raison d'etre*. It is a relatively new idea which was pioneered by Gerald Durrell at the small Jersey Zoo about 15 years ago when there began to be more public concern about the extinction of species [118]. Since it is usually considered of particular importance by zoos themselves, it is the subject of a separate section (pages 172-173).

2) Research

If zoos argue that they contribute to our knowledge of animals, then how much research have they done and are they doing, and what type of research is this?

The truth of it is that although in principle most zoos are in favour of having some research continuing on the behaviour of their animals, particularly now they have come under attack, very few zoos have financed research, even that which might lead to their own animals benefiting. Several American zoos have financed research personnel to go and work in the field in Africa and Asia, (e.g. The Smithsonian in Washington; The Bronx Zoo in New York), but very few have even one research person on their staff. Some zoos may encourage students and research personnel to come into the zoos and do some short-term work on their animals, but normally the money for this work has to be found from other sources.

Some of the financing is for 'high profile' research, such as the tiger reproduction project at Minnesota Zoo, or the artificial insemination of giant pandas at London Zoo [9; 10]. This is research which comes under the auspices of Biological Research but is more biochemical/physiological. This research is often not involved with the whole animal even as a representative of a species, but rather one system. Although in the field particularly of veterinary science, such research **can** contribute to the welfare of animals in zoos, the use that is sometimes made of the zoo animals as laboratory specimens is not often known or exposed to the public. This type of research is suspect for two reasons:

i)   there is often no clear likelihood of the species or the individual benefitting from the pain and suffering caused;

ii)   there are a host of immediate problems in terms of how to design the animals' environments to cater for all aspects of their behaviour, and overcome behavioural abnormalities.

Zoos are becoming a little more conscious of the need to be seen to be financing research - and relevant research. There has recently been some advances in this areas [95; 97], but this remains an area of valid criticism [35].

Circuses have not usually considered research as an area where they could contribute. However, there are three areas where they are uniquely placed to do this, that is in research on:

i)   differences between individuals: personality profiles, etc.
ii)   training and human animal interactions; and most importantly
iii) in the field of animal cognition.

One British circus proprietor has mentioned as a priority that she would like to see more research being done on the behaviour of animals in circuses [119]. This may result in further financial contributions in this direction. Some European circuses have certainly encouraged research on their animals [120], but again there is little evidence that they have financed directly any research to date.

3) Education

Lately, many zoos have been taking this issue seriously, and many have educational officers whose job it is to think up and publicise interesting and stimulating educational activities and displays for school children and families. Some zoos, for example the Bronx, New York, also have 'high tech' teaching aids to try to put across environmental messages to adults.

This education almost exclusively concentrates on environmental issues, such as the destruction of the forests, loss of habitats worldwide, climatic changes, and species information. The 'exhibits' in the 'collection' are simply representatives of a species whose habitat and habits are described briefly. There is in this way a heavy emphasis on 'science', although some rely on imaginative imagery and originality in putting across conservation messages and general zoological information.

Occasionally the animal's name will be displayed on the cage or enclosure (because otherwise keepers are pestered constantly by the public wanting to know what the animals' names are), but more often than not the animals do not have names and the keepers are discouraged from any handling or direct interaction with an individual animal. This leads to many problems with the care and maintenance of many animals, and has in fact led to the death of some animals at well-known zoos (e.g. an elephant at London Zoo in the 1980s). In fact, a couple of zoos have now dropped their 'zero-handling' philosophies (e.g. Chester Zoo) in favour of the handling of some animals. The rationale of which animals should be handled and which not does not seem to have been very clearly defined.

I have only come across one zoo, and that a particularly interesting small private zoo (Twycross), where, although environmental messages are frequently and imaginatively displayed, the central concern is with the individual. The management began the zoo originally, not with ideas of having displays, collections, and zoological gardens, but rather to provide a home for unwanted pet primates. Although the zoo has grown and is apparently in line with the mainline establishment thrust of zoological gardens, the fundamental philosophy is very different and permeates through the general atmosphere and to all working there. The concern is **primarily** with the individual rather than the species.

Concern with the individual as opposed to the species may result in emotional bonds establishing between animal and handler or keeper. In general in zoological circles such an approach is considered 'unscientific', and mainline zoos like to be considered primarily 'scientific' establishments. Concern with the individual smacks of pet keeping, empathy, and emotional involvement... although why behavioural science should deny or ignore emotionality is mysterious. Nevertheless, there is now a growing awareness of the importance of individual differences in ethology and the behavioural sciences [131]. Emotional involvement of humans with animals does not necessarily indicate human inadequacy, is not necessarily a substitute for human-human emotional involvement but can be something enriching and important in **itself.**

Much can be learnt both about the animal and its species, and about oneself and other humans. As a result, changes can be made in human beings' attitudes to animals, and their own place in the biosphere by developing and encouraging emotional attachments and studying individuals. In addition, the general public often find this a much easier entrance to general environmental education (note the large number of children's books about animals) than the perhaps more immediately intellectual interest in species and 'environmental issues' which is usually adopted by zoos. The reason why Virginia Mackenna and Bill Travers founded 'Zoo Check' was because they had become involved with **individual lions.**

Circuses **by their nature** emphasise the individual, the training is individually done, and the performances rely on relationships between individual human and animal. Thus they are uniquely placed to educate the public in both individual and species differences and similarities, and those between humans and other animals. At present very little education of this nature is done in the circuses, although many would like to see it (Appendix 3). If circuses are going to continue to exist, then it is important that they take their educational role seriously and develop it.

4) The provision of recreation and entertainment

This is where both zoos and circuses began. Provided the animals do not suffer, and the environment and their survival is not threatened by providing for human recreation and entertainment, there seems little reason why this should be condemned.

Zoos often combine their animal 'exhibits' with the provision of playgrounds, fair grounds, picnic areas, gardens, restaurants, and status architecture, the idea being to draw as many people in as possible. Like everything else in the zoo these are sometimes done well and thoughtfully, and sometimes not. Occasionally further entertainment is provided by the animals giving rides, pulling carts, or giving displays, chimpanzees' tea parties or dolphin and whale displays. Here there is a combination of zoo and circus, and they are often very popular. The acceptability or not of such displays from the point of view of the animal has been discussed in Chapter 6.

Similarly the circus, although fundamentally there to entertain and perform with their animals and human acts, often has a menagerie, or small travelling zoo. This attracts people to wander round the encampment during the day, to attend the training sessions (if there are any), and that in turn will encourage them to come to the performance.

Provided the animals' acts are appropriate for the animals and designed to make people respect them, and they and the environment do not suffer as a result, there is little reason to condemn travelling menageries and animal performances. One of the arguments used against circuses is that the animals lose dignity by performing and this undermines humans' attitudes to them. We have discussed this already on page 129 *et seq.*.

What evidence is there that by providing recreation for humans, zoos and circuses are having a beneficial effect on humans or animals, directly or indirectly? There are obvious advantages, for example they can provide pleasant surroundings where families will go to relax and enjoy themselves away from day to day life. Although such environments are not completely rural, they can introduce the urban dweller, often for the first time, to the real experience of other sentient intelligent beings and other aspects of the natural world, and offer facilities for her to ponder on her ideas, attitudes to and understanding of the living world outside her own.

Often they provide experiences of the live animals, their smells, their presence and size which cannot be gained from television wildlife films. Particularly in circuses and perhaps the children's zoo, the public can often touch and directly interact with individuals, which is possibly the best education of all, and certainly the most popular. Humans seem to want to do this. They will immediately ask the name of an animal, and then they will want to feed him or her in order to have a direct interaction with the animal. In the circus most of the audience will go out the back after a performance to see the animals close to, perhaps even touch them and interact with them.

These are things that the wild animal, the animal in a safari park and the television film cannot provide. Perhaps the most important way to change humans' attitudes to animals is by increasing their familiarity with them, not to admire the animals from a distance as beautiful paintings, but as intelligent beings that love or hate, learn and think, eat and defecate, and in many ways are more similar than different to human beings.

5) To make money, and run an efficient business
Although this is rarely if ever a stated aim of either zoos or circuses, unlike farms who often give their *raison d'etre* as money making, nevertheless it usually has to be a central criterion. Certainly zoos, except in some Eastern-bloc cities, are not considered as a service like schools or research institutes which are not expected to

make any money or even cover their costs. Some zoos are sponsored in some way or another, by city councils or foundations, but they are usually still expected to cover their running costs from gate fees and other money-making activities.

The majority of zoos, though, are entirely self-financing and they must not only finance their running costs, but any capital improvements or changes that they require. One is constantly reminded by the management that the economics are a key issue in many zoos when suggesting changes or improvements to animal housing or management. Yet some zoos spend very large sums on 'status' buildings which receive much publicity and are often used to enhance national standing, for example the Snowdon Aviary or Hugh Casson's Rhino and Elephant House at London Zoo, the Jungle World at the Bronx and many others.

In urban zoos (usually because of the need to make money by increasing the gate), there is a constant competition for space: people versus the animals. Often the result is that more space is devoted to people for their pathways, toilets, restaurants, play areas, picnic areas and gardens than for the animals' housing and runs. This is a difficult problem to resolve, but with good planning and a real commitment to improving the conditions for the animals, it usually can be, and it does not necessitate large expenditures.

The rising land prices, particularly in inner cities, has ensured that many zoos have considerable capital assets. Some have cashed in on some of these assets to buy land outside the city and start wildlife parks, such as London Zoo and San Diego, California. However, one cannot help thinking that if their priorities really **were** conservation, conservation education and research, that they might do more good for these causes by selling out and giving their money to organisations which exist only to do these things, or otherwise to start their own foundations or conservation centres where the animals can be in their native habitats.

With the exception of the Moscow State Circus, and possibly some other Eastern-bloc circuses, the circuses throughout the world are self-financing and usually they make this quite clear. They are run as businesses: one of the major reasons for running a business, for some animal businesses often the only one, is to make money (e.g. farming).

Recently circuses in Britain have had declining audiences and have had a hard time financially. If money making was their only, or their prime, motive for running circuses, many would have quit. With their considerable capital assets (trucks, tents, animals, and often land for winter quarters) they could successfully have gone into other businesses. However, few of them have and this would seem to be because circus is a unique way of life; the only type of life which many circus people have experienced since they tend to be born and remain in the circus all their lives. In fact, some circuses do run other businesses to help finance the travelling circus in hard times: making and hiring out tents is a favourite one; others run safari parks and animal-training businesses.

Nothing succeeds like success in circus as in other businesses. As a circus begins to become prosperous, the standards go up, the performance improves, the atmosphere becomes positive and this attracts more people. It also allows improvements in, for example, the animal housing and transport facilities, the tent seating, hiring of a band instead of having taped music, and so on. This difference was very obvious when I visited Circus Knie in Switzerland which is considered a very respectable, commendable institution. There is a children's matinee, but adults attend the evening performance and it is treated rather like going to the opera or ballet.

6) A way of life

Only a few zoo directors or keepers (and those of small zoos that they have usually started themselves), say they run the zoo because it is a way of life. As a rule they do it because it is a job which allows them to exercise their particular skills, and they leave their normal house in the suburbs and go to work and come home in the evening to their families in much the same way as the vast majority of people.

On the other hand, the circus proprietors and directors, as a rule, travel with the tented circuses. This is a different way of life. They are nomads and live in trailers or caravans, and apparently have no wish to have houses. Indeed often there are houses at their winter quarters, but in almost all cases the houses are not lived in but are used for storage. When the circus people move to these quarters for their short winter break (December to March) they usually stay in their trailers. Rather than being relieved to be in one place for a time, they often complain after a few weeks and develop 'itchy feet' aching to get back on the road.

When on the road, the circus people live 24 hours a day at the encampment. Then after a short period they take the whole thing down and pack it all into trucks to erect the whole 'village' - or in some cases, township - in another place that night. The logistics, independence, self-reliance, ability to cope with all contingencies, entrepreneurial skills, and sheer hard work are very impressive.

All sorts of people, from ex-criminals to bank managers or lawyers, may join the circus for short periods of time to help in lowly capacities - such as ring boys and grooms. The circus forms its own society and although they must mix easily with people wherever they go, nevertheless the close-knit circus community functions like an extended family and they look after each other. The very young and the very old travel with the circus, and there is always a job that person can do. It is not unusual to find four generations of a family with a travelling circus.

Despite the hard work and often primitive living conditions, this way of life is very attractive to some from outside the circus. Several who have joined the circus said that they feel that at last they belong somewhere. Another attraction is that it is a classless society - one's background and status outside the circus become irrelevant, what matters is your performance within it, and commitment to it: 'The show must go on'. It is possible in a relatively short time to work one's way up from being a tent hand, ring boy or groom, to being an 'artiste' and then to being hired by other circuses, maybe in other lands. There is a constant exchange of artists and acts around the world, and circus people always know, or often are related to, other circus people the other side of the world. Even small British circuses touring around village greens will have some artistes from romantic-sounding places - Morocco, Italy, or wherever; circuses are truly international communities. As a result of these things, and because the circus will often give a chance to a young person who would like to try out his/her own creativity, animal training, or acting abilities, there is a constant recruit of people joining the circuses annually. Not all stay there for life, but a fair percentage do, often by marrying into an old circus family.

Another characteristic is that the circus people live all the time with their animals. The result is familiarity with, and treatment of each animal as an individual. Young animals of many species are often raised in the trailers, and with the exception of a few of the large cats, all the animals are handled daily.

It is more than a 'sub-culture'; it is rather a 'culture' of its own with its own priorities and value.

There is much to admire in circus culture and in this age of increasing uniformity of human culture, there would be much to lose if circuses were to go. If it can be retained, while also allowing the animals to have a high quality of life and suffer minimal distress, then why should circuses be banned or outlawed?

To conclude, there is no insurmountable reason why all of these aims should not be fulfilled for circuses, with the possible exception of 'breeding endangered species' which it might be argued is likely to be more successful in the animals' natural habitat. The type of research needs to be examined carefully, with the **individual** animal's interests paramount. This is not always the case in the zoos. It could also be argued that **environmental education** might be better achieved in different surroundings, and with different modes than 'displaying exhibits in collections'.

There is a very neglected area of education and research in zoos which would make a better argument for zoos, although circuses are probably generally better placed to do this: this is to emphasise the uniqueness, intelligence and abilities of individuals as representatives of species. Their similarities, in terms of emotional response to human beings, and the sophistication of possible communication between humans and other species can be best displayed in training and thoughtful animal performances.

The degree to which these criteria are actually fulfilled varies greatly, as do the priorities which different zoos and circuses give to them.

The zoos are least good at the argument they make most of: breeding endangered species. Although some species have been bred successfully in zoos, for every species bred, zoos over the course of history have contributed to the extinction of another by creating a market for their capture. Indeed the trade in rare and endangered species to 'exhibit' and try to breed continues to exist. The foetal transplants and similar biotechnological advances are open to severe ethical and scientific question in this context and should **not** be used by zoos to support their existence. The individual animal's needs should be considered, as they would if such techniques were to be applied to human beings.

Environmental and ethological field research is being conducted by a few zoos, but zoos may not be the best place to do this. What is happening in only a few zoos is research on optimising the animals' environments and fulfilling their physical and behavioural needs within the context of a zoo. Thus there should be no evidence that the animals' life within the zoo is of low quality or that the animal is distressed or severely restricted behaviourally. This is an area that requires an inter-disciplinary knowledge and a holistic approach, as well as originality, creativity and practical expertise. The case for the continual existence of zoos would be strengthened infinitely if such research programmes were more frequent and seriously embarked upon, and such work was not left to those outside the zoos to finance.

Although zoos have recently developed interesting environmental educational programmes, nevertheless it has been argued that this can be better done by television and films without the animals having to be confined in artificial environments [35]. Again one feels that their jumping on the environmental bandwagon in justifying themselves might be misplaced, and opens their approach to more criticisms than achievement. It might well be that zoos, as well as circuses, should rather concentrate on giving experiences and education that the television and film cannot do.

Zoos do provide recreational facilities which are often much appreciated by the public. These are nowadays better designed and in keeping with the environmental philosophy. However, one is somewhat suspicious about whether the priorities are right when the zoo is famous for winning prizes for its rose gardens (Chester Zoo, England)! A careful, self-critical eye should be directed at themselves from time to time by the zoo directorate. The environmental impact both locally and globally must be assessed. Using imported timber from equatorial forests in the construction of the 'save the equatorial forests' exhibit is not what most people would consider appropriate (see Chapter 9).

That one of the main aims of zoos and circuses is to make money (however this is spent) is a truism, and it would be silly to deny it. It might well be that the business is not always particularly well run and that a saving in one direction, such as carrying out certain animal management practices which require less labour, could free money to be used in a better way for the animals' welfare. 'Good' animal management is not necessarily more expensive. In fact, one of the ways in which improvements in the animals' management are being made in the circuses is by such suggestions.

Circuses are now beginning to think about arguments, other than providing recreation and entertainment and making a living, to justify themselves in the public's increasingly critical eye. They are uniquely placed to contribute in many ways, but must do more of this.

Conservation and zoos and circuses

Arguments for the care of the environment tend to get thoroughly muddled up with arguments either for or against zoos in particular. Their relevance is not always clear [e.g. 9; 35]. We will try and make some sense of the arguments here, and their validity, or not as the case may be.

In the last decade or so, zoos have come under attack from animal welfare and environmental organisations, which are not necessarily the same. Many zoos have, as a result, argued that their real value to the world at large is to preserve endangered species. This argument can be assessed on various grounds: whether or not they can and are doing this, whether this is a good thing anyway, and whether there will not be other environmental effects as a result of zoos doing this. There is also the effect on individuals: should individuals be considered as gene-preserving machines or not? There has been much written about all of these points in the last decade [9; 35]. It is not our intention to re-examine all these in depth. Given that the preservation of endangered species is not necessarily a bad thing, how should it be done? Are there other considerations here? The main points which emerge are:

● If having zoos and circuses creates a market for captured wild animals, this may encourage the capturing and perhaps the killing of some animals, endangered or not, when otherwise they would not be threatened. This then is unacceptable, both on a species and individual level.

● If in the construction of the 'exhibit' in the zoo, or 'act' in the circus, resources such as building materials, non-renewable energy and so on are used which will cause environmental denudation locally or globally are employed, then this is not acceptable.

● The other needs of the animals, such as their food supply and type must not cause global or local environmental disruption, but it must also remain suitable for the animal (e.g. feeding high-protein foods to cellulose converters is inappropriate).

- If the presence of the animals in zoos and circuses cause other local or global problems (e.g. by disease transfer, pollution, smells etc.) which will be derogatory for existing populations (of any species), then the positive and negative effects must be considered very carefully.

- The animals should be kept in as appropriate an environment as possible with close and studied reference to its natural habitat, (particularly if they are captured as adult), as they are likely to do best in such an environment.

- Finally, if it is clear that the individual will benefit from such a change in lifestyle then this is acceptable. The obvious case here is one in which the animals would have been slaughtered or would have died, for example, as a result of the destruction of their habitat if they had stayed in the wild.

This still leaves many areas for decisions to be made in individual cases, and vague areas (e.g. who is to say what is a similar enough habitat?)

The end result of such thinking will be towards breeding self-sustaining populations of animals in zoos and circuses.

Meanwhile is it acceptable to consider that breeding endangered species is the most worthwhile aim of the zoos? Midgeley [103] argues against what she calls 'keeping animals on ice'. If the animal's individual needs and desires are thwarted in order for it to be 'displayed' in a similar way to works of art, or something to be admired from a distance and kept around (despite the fact that we have destroyed their habitat), then this would not be acceptable.

It would seem that if this was the **only** argument for zoos (and circuses) then they would do much better selling all their real estate (some very valuable stocks) and giving all this money to establish and maintain wildlife conservation areas in the animals' countries of origin in their own habitat.

To go to the level of attempting artificial insemination of tigers, involving frequent immobilising, surgery, drug treatment and so on in order to try to keep a particular sub-species going [9] is not really concerned so much with conservation as with experimenting with reproductive physiology.

The origin of zoo and circus animals

One of the important aspects to look at, therefore, is the origin of the animals in zoos and circuses and in particular to find out how many have been wild caught. I have not done this for zoos, but there are good records and it could be done. Figures 23, 25 and 26 show the origin of the animals in circuses dividing them up into those wild caught, zoo bred, circus bred and other origin (such as pets, sale yards, private breeders).

More than half of the carnivores were circus born (54%), 40% came from zoos, and none were wild caught.

The elephants are the most important wild caught group. The majority of the Indian elephants were between 20 and 30 years old, and it is unlikely that more will be imported because of legislative change to prevent it. Young African elephants are still being imported, but these are from populations that are being culled due to human population pressures and environmental demands. It can be argued that their importation is of benefit to the animal as at least they are alive rather than dead, provided the environment they live in thereafter is appropriate, and they show no signs of prolonged distress.

Of the rest of the wild ungulates, 27% were circus born, 5.7% were from zoos, and some unknown in origin.

Relevant to this debate is the number and types of animals found in the circuses. Figures 23, 25 and 26 give a list of the 41 species of animals we found in the circuses.

Twenty six (63%) of these species are generally considered to be 'wild' species, the remaining 37% 'domestic'. The numbers and types of animals in circuses is not stable, and this represents the position from winter 1987 to winter 1988. Animal acts are exported and imported frequently, and the animal species represented in the circuses also follow fashions. However there are not a great many animals in circuses anyway - a total of 513, of which 50 were canaries and pigeons, 128 horses, ponies, donkeys and mules, and 43 dogs. A total, therefore, of 292 traditionally 'wild' animals.

The mammals

The figures give the relative representation of the different species. By far the most popular mammalian species were horses and ponies which were present in all circuses (75 horses: 17.7%, and 49 ponies: 11.6%). Dogs (43: 10.2%) were also well represented, although not all circuses had performing dog acts.

The most common of the wild animals were tigers (58: 13.7%) and lions (43: 10.2%). Five circuses had elephants and they represented 8.4% of the mammals in number.

The camelids (camels, llamas, guanacos and alpacas) are also popular circus animals, and together represent 9.1% of the mammals. Zebras were also relatively numerous, and represented 3.7% of the mammals.

The other species were relatively rarely represented with often only one individual present.

The birds and snakes

There was only one emu, but the other birds - canaries, macaws and pigeons - were in large breeding groups which is why their figures are high. Two circuses had acts with only a few pigeons or macaws.

There were only two snakes in the circuses at the time when the survey was conducted (winter 1987 - winter 1988).

As stated, the total number of animals in all circuses visited was 513, less than in one of the medium sized zoos.

Breeding of animals in the circus

Many consider that the travelling show is not conducive or appropriate to animal breeding. It is not evident that this could **never** be the case, but it certainly might be more difficult to provide the necessary suitable quarters for maternity and raising the very young. One circus, as well as having a static training ground and a travelling show, also runs its own safari parks where many of the animals are bred.

It is in the winter quarters that much of the breeding and raising of the replacement animals takes place. The circuses' record on animal breeding is not at all bad. We can see from Figures 23, 25 and 26 column 5 that they bred 28% of the carnivores, and 13% of the hoofed stock - a total of 41% of their mammals. The snow leopard had a litter of four cubs, and one circus was trying to breed lynx, leopards and puma all of which had bred successfully before. The bears, guanacos, alpacas and zebras have also bred in circuses.

The breeding record for elephants, both in zoos and circuses, is bad but little serious effort has, until recently, been put into it. One Indian elephant was born in a European circus in 1984, but she died in 1988. It is no longer acceptable with the elephant on the endangered species list that so many cows of reproductive age should be in either zoos or circuses and not be breeding. It is of urgent priority that at least the Indian elephants in the circuses should be allowed to breed. There are at least three adult bulls at stud (or who could be) in Britain today. It may not be possible for many reasons to breed all the females in one year, but at least the cows should go to the bull in sequence, and every effort be made to breed and raise as many calves as possible. Every encouragement should be given to their owners.

The inter-relationship of zoo and circus animals

Recently zoos have been over-producing Burchells' zebra and these have been bought by several circuses. Over 66% of the zebras in the circuses are of zoo origin. It is particularly silly to find that several zoos will not admit to this trade; indeed they often proclaim that they would not 'sell their animals to circuses or any travelling menagerie' [9]. This implies that the zoos are in some way superior in their animal management to circuses or travelling menagerie. That this will

Fig. 64. A breeding group of elephants in a zoo.

Fig. 65. Mating in elephants, and breeding is quite possible in circuses and zoos.

Fig. 66. A tiger family (mother and cubs in one den, father next door) in a travelling circus. Outside exercise runs with objects to play with and manipulate, and good views, should be provided as well as social contact with humans, such as seen here.

177

necessarily be the case is not clear either in theory or in practice. In some cases, the reverse might be true.

Selling off the zoos' surplus to circuses can often offer life to that individual instead of death. It would be possible for the zoos and circuses to work more closely to provide a home and a job for as many animals as possible that are born in the zoos. In fact, this can work particularly well for placing spare zoo-born males who are not required for breeding and the zoo may not be able to keep, but who would be welcome in the circuses who often prefer males.

Sex ratios

The ratio of males to females in many species in the circuses is heavily weighted in favour of males (see Figures 23, 25 and 26). The reason for this is that males are often more spectacular, and show themselves off better than females, for example stallions compared to mares. They can be slightly more difficult to handle, and require more individual attention in order to adapt well to the environment than some females. For this reason as well they may be more suitable for the circus where there is a concentration on the individual and they have more professional handlers and trainers than in the zoo.

Conclusions

Thus it can be concluded that provided the animals are kept in an ecologically, ethologically and ethically sound environment, and that the costs and benefits to the individual and the environment at a whole are seriously considered there is no reason why animals should not be kept and bred in captivity.

Although the preservation of endangered species is used, particularly by zoos, as their central *raison d'etre,* there are other reasons which make better arguments for the existence of appropriate zoos and circuses. Having said this, though, there is no reason why circuses as well as zoos should not contribute to conservation aims and breeding of endangered species. Circuses can and do breed various endangered species and a relatively high percentage of all their animals. They also can offer a chance to life to animals surfeit to zoo requirements. It would seem that zoos and circuses should work more closely together and make better use of each other's knowledge and skills to improve along appropriate lines.

Chapter 9

Symbiotic animal management

This is a summary of a longer paper concerned with agricultural strategy in which all the arguments are more fully discussed: Kiley-Worthington, in press, 1990, Food First Ecological Agriculture.

We have examined the arguments for and against circuses and zoos and we have suggested that with certain provisoes both zoos and circuses can be mutually beneficial to the animals and the humans in them. There is no reason to suggest that this will not be the case with other animal husbandry systems as well. In this chapter we will outline what these provisoes are. We have already discussed how we can tell if we have got it wrong for the animal: he will show evidence of distress (Chapters 3 and 4).

However, there are other considerations which we have touched on (e.g. Chapter 8). For example, should we not think of the wider environmental connotations of the animal management system, as Shumaker [122] said: 'Think globally, act locally.'

If so, what does this entail?

Ecologically sound environments for animals

There are two initial points which are relevant here:
● When designing environments for animals, their natural habitats should be considered rather than ignored;
● To date the global implications for the development of various animal husbandry systems (e.g. intensive pig and poultry houses) has received little attention.

In order to understand the importance of these points and to fulfil them in animal husbandry systems, an understanding of two fundamental ecological principles is required. These are:

1) The inter-relatedness of living things with each other and the environment

Although the inter-relatedness of all living things with all others in the biosphere has been stressed in recent times [92], it is as well to remember that the biosphere is made up of relatively discrete ecosystems (e.g. the pond at the bottom of the garden, the Sahara desert, the Amazonian forest, and so on [123]). The boundaries to each of these ecosystems are not obvious. For example, one can study how the ecosystem of a rotting log operates (as many ecology students do) the species that live on it, their food habits, population dynamics, and how the nutrients circulate. Alternatively, one can study the ecology of the forest where the log is found, or the island where the forest grows, and so on. Thus, although all things within the biosphere are to some degree mutually dependent, there are within the biosphere many ecosystems. Within ecosystems the **mutually dependent relationships between different species are stronger than those between ecosytems.**

2) The self-sustaining nature of ecosystems

The dependency relationships within ecosystems are crucial. The log can go on rotting long after the wood has burnt down. This is because one of the fundamental characterisitcs of ecosystems is that they are to a large degree **self-sustaining**; understanding this is fundamental to developing ecologically sound systems of land management (Figure 67). It implies that, for example, there are almost no inputs to a farm, and all the animal fodder is produced on the unit [124]. This idea does

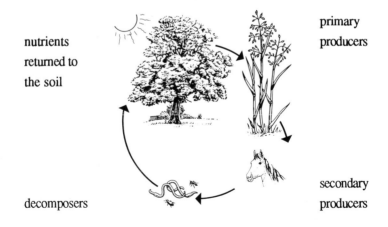

nutrients
returned to
the soil

primary
producers

decomposers

secondary
producers

Fig. 67. The self-sustaining characteristic of ecosystems.

not have to be confined to agriculture; a city could be both diversifed (they often are) and largely self-sustaining in this sense. Indeed for generations the city of Peking (Beijing) grew all its own vegetables on the night soil (human faeces and urine) which was collected, composted and returned to vegetable plots.

Understanding such basic ecological principles and applying them to land management systems is important if we are to be able to overcome many problems that confront us today. An approach based on an understanding of this, and other ecological problems can help with conservation, biological, social, political, ethical, aesthetic, economic and problems of resource utilisation and distribution [92; 93]

How can zoos and circuses more nearly fulfil these aims?

a) What the animals eat must be considered carefully. It would be ecologically sound to some animals' waste products from the system (e.g. scrap bones and meat from animals, themselves raised in ecologically sound environments). If, on the other hand, the animals contribute to a large-scale change elsewhere in the world - for example, by being fed whale meat which threatens whale populations, or beef raised where equatorial forest has recently been cut down, then it is not ecologically sound.

It is possible for many zoos to grow a considerable percentage of their own animal fodder using the manure produced by the animals. (This I suggested to Jersey Zoo in 1979, and they are now quite successful in this direction.) It is also quite possible to use existing micro-climates for this; for example, tropical aviaries can be used to grow some tropical food crops for the herbivores.

This is more difficult for the travelling circus but they can insist on buying fodders that are locally produced and grown causing no ecological problems (e.g. without the use of high chemical inputs, insecticides and herbicides), rather than processed feedstuffs made from imported high-protein feeds such as soya and fish meals. They can (and usually do) use waste products from greengrocers, supermarkets and butchers.

b) The animals may endanger the survival of other species in the urban habitat (e.g. by the transfer of disease), or create a nuisance to other species (e.g. by smells or noise or defaecating and urinating in the wrong places).

The answer is **not** to ban zoos and circuses, for they contribute in many ways to the survival and happiness of human beings who create urban environments (Chapter

8). The solution may rather be to think how to overcome the problems for example by:

- providing suitable facilities and training for animals to defaecate and urinate in the right places and training for their use (see page 210). The muck can then be disposed of in a suitable way, by for example being made available to gardeners (as it often is). Groups of keen allotment holders can often be seen around the manure skip discussing the relative merits of elephant or lion muck for their brussel sprouts!

- investigate properly the alleged disease risk, and issue advice to the public on prevention and control.

On the point of disease transfer, the most dangerous creature to associate with is another member of one's **own** species; this, however, does not result in human beings living as hermits. They have considered carefully the various modes of disease transfer and have developed preventive and curative medicine, and better levels of hygiene and nutrition. This approach has been remarkably successful over the last few decades. Surely the same approach can be used for other species.

Ecologically and ethologically sound animal management results in smaller numbers of animals overall in most enterprises and an effort to provide the appropriate 'niche' on the farm, in the zoo or circus, which they have evolved to live in. If the animals are omnivorous scavengers, like pigs, then they should be fed appropriately rather than on high-protein imported feeds, and so on.

3) The importance of diversified systems

The more diverse the system in terms of the number and type of species within it, the less likely it is to succumb to large changes. The system will, on the whole, tend to be more adaptable although it is dynamic (e.g. changes in population numbers within species).

Specialised monocultural systems of plants or animals tend to be more disease-prone and, in addition, there is more intra-specific competition. Thus diversification, as a general rule (although there are exceptions), leads to less competition between species and to more easily balanced sustainable systems. Usually neither zoos nor circuses have any problem with this. In fact the problem is sometimes towards too much diversity of species kept in inappropriate environments, particularly of zoos.

Both zoos and circuses should be careful to restrict the numbers of their species to those which can optimise the local environmental conditions. It is possible to have very large collections of different species, or to transport water-loving species such as sea lions or penguins, but it is much more difficult to fulfil all these criteria by so doing.

In the last 15 years, the importance of endangered species and active interest in conserving them has risen dramatically. The usual reason for this interest is aesthetic (it is a shame to lose irreplaceable and beautiful species). Although this is a serious consideration [9; 23], there is also a vested interest in conserving species in order to maintain the stability of the bioshere. As Erlich and Erlich [92] put it, loss of a species is like 'rivet popping': it weakens the biospherical structure.

Many zoos justify their existence on the grounds that they are breeding rare species, extinct or nearly so in the wild. In so far as this is true, and the animals are kept in ecologically and ethologically sound environments, then this is acceptable. For it must also be considered that zoos and circuses can sometimes offer a chance for life to wild animals where culling has become essential to maintain the wild biotype. For example, there is at present an active trade in East and Central African elephants to zoos and circuses. These animals would otherwise have been shot since their wildlife parks are overpopulated, and poaching is out of control.

The buildings the animals are kept in, materials for their construction, the way they are heated and so on must be considered in terms of their effect on the local and global environment. Zoos sometimes go in for high-status permanent architecture, or even for investing huge sums and sometimes scarce and theatened resources into creating 'naturalistic' environments to put across conservation messages (e.g. Jungle World at the Bronx Zoo, New York). The environmental costs and benefits here must be assessed very carefully.

Circuses often used a minimum of materials of this sort. However, even what they do use must be considered carefully in respect to their environmental effect. For example, how the tents and so on are heated must be considered. Renewable heat and energy supply from solar or wind generators might be appropriate for some.

A more holistic, ecological approach for all animal husbandry systems is necessary. If animal husbandry systems cause serious environmental problems locally or globally, even if the animals are well fed, well kept and experiencing 'good welfare' (whatever this is!) they remain unacceptable.

These ecological concerns are not usually raised in welfare debates. It is curious that this is the case since they are fundamentally involved. As a hog or a human I am concerned with my own personal present and future, staying alive and preserving some quality of life for myself (what is usually called welfare). I (the hog or the human) am also concerned (conciously or not) with that of my offspring: future generations. Both the present quality of life, and that of future generations, of hogs and humans is threatened if ecological considerations are not taken into account.

It is true, I am assuming here, that life itself is important. For example, it has been argued that if there is no life there can be no suffering. If there are, for example, no foxes, there can be no suffering foxes. Here it is argued that the existence of foxes is important, even though they may have to take the risk of suffering. This is in part because all forms of sentient life have some rights to life [9; 20; 24], and in part because the interaction of living systems with each other and the non-living environment ensures that having no foxes will cause other changes in the ecosystems, and this may eventually affect my (and other individuals' and species') quality of life. We may not know exactly what the consequences will be, but it is sensible for our own survival and that of our offspring to be cautious.

Neither an individual nor a species can exist independently of its environment; these ecological considerations are concerned with the animals' or the species' relationship with the environment. They are fundamental to any debate on welfare: the quality of life.

Aesthetic considerations

It is important not to ignore aesthetic considerations in the design and management of animal husbandry. From the human's point of view, Shoard [125] outlines many aesthetic concerns in the countryside: deafforestation, ugly farm buildings, industrialisation of agriculture, including destroying wild flowers and birds. It is possible to site and design even large farm buildings, zoos, kennels, stables, circuses and so on so that they are aesthetically acceptable, but it is something that needs much more thought.

The aesthetics of animal husbandry systems are complicated by the possibility that the animals themselves may have some form of aesthetic appreciation or objection. For example, horses appear to dislike strong human smells, and like to choose to be where they can have a good view (personal observations). A distinction here between uncomfortable or deprived environments and aesthetically unpleasing ones for the animals is difficult. This is not the place to take this further, but it is a possibility that cannot be ignored.

FIGURE 68. CRITERIA FOR ECOLOGICALLY SOUND ENVIRONMENTS FOR ANIMALS.

They should cause no long term or irreversible environmental change by considering the local and global environmental effect of all aspects of the husbandry. In particular:

1) The effect on other species of plants and animals.

2) The long term and short term effects on the physical environment, eg. soils, tree distruction etc.

3) The effects on local humans of the husbandry (eg any 'nuisance' or environmental value).

4) Provision of appropriate food which causes no adverse ecological effect locally or globally.

5) Provision of other environmental needs of the animal. For example supply of materials for shelter, shade, nesting materials, heating etc and their environmental effect.

6) Appropriate climate and ability to adapt to chances.

7) The origin of the animals, and its local and global effect (particularly if captured from the wild).

Ethologically sound environments for animals

Ethologically sound environments are those which reduce or eliminate prolonged animal suffering. Many environments that have been designed for animals in the last few decades have concentrated on meeting the requirements of the human handlers, rather than giving first priority to the physical and psychological 'needs' of the animals housed therein.

That animals feel pain, can suffer, and that they feel emotions - terror, fear, happiness and joy among others, albeit that these states may be somewhat different from those typically experienced by human beings (whatever that is) - is today, in general, agreed by ethologists seriously concerned with animal welfare (see Chapter 7). The problems arise in defining for each species and individual what is prolonged suffering, and what are their behavioural needs (see Chapters 3, 4 and 5).

It is **not** argued here that if at any time any of these criteria are not fulfilled, the animal is distressed and therefore its environment should not be considered appropriate. A certain amount of stress and distress is inevitable, and perhaps even desirable during a being's life. It is rather the intention here to point out possible indicators which could be used (perhaps in conjunction) as an aid to making decisions concerning environmental design and acceptability for all types of animal husbandry.

Thus, if we are to be concerned not only with an animal staying alive but also having some quality of life, then I suggest we already have sufficient information to design its environment. It may be that certain judgements we may make prove later to be incorrect, but the rational starting point is to use our existing knowledge in designing ethologically acceptable environments.

Invention and substitution can and must often be used to fulfil these criteria, in much the same way as some wild animals use them in adapting to new environments. For example, seagulls usually live near the sea, eat fish and carrion, nest on cliffs and swim on the sea. However, they have in some cases adapted to living at some distance from the sea, eating from garbage tips and nesting on buildings. All their behavioural needs are apparently met in such areas, and they continue to perform all the behaviours in their repertoires, including flying and swimming. Another interesting example of adaptation to 'unnatural' conditions is the

South African butcher bird (shrike) which naturally hangs its prey on the thorns of certain species of acacia but nowadays also uses the barbs in barbed wire fences [127].

It is a question of where the limits to adaption are for a particular species or individual in different environments. It is argued here that they are **where there is behavioural restriction, and where there is evidence of distress.**

Since there is little evidence that domestication has changed fundamental behaviour (Chapter 7), we should give the animals the benefit of the doubt and design both domestic and wild animals' environments to fulfil their ethological needs. These are summarised in Figure 73 and discussed here.

If then we have ways of assessing when the environment is apparently unacceptable to the animal, how should their environments be designed? There is a basic blueprint and that is to consider first **the species'** evolutionary background by taking account of:

a) social organisation

b) habitat

c) the natural food, its nutrient content and textures

d) the performance of the entire behavioural repertoire

e) the species' specific characteristics of the receptors

f) the species' specific brain anatomy

g) the species' communication system - in detail

h) how the animals learn, and what that species might be expected to learn

Let us look at each of these in turn.

a) Taking account of social organisation

The animals should be kept in the social groupings that they associate in with in the wild, and that they have evolved to live in. Different species have different requirements: pigs live in family groups and cats are semi-solitary. Horses and cattle are social herbivores but have rather different social organisations; for example, horses live in family groups which can join together into larger herds, the strongest bonds appear to be between generations (mother to daughter). In cattle, the bonds between peers - within generations - are very strong. This difference is illustrated in Figure 74 where the distances between mother and young of these two species are contrasted. Consideration of such factors should give rise to different types of management for each species. For example, separating post-weaned youngsters into peer groups is reasonably appropriate for cattle, but for horses it is extremely traumatic and can trigger the start of behavioural problems and abnormalities [29] because the bond between mother and young is particularly strong.

Fig. 69. The social lion, who normally spend much of their day sleeping or rolling around, can be relatively easily catered for in the circus or zoo.

Fig. 70. The social sea lion is relatively easy to cater for in terms of his social needs, but must have proper water living and swimming facilities which are more difficult to provide in a travelling show, although not impossible.

b) Taking account of habitat

The place where the animals are kept should approximate the type of habitat they have evolved to live in. For example, keeping forest-living animals in large open environments with little cover is likely to cause them trauma. With thought, it is almost always possible to cater for the species' demands in this way. For instance, by reversing day and night hours, it is possible for nocturnal animals to be seen active by diurnal human beings (e.g. in the Charles Clore pavilion, the small mammal house at London Zoo).

c) Taking account of animals' food

The food animals are fed must also be appropriate. For example, the practice of giving high-concentrate protein diets to some herbivores - which is considered 'good management' is often inappropriate. Cellulose converters have evolved to convert cellulose and they should be fed diets high in cellulose. If this is not done, physical and psychological problems can result. Some of the zoo antelope are now at risk from 'mad cow disease' because of the practice of feeding them high protein concentrate foods made from other infected cattle brains!

d) Allowing for the performance of the entire behavioural repertoire which does not cause suffering to others. (Chapter 4).

e) The species' specific characteristics of the receptors

For example, the horse's eye differs from the human's in its anatomy and physiolog. What 'view of the world' does the horse have that might be different from the human's? (Figure 71). Whales and mice (and maybe many other species) can hear ultra-sound; electric fish pick up electric signals, and bats eco-locate.

f) The species' specific brain anatomy

This can tell us something about the relative importance of different brain functions for the species (Figure 72). Here we need much more information on species' specific differences. Nevertheless what differences in the gross anatomy, or indeed the size of the brain tells us is still debatable [132]. However, the mutilation or sacrifice of many animals in order to find out more about such questions would not be ethically

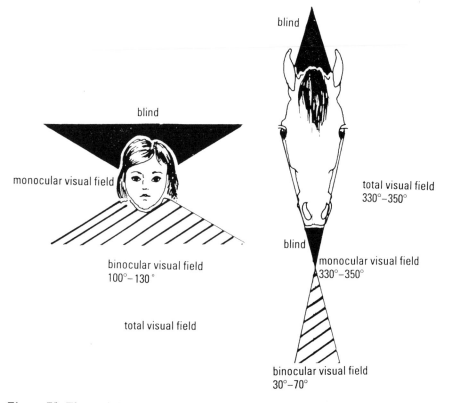

Figure 71. The visual fields of a girl and a horse contrasted. Note the much greater binocular field on vision for a girl, but a much more restricted monocular vision. Some horses can see right around to the person on their back if they put their head up.

desirable, or ethologically sound. There is great scope for further anatomical studies on animals already slaughtered, and much more could be discovered using simple behavioural techniques, such as discrimination tests.

g) The species' communication system

This is particularly important for animals that are trained and are used to help humans with tasks, or perform in one way or another, such as guide dogs, police or sheep dogs, horses, and circus animals. For successful working relationships between species (humans and others) reciprocal animal/human communication is central. Proper knowledge of inter- and intra-specific communication is also essential for the

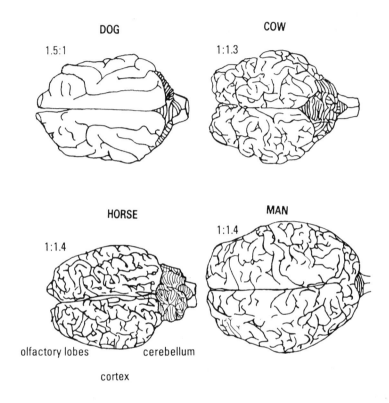

DOG
1.5:1

COW
1:1.3

HORSE
1:1.4

MAN
1:1.4

olfactory lobes

cerebellum

cortex

Figure 72. Differences in the gross anatomy of the brains may or may not tell us something about the mental abilities of the species. The size of the forbrain (the convoluted part) is often considered to indicate 'intelligence' and ability for rational thought. If this is the case, then the dog's abilities in this direction are much less than the horse's! Indeed, the horse's cerebrum has more convolutions and therefore greater surface area than that of humans, and the cow's is not much different. What all this means we don't really know, but perhaps we should not underestimate animals' cognitive abilities.

good husbandry of any animal. This can be taught, although some humans will be better than others at this as in everything else.

Individual animals have their own personalities (see (i) below) even within an age or sex group, but until the species' communication is reasonably well known, it is often very difficult to understand this, and to predict possible actions. One example is the sophistication of the visual communication in horses. They are able to pick up subliminal visual cues that humans find difficult or impossible (this is called the 'Clever Hans effect'). An understanding of this aids all training and working with horses [29].

h) Grasping how animals learn, and what they might be expected to learn

This is particularly important if the animal is to be a companion or be trained. Learning plays an important part even in the everyday husbandry of large numbers of food animals. Appropriate learnt responses can simplify husbandry, and reduce trauma for the animal. For example, sheep or cattle can be trained to come to an auditory signal, instead of having to be herded or even chased to the desired point. However what, and how quickly, animals of different species learn varies, so one must have a grasp of the species' specific characteristics. Little is known about this from the scientific literature at present, but there is a considerable amount of knowledge among those looking after and training different species. [See 107 for a thought-provoking critique of the scientific approach.]

The factors mentioned above are important to **the species** and must be taken into account when designing appropriate ethologically sound environments, but there are also factors concerned with **the individual** that must be considered. These are:
i) the individual's past experience
ii) individual personalities.

i) The individual's past experience

Animals, like humans, become accustomed to particular types of environments. Battery hens have usually never had to compete with many other hens to find food, to obtain shelter and so on; nor have they been able to move around. When they are released from their batteries, they often find the change extremely traumatic and some even collapse from the stress. This is not to say that battery hens' environments are ethologically sound, nor to say that they should not be allowed the opportunity to experience the great outdoors, but rather to emphasise the effect of past experience. Good or bad experience in their past will affect the animals' behaviour: as a human, for example, weaning too early in dogs gives rise to difficulties in socialising [110]. A horse, elephant or an eland that has been frightened at some time going into a trailer may show great resistance to going in again.

ii) Individual personalities

Even within an age or sex class, animals, like humans, have individual personalities. This is the result of their genetic inheritance, and past experience. Individual differences and personality profiles have not as yet been the subject of much study in ethology, but an understanding of this is central for any successful trainer [29; 107].

A consideration of **all** those factors (summarised in Figure 73) related to species and individual characteristics is fundamental for designing ethologically sound environments for animals. If these criteria are correctly fulfilled, then the animal should show no evidence of distress.

FIGURE 73. **ETHOLOGICALLY SOUND ENVIRONMENTS FOR ANIMALS.**

The Criteria that must be taken into account:-

1) The animal should be allowed to perform all the behaviour in his repertoire which does not cause prolonged or acute suffering to others.

2) The animal should be able to associate in the appropriate groups size and structure to his species and past experience.

3) The animal should be in an appropriate physical environment (eg forest or simulate forest if forest dwelling etc).

4) There must be no evidence of prolonged distress (as defined on page 76).

5) The animals 'telos' must be catered for by:-

a) Considering the way the animal perceives the world, his receptors; his brain anatomy, his cognitive ability, his specific learning abilities and his communciation system.

6) The animal must be considered not only as a representative of a species, but also as an individual and his past experience must be assessed in order to design the most appropriate environment for him as a) a member of a species and b) an individual.

Ethically sound environments for animals

Opinion concerning what humans' attitudes to animals and the environment should be have varied with history. In the early days, during the era of human hunter-gatherers, it appears that humans lived very much in a give-and-take situation with Nature, as they do today [115; 133]. The humans must have a certain respect for the natural order of things, and how nature works, but at the same time, they are dominated by it and are aware of this.

The first agriculturalists, it seems, had much the same attitude, a very definite respect, and in addition the beginning of efforts to dominate and twist nature for their own ends.

Self-sustaining peasants have retained much of this attitude today, for obvious survival reasons. Nature and animals are respected, sometimes admired and/or worshipped. It is understood that in order to survive the human must work with nature and have some understanding of her controls. **There is no question of complete domination of nature,** but rather one of a symbiotic relationship with nature. Peasants would dearly love to dominate nature, but know that they cannot.

Among many other populations of humans, particularly urban ones, a war was declared on nature throughout the 16th-21st centuries. This has its origins in part in the Judeo-Christian and Islamic philosophy of the superiority of humans [24]. The result has been that humans have made real efforts to overcome and to subdue and dominate nature and animals, losing any real respect for other living creatures but themselves. In fact, with the growth of industrialisation and urbanisation, even of the farm, zoo or wildlife park, the predominant cultural attitude in the west has been, and still is, extremely anthropocentric. Nowhere is this more obvious today than in the conventional teaching of agriculture, veterinary and medical sciences and animal management. This is illustrated by the French verb to farm or cultivate: 'exploiter'.

If we really did have dominion over nature, then we would not suffer from earthquakes, storms and floods, plagues of locusts, diseases and even death. Technologically we do have a great environmental effect, but we certainly don't have control and rarely have much comprehension, particularly of the long-term effects of some of our manipulations, as is becoming abundantly clear. The world is too full of examples from the Ganges floods to the generation of nuclear waste, from Ethiopia to Brazil.

On the other hand, the radical Respect for Life philosophy is, although thought-provoking, impractical without very massive changes in all aspects of modern human lifestyle. It is not possible to survive without destroying life or potential life, every time one eats a cabbage, or even a fruit or nut. A modified edition of this theory has some relevance however. Others have suggested [22] that a respect for life position does not necessarily mean that nature is sacred, or that all living things have unqualified right to life. However this approach can lead to species separation - 'Animal Apartheid' (Chapter 7). As I have argued, I am not convinced this is always (or even sometimes) desirable and mutually beneficial for humans and animals.

Some argue convincingly that animals must be objects of moral concern (Chapter 7). However, Rollin [23] recognises that the interests of one species do trump others; thus the right to life is not absolute, as Regan [24] maintains. More importantly though, he does point out that the killing of animals or causing of their pain and suffering is a moral decision.

Each individual should have the ability to fulfil their 'telos' [134]; that is, their species and individual characteristics and so they may serve and be served by others, so long as the relationship remains symbiotic. As well as cooperating and benefiting from the presence of others, each individual also manipulates and profits from them.

Passmore [135] and, in a more watered down form, Attfield [136] propose an attitude of stewardship towards animals and nature. Such an approach implies both comprehension and knowledge of the animals or natural system, and management, which although we at present do not have a great deal of this, we could achieve. A less attractive aspect of this stewardship approach is its implication that 'big brother knows best' approach, and the judeo-christian assumption that humans' interests will always trump those of other species, this cannot be accepted without much more thought.

The close association of some humans with animals that comes from farming, pet keeping, sport animals, zoos and in the training of animals for various forms of work (guide dogs for the blind, sheep dogs, stock horses, draught buffalo, timber elephants) including entertainments, such as in circuses - provided the animals' physical and behavioural 'needs' are catered for ('telos') - can increase enormously the quality of life for both humans and for the animals. This also educates the humans to understanding that there are other skilled able and interesting beings who inhabit the world, as well as humans, and to whom s/he can relate too closely. Why should for a human a close relationship with any other animal but a human be a sign of that human's sickness or shortcomings?

From the animal's point of view such a relationship may be equally rewarding and exciting. In humans, an increase in the quality of life as a result of education is taken for granted by all human societies, although they may educate their children in very different ways. Why should this not be the case for animals, provided it is done in such a way as to fulfil the above criteria? At least **until proved otherwise**, it would seem sensible to consider this to be the case.

Thus there is no rational reason why animals should not be used by humans, and humans used by animals, for most activities, provided the animals are kept, trained and so on in ethologically and ecologically sound environments. The fact that they are not always, simply indicates that changes should be made, not that we should ban the use of animals for certain things, or assume that they would be 'better off dead'. We do not have this attitude generally to other humans!

'Good' animal management today is still modelled on the patronising stewardship attitude. Thus it involves much interference 'for the animals' good'. The well-meaning but misplaced parallel in treatment of infants or imbeciles and adult animals is in part responsible for this: adult animals are **not** children or stupid adults. That is not to say that they should not have equal consideration [21].

There is a fine line to be drawn between 'over management' and resulting interference with the animal 'for his own good', and 'educating' the animal so that he had certain skills and abilities. Education is intended to enhance the animal's abilities, knowledge and understanding of the world so that he can improve his enjoyment of it in one way or another. As far as animals are concerned, the wider the appropriate experience of different situations, the more able he may be to cope with them.

Over management and the somewhat patronising 'stewardship' attitude, by contrast, results often in over protection of the individual, and has the opposite effect; it can be self defeating. For example, a valuable stallion is not allowed to associate with mares and court and mate them in a natural way **because he may be injured by the mares**. He is kept isolated from them, and only mates them when they are restrained with hobbles, switches and so on. The result of this is that he becomes inept at normal equine communication, he has not learnt to be sensitive to and to interpret all the mare's signals during courtship which will tell him of her next action, and he is much **more** likely to be injured as a result. The more animals are kept confined and restrained **for their own good** the more they are likely to cause havoc or be injured. The same is of course true for educating human beings. If the child or the puppy is always protected from being anywhere near the fire, he will not learn that it hurts and sooner or later may well be seriously burnt. He must learn by experience and with the help of a good educator that fire hurts so that he will avoid being burnt.

Exactly where the lines are drawn between education and over management or protection will remain an area of debate. We must recognise that they are not obvious or clear in every case, and they have been drawn in the wrong place if the animal (or human) shows any sign of distress as defined here.

FIGURE 74. **The distance typically maintained between cow and calf compared to those between mare and foal**

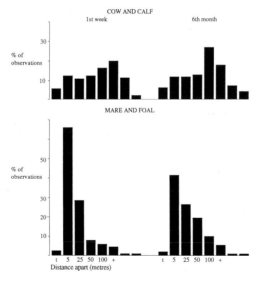

In practical terms, how then are we to conduct our relationships with other animals, and how should we design their environments? Is there a practical alternative that fulfils the criteria set and reduces the problems to the individual human, animal and the biosphere as a whole and which will in the long run benefit us individually?

The symbiotic approach proposed here implies a healthy respect of evolution and the complex and intricate workings of the biosphere. It recognises that humans are the most manipulative species of the moment, but also that they have as yet relatively little comprehension of the workings of the biosphere, or the individual living things. It is a rationalistic holistic approach, but also cautionary: it is wiser not to rock the biospherical or ethological boat. Causing change is more likely to be disadvantageous than advantageous, even though it might be ingenious or amusing and apparently show short-term advantages. It is in the long run more likely than not to be disadvantageous to my own, or your, survival, and that of our offspring.

We are now in a position to design practical housing for most animals with these criteria in mind. There is a growing literature on how to do this for different species [29; 137; 138].

Thus to summarise, the 'right' or ethically acceptable husbandry system for animals is one where:

1) **The local and global ecological effect of the system is considered in relation to the biological, environmental and aesthetic value to humans and other animals (Figure 68).**

2) **The animal is in the type of environment which is ethologically sound (Figure 73) where he is 'happy' and not showing distress, and able to perform all the behaviour within his repertoire provided this does not cause suffering to others.**

3) **Consideration to him as a sentient being of moral concern is shown.**

4) **The animal, human and rest of the environment have a symbiotic relationship, which is of mutual benefit rather than competitive. The relationship of the human to the animal could be considered rather as one of an employee than a tool or slave.**

These criteria add up to what might consitute a 'Bill of Rights for Mammals and Birds'.

Chapter 10

Recommendations

The widely held position that circuses, and sometimes zoos, necessarily cause suffering to animals because of their nature has not been found to be the case. In fact it has been argued that the possible positive aspects of what zoos and circuses could do for the animals under their care, and for humans' perception of animals, outweighs the negative aspects of possible suffering of the animals in circuses and zoos.

However, there is evidence of distress in the animals in circuses and zoos, and in almost every other husbandry system. The question therefore is how must zoos and circuses be changed to reduce this distress and eventually to be able to design and manage animals' systems so, as a rule, there is no evidence for prolonged suffering of the animals in them?

As a result of examining all the various arguments and the empirical data I have collected, it is my opinion that the efforts and money of animal welfare organisations should **not** go into trying to ban circuses and zoos. Instead they should put their efforts and money into reducing animals' suffering, by research on these improvements and learning more about the behavioural and other needs of the different species, individuals, their cognition, and the education of humans to further respect and understand animals.

It **is** possible for circuses and zoos, as for any other animal management system, to achieve the aims outlined in the previous chapter. For circuses it may be, in some respects, more difficult because, for example, animals are transported around and therefore appropriate housing must be reconstructed quickly at each location. On the other hand, it may be easier in other respects to fulfil certain psychological needs than some other husbandry systems, such as zoos. This is because circuses **by their nature** specialise in handling and educating animals, and are primarily concerned with the individual.

I have argued that there are ways in which inappropriate environments which interfere with the animals' 'rights' and are likely to cause prolonged suffering can be quickly assessed. The criteria for doing this are outlined in Figures 68 and 73. It will not be possible to fulfil all these criteria immediately, nor will it be desirable for certain individual animals (for example, an elephant who has lived on her own for many years might find it traumatic to be thrust into a group) but in general they are the goals we should work towards in all our animal husbandry systems, particularly for the next generation of animals.

There are also ways in which we can assess if the environment is inappropriate for the individual: whether or not it is suffering or distressed. This can be done by assessing:

1)   If the physical condition is poor, disease frequent, mortality high, or where drugs or surgery are needed to maintain the system (Chapter 3).

2)   Where there is evidence of distress in the behaviour of the animal (Chapter 4). The frequent occurrence of abnormal behaviours which may indicate inappropriate environments, such as atypically high levels of aggression for the species, neuroses and pathologies. Stereotypies are ready evidence for environmental inadequacy.

3)   Where there is severe behavioural restriction so that the animal is unable to perform a number of its social and physical behaviours normally in its repertoire (pages 63-70).

Inevitably there are grey areas in making these assessments, and in some cases more knowledge is required. For example, we have little information on normal time budgets and the amounts of aggression and affiliative behaviour, or behaviour often related to frustration and conflict for some species in unrestricted environments, so it is difficult in some cases to make judgements. Nevertheless, we do have enough information to make some assessments of 'suffering' and 'cruelty'. It is important, however, that skilled personnel implement these criteria. This requires detailed knowledge of practical stockmanship, ethology and some basic veterinary understanding.

The next question is, having assessed that there are problems in relation to these criteria for certain animals, in what respects do we change the environment to try and reduce or eradicate them?

The most important points here are:

1)   The environment must be constructed to at least resemble the environment which the animal has evolved to live in, both in a physical and a social sense. The use of natural and living materials, as opposed to artificial ones, is

preferred but not essential. With a little innovative thinking this can often be achieved.

The construction of the social environment is also important - solitary or semi-solitary species should be catered for and not always thrust with others. How the species' groups are structured must be considered in detail in order to fulfil this requirement. It is best for conspecifics to be kept in groups if social; however, in circuses, because of their emphasis on the individual, there may be few animals, and those representing a range of species. In some cases (see below), it may be acceptable to have mixed species groups, provided the specific needs of the different individuals constituting the groups can be catered for, and there are no signs of prolonged distress.

2) The species' characteristics in terms of how they 'perceive' the world, their communications system, and cognitive abilities must be seriously considered and catered for.

3) The individuals' past experience and consequently the mixing of nature and nurture which gives rise to the individual personality must be catered for.

4) The handling and educating of the animal for its particular tasks which should enhance his "telos" must be considered carefully and done skillfully. There is no reason why the animal should not be taught to perform actions or behaviour that are not normally within his repertoire, provided he does not suffer as a result.

Although there is not a great deal of information on many of these aspects, these are not vague concepts, but important criteria that must not be ignored if we are going to progress in our considerations of ethically acceptable environments for animals. It is the duty of those involved in animal husbandry to use all existing knowledge, and help to finance further research. Inevitably, this approach requires a consideration of individual cases. Here we can give some more detailed guidelines that might be appropriate for the most common circus species.

The elephants

The physical environment

It is not ethologically sound to keep the elephants shackled for prolonged periods. Quickly constructed safe enclosures can be made using electric fences and the elephants should be allowed access to these for the majority of each 24 hours. They should also be taken out, allowed to roam about at will and on walks, parades, to the sea, river, beach or woodlands whenever and wherever possible. They must be properly educated so that this can be achieved without undue risk.

When in their living quarters the elephants should have access **for the great majority of the time** to high-fibre food, and preferably objects to manipulate, leaves to eat and so on. They should have plenty of bedding, and space to lie in (at least twice their own body size). Lying on bare concrete or wooden slats is unacceptable.

Shackling should gradually be phased out, although it is advisable to train the elephants so that they can be shackled if essential. If it is not possible for certain managers to keep elephants safely without shackling them for prolonged periods, then they should not be kept.

The social environment

The elephants should be kept in social groups, preferably family matriarchal groups including animals of different ages. If an elephant has always been alone, then it may well be that she is socially inept and would find close company distressing. Thus for her lifetime it may be suitable for her to remain alone, although she should have the opportunity to breed. This does not argue for keeping young elephants isolated in the future.

Breeding

Each elephant (particularly the Indian elephants) should breed at least once in their lifetime in order to ensure the next generation and also to allow the existing animals to have and bring up young.

Training

The elephants should be given training or education sessions daily so that they are learning **new and different things** and having to think. They should also be exposed to as many different situations as possible so that the risk of them becoming frightened and panicking is reduced. The handling and training of the elephants is particularly important and requires great dedication and skill, but the rewards in terms of the possible relationships between humans and elephants are very great.

The elephants might well benefit from helping around the circus moving heavy objects and so on, and the circus could certainly benefit from such activities. Elephants can be trained to perform certain tasks to make life easier for themselves and their human associates. For example, they can be taught to urinate and defaecate in certain places or even in a bucket or wheelbarrow; they can help to erect their own tents, to load the Big Top and so on.

Performance

The elephants should be taught to do appropriate acts to display their unique abilities, for example the manipulative ability of their trunk, their strength, the love of playing with objects and each other, and their great cognitive abilities and willingness to work. Their apparent fondness for each other and their handlers and trainers can also be shown.

Carnivores with particular reference to the big cats

The physical environment

Confining the cats to beast wagons or cages indoors for all or the majority of their time is not acceptable. The environment is dull, confined and restrictive. Even though circus animals (unlike zoo animals) leave the wagons or cages for some time each day for training or performance sessions, this is insufficient to allow them to perform all their behaviours. It is important that the conditions are improved not only when the circuses are on the road, but also in the winter quarters or on breeding and training farms.

All the cats and carnivores should have access to exercise yards or pens outside (unless the animals are sick and it would be bad for their physical health), for the **majority** of each day. Cages that allow the animals to leap, chase, bound, climb and perform other athletic activities in their species' repertoires are required. In addition, these cages must be quick and easily constructed and taken down, and they must be safe for both the animals and the humans. This is not impossible to achieve; exercise ring cages can be constructed in the compounds with tunnel access for the different cats, or mesh cages constructed adjacent to the beast wagons which can then act as large extensions of their living areas.

There must be a greater provision of cage furniture in the beast wagons, particularly for the climbing cats. Shelves, climbing bars and logs which allow the cats to use the third dimension are essential. In addition, objects to manipulate, chew and play with should be provided for all. Natural vegetation, because it is aesthetically more pleasing, and possibly something that the animals might find easier to relate to, and is replaceable, could be used more widely. For example, tree branches with leaves can often be purchased on arrival at the new site.

Details such as the direction to which the wagon points, and thus the amount of sun the animals will receive; the outlook from the wagons; their positioning where there is sufficient interest and action around must also be considered, and may well make a large difference to the life of the animal.

The beast wagons should not be shut up at night when the weather is suitable. If they are shut up then the period of enclosure should be minimised, and certainly should not exceed eight hours. There is no excuse for the carnivore grooms not getting up early to allow their animals access to the light and the exercise yard. This is particularly necessary for animals such as the tiger, leopard and wolf who are often crepuscular or nocturnal in the wild.

The social environment

The social structure of the groups in which the animals are kept should be considered carefully. For example, if social and non-social species are going to be in the same act and therefore kept together -such as lions and leopards - then suitable and different living accommodation should be provided. Again this is not necessarily impossible. For example, the smaller leopard can have an escape door through which only he can slink, into a private apartment, perhaps where he cannot be seen from outside.

All the carnivores should be allowed to breed at least once in their lives and to raise their own young. The groups should be constituted to allow this.

Handling and training

All the animals raised in the circus should be handled, preferably daily, and they should also have training sessions as well as give performances. The presenter/groom of the big cat acts usually has few, if any, tasks other than looking after his animals, and therefore s/he often has plenty of time to handle, play with, relate to and educate the carnivores. The training/educational programme should be appropriate to the species and the acts designed to show off the animals' particular physical and behavioural abilities, whether it is climbing, balancing and leaping, or rolling around and playing - innovation in the acts is needed here.

Similar but species-appropriate criteria should be applied to all the other carnivores in circuses - bears, wolves, hyenas and domestic cats and dogs. Specific recommendations could be made for each species.

There were many domestic dogs in the circuses - some performers, some pets and some guard dogs - and it is worth emphasising that the same criteria must apply to them. There is **no excuse** for the dogs of any of these categories not being able to run free for at least part of the day, to be housed in trailers perhaps but with outside runs available all of the time, and to have social contact with conspecifics and with their human trainers or handlers. There is no reason, for example, that the dogs should bark persistently other than because the environment is in one way or another inappropriate. If this is what happens when they are kept outside, then all aspects of their environment must be reconsidered carefully, including their training which may not be up to standard. There is a widely held belief that good working dogs cannot be pets as well. That there are leading sheepdogs, circus performing dogs, retrievers, guide dogs for the blind and so on who are also pets (that are allowed to share the life of their human handlers to a great degree, and have profound emotional relationships with them) gives the lie to this statement.

If we are to work towards symbiotic relationships with animals, then this must also involve increasing the liberty of the animal so that he stays around and does what is required because he **wants** to not because he has no choice. There is no doubt that this can and does happen for dogs. In a circus where animal training is their profession, this should be seen to be the case. Where better to begin than with the dogs?

The hoofed stock

The physical environment

The tendency is to keep many of the exotic hoofed stock stalled and only to take them out for training and performance - this is unacceptable. In order for the animals to be able to perform more of the behaviour in their repertoire, it is necessary for them at least to be taken for walks, tethered outside, and allowed loose into enclosures daily. Again these enclosures can be constructed quickly using electric-fencing equipment, and could be attached to the stable tent so that the animals can go in or out as they wish (Figure 12, page 35).

Most of these animals are well adapted to eating a high-fibre diet, and normally spend a large portion of each day in the wild eating. They must have access to high-fibre food all the time. The best system is probably to feed hay *ad libitum* placed in racks or nets so that the animals have to work a little to obtain it. If water is on offer all the time, this is preferable but not essential as taking the animals to a central water butt twice a day can ensure that they are handled, and come into contact with others.

Rolling and scratching facilities

Another important feature that was universally neglected in the management of circus horses and other hoofed stock was the provision of suitable time and place for the animals to roll or scratch. These activities relieve skin irritation and may have other functions (e.g. leaving pheromones). In order to roll, horses and llamas in particular need an appropriate substrate (this can be grass, sawdust, straw etc.) and room to move, to pick their place and to get up afterwards. Horses, and probably llamas, can be taught to roll on command at suitable times, such as after exercise, in just the same way as they can be taught to defaecate and urinate in certain areas (see page 210). It is not difficult in a circus to provide the right time and place to encourage horses to roll, but I saw no evidence of this. Hediger [48] points out the importance of providing scratching posts for zebras and other animals. This can be done easily by knocking in a firm post in the enclosure, if there are no other suitable objects in the environment.

Exercise

This is another important criteria for the hoofed stock. Generally, the animals were out of their tents for insufficient time each day (10 minutes - 2 hours) and during this time they did not have remotely the same amount of exercise that they would normally have in a feral or wild state or even at pasture or in a yard. Exercise will be increased if training, educating and taking the animals for walks and parades is increased. If the animals are loose in reasonable sized enclosures, which at some grounds is not difficult to arrange, they will exercise themselves more and this will also help.

Looseboxes are not necessarily better from the horse's point of view than stalls since they often isolate the animal more from conspecific contact, and from the environment as a whole. The public and management often like the idea of hoofed stock, particularly horses, in individual stables with doors, and grating between the animals. Such systems are traditionally associated with what are usually considered 'quality' animal breeding establishments. One must be cautious here if one is centrally involved with the **animals'** welfare as opposed to the public's view of what is best. Graphics can often achieve much in this direction. They are sometimes used to good advantage in zoos but could be much more widely used in circuses.

'Holiday periods'

These requirements are important. At the winter quarters there **is** sufficient space to be able to allow the hoofed animals out into fields. If there is difficulty catching them for training sessions, then the approach must **not** be one of confining the animal as a result, but rather one of self-questioning the training and catching techniques. It should be considered a pre-requisite of all circus hoofed animals (as for all other husbandry systems) that they have some period each year, say for 1-2 months when they are out in semi-liberty in large enclosures or fields. This is not difficult for most circuses to organise out of season as almost all have land available at their winter quarters.

The social environment

Most hoofed animals are social species, but they have rather different types of social organisations. For example, some live in multi-male groups (e.g. cattle and bison), some in groups with one male (e.g. many of the equids). The majority of the species have home areas although they vary greatly in size from the quarter of a square mile of a bushbuck to the two home areas joined by a hundred-mile migration route of the Serengeti Wildebeest; or the several square mile areas in which eland live. Many other elements of their social organisations vary too.

Despite these differences it is possible, with thought, to cater for the individual animal's and species' needs in this regard even where there is only one of that species. It is, by definition, always better to have more than one individual of any social species. However this may not be always possible, and with care suitable relationships can be substituted by other species, including human beings. Thus close relationships and apparent companionship was provided by goats for ponies, cattle for eland, horses for zebras, and so on. The encouragement and development of these arrangements have to be managed with care. It is often best to start with young animals, who should be mother-raised to avoid the possibility of inappropriate sexual imprinting or other behavioural abnormalities.

Because of the most common management system at the moment which involves keeping many of the animals tied in stalls, the integration of old animals who have all their lives been prevented from free social contact with conspecifics is likely to be difficult and need particular care. This is not to say that it **cannot** be achieved, it is just a question of working out **how** it can. There is, however, no reason why more physically and socially appropriate environments should not be achieved for the next generation of hoofed stock; for example, feral stallions, which do not have harems, live in batchelor groups. With suitable social upbringing and careful introduction domestic stallions can be so kept [29]. The majority of horses in circuses are stallions. Efforts should be made to gradually allow them free social assocation together in social groups in enclosures for at least part of each day.

General considerations

Breeding

The breeding of rare species, in particular, should be encouraged by careful formation and management of the groups. Breeding of other species, at least once during each animal's lifetime, allows the individuals to exercise this aspect of their behaviours, and has the added advantage of keeping different genes in the populations [see 9 p. 46 on for simple discussion of the need for all individuals in small populations to breed).

The aims, however, of the circus are different although not necessarily inferior to those of most zoos whose main self-publicised aim is for the survival of the **species**. The emphasis in circuses is on the **individual** and its breeding must be considered in respect of the costs and benefits to the individual mother and the individual offspring. It may be that in certain cases, there will be no need or facilities for keeping and training more youngsters; in which case, temporary birth control may well have to be exercised. However irreversible surgery, particularly that with accompanying endocrinal and behavioural effects, such as castration or hysterectomy, is not recommended for either zoos or circuses. Mothers should be allowed and encouraged to raise their own young. In order to achieve this it is often important to be able to handle the mother safely as it is often easier to **help** the mother, but not be a substitute for her, even though, as is the case with so many captive-born females these days, she has had no experience of being mothered (she was herself hand raised) and therefore possibly less likely to be a good mother.

Only if natural mother rearing will cause the death of the young should they be taken away and hand reared. This is rarely the case if the mothers can be handled by experienced and skilled people. Inappropriate management often causes infant rejection by taking the infant away too soon or interfering too much with inexperienced mothers [author's animal behaviour consultancy results].

If infants are hand reared, although they may live closely with humans, they **must** also become integrated into their own species group and learn the appropriate species' specific behaviour and organisation. If weaning away from the human rearers is then desirable eventually, this should be gradually and carefully done so that the animal does not show obvious signs of distress or behavioural restriction.

Training

The training of all the animals should be taken more seriously, more regularly and preferably be more innovative, particularly with regard to educating the animals to perform activities which enhance human's respect for them by demonstrating their unique abilities and differences. Perhaps this could be done with suitable educational programmes for the animals, which could advance our understanding of the different species' abilities. Time must be made available for daily training, handling and exercising of the animals. This can be done by:

- suitable management changes;
- increasing the number of people, or their expertise and skills;
- establishing a circus training school to pass on and increase our knowledge of training.

There are many ways in which the further training of the animals for appropriate behaviour **outside** the ring could cut down labour and the time required for routine jobs. For example:

a) Controlled defaecation

It is not impossible, or even difficult, to train horses or elephants to defaecate in specific places. This was done at three circuses to avoid them defaecating in the ring. An extension of that training to their living quarters is possible (particularly for stallions). Thus there could be specific places where the horses or elephants defaecate, or particular times so that the mucking out would become a quick and simple operation. One elephant had in fact already been trained in this way, and her handler simply presented a bucket or wheelbarrow to her at the appropriate times for her to muck or urinate into. An extension of this approach to other stock could be quite possible - dairy cattle, for example, can be trained not to defaecate in the milking parlour [P. Savage, Colin Godman's Farm, and other dairy farmers]. There is no reason to suppose other artiodactyls could not also learn such control.

b) Animals working

The animals could help with the work around the site. This could provide employment for them, is good advertising (since the majority of people like to see the animals doing something), and if it were sensibly organised could cut down human labour. For example, the elephants could help erect the tents, the horses and ponies and llama could pull small muck carts around, the dogs could help to herd appropriate hoofed stock, and so on. At one circus/zoo, horses pulled a tram around and elephants give rides at several circuses and one or two zoos (Figure 75). These are a few suggestions on the direction in which changes should be made.

Fig. 75. An elephant 'working' by giving rides.

Although I was often impressed with the ring training of the animals, not often was the same degree of commitment and skill employed in the management of the stock outside the ring. This would be advantageous for the wellbeing of much of the stock and grooms, and is quite possible with the existing skills.

As with all animal management systems, good management involves constantly reassessing the system and the animals' physical and mental health within it, as well as considering economic and other controls.

Sensible priorities

A useful concept here is one of 'sensible priorities'. It is always possible to have different priorities in assessing animal management, but if one is centrally concerned with welfare (both physical and psychological) often the conventional priority list may have to be reviewed. This is true in circuses, as in any other husbandry (see for example Figure 27, page 58) which shows how very common behavioural signs of distress are in racehorses or horses used for teaching, managed to what are normally considered the highest standards. Clearly changes from established traditional practices are badly needed for horse management outside circuses as well as within them. Most of the management systems in zoos and circuses are tradition bound, and although the managers often seriously have the animals' health and happiness as a central consideration, the priorities on **how** to achieve this were not always sensible. For example, there is a universal concern that all the animals should not be out in the rain, mist etc., even in the summer, despite the fact that summer rain showers are highly unlikely to cause physical illness to normally healthy adult mammals who are used to the European climate. The result was that animals were confined unnecessarily, and there was some coughing in the horses. The same type of problem is often encountered in zoos where until very recently the physical health of the animal, even at the risk of housing the animals in dull sterile conditions, has always taken priority [e.g. 53]. This has not been conducive to the animals' psychological health and their ability to exercise many behaviours in their repertoire.

There are other odd practices which might, if nothing else, reduce the time spent by grooms doing repetitive, pointless tasks and thus liberate more time for them to spend with the animals, exercising, training and so on. Here are some examples:

- Why is the water taken to the animals, rather than the animals taken to a water butt? Walking the animals out to a water butt would ensure that all the animals are taken out twice a day, that they are handled and that they meet others frequently. It would save much time and energy spent in carting buckets around.

- Why is the hay always put in hay nets which take time to fill, rather than into easily erected hayracks which can be filled in an instant?

- Why is all the mucking out done by hand when it could be possible to use good clean deep litter or sawdust beds for the period at the campsite and muck out mechanically with existing equipment at the end of the stay?

The conventional stable management, on which British horse management manuals and much of the circus animal management is based, was designed to keep **all** the cavalry men (and these days working pupils) employed all day in the stables in order to keep them out of mischief [see 29]; so jobs were constantly invented for the grooms. All of what they do does not necessarily benefit the physical or psychological wellbeing of the animals. Of course, some practices are crucial, but others are not, and the good manager, particularly where labour is expensive and short, will understand this and decide on his/her priorities.

The health and happiness of the animals must always take priority however. If there is a conflict between these two, then the individual cases must be considered very carefully, and it must be understood that psychological health should not always play second fiddle to physical health, nor should the management become so intrusive and concerned that it becomes self-defeating and actually creates problem. This is often the case with modern horse and pet management. 'Good management' is often synonymous with 'interfering and restricting the animal a great deal'.

If the relationship between animals and humans is to develop along lines of symbiosis rather than exploitation of the animals, then it is important to have sensible priorities which examine and carefully balance the different pertinent factors. These priorities may well need reviewing as knowledge increases or conditions change.

Grooms and stockpeople

Although some grooms may spend their entire lives in circuses, the majority of the grooms are casual employees who for various reasons want to join a circus for a time. Therefore not all the people looking after the animals are genuinely interested in them and committed. This does not matter as long as there is good supervision, and regular training, and the supervisor has sensible priorities.

If the public are going to be educated and have their awareness, interest and respect for the animals enhanced, the first impression must be one of professionalism, cleanliness and tidiness.

Most circuses are aware of this now. There are, however, problems that would daunt any but the committed - such as having to put the show on in a muddy field because the council has banned the circus on a better site. Such occurrences (I witnessed four), are not conducive to the animals' welfare either, however hard the circus personnel work.

Around the time of the performance, the campsite is well ordered and tidy with the animal tents, mucked out and the stockpeople in their uniforms. For the rest of the day, however, when there may well be members of the public still wandering about, the tidiness standards may lapse. There are a few basic recommendations here which, if circuses are going to achieve they must attend to: for example, the stockpeople and public should have access to good clean toilets, and grooms should be provided with working overalls and good washing facilities.

Because the animals are on public view at performances twice a day, they are usually all regularly groomed and presented looking their best. It is easy (and often happens in horse stables and showing kennels) that the obsession with the cleanliness of the animals causes further restriction. For instance, horses or dogs may not be allowed out or let loose in a field because they will roll and get muddy which causes extra work for the grooms. This can be a problem for circuses too, but not an insurmountable one; for example, the use of rugs or washing on occasions for the hoofed stock, and electric groomers helps cut down grooming time so that the animals are not restricted in order to keep them clean.

Training circus grooms and trainers

It is recommended that a Circus Animal School should be started which would give apprentices a basic introduction to animal husbandry and particularly the theory and practice of animal handling and training. This would be the first of its kind, and it could attract students from many animal husbandry systems, including zoos, stables, kennels and so on. After a course, the students could be apprenticed to different circuses, and sit a qualification at the end, along the lines of a City and Guilds certificate. A similar system already exists for zookeepers, but the animal training school would, in addition to teaching normal husbandry requirements (such as nutrition, recognition of disease and prophylactic treatments), concentrate on handling and training.

The constant plea in circuses has been that the trainers who are often the proprietors, mechanics and/or general organisers as well, have insufficient time to do as much training as they would like. In order for training/educating of the animals to progress, and fulfil the necessary criteria, circuses should have a registered apprentice trainer/stockperson whose main job is to ensure that the animals are given sufficient individual training, exercise and so on. Such a person would be under the direction of the head trainer, and this would be an extra post, not someone doubling as a groom.

214

Performance

Fig. 76. A dolphin playing ball with some children voluntarily, not in a performance.

There are general recommendations here which have already been suggested in previous chapters. In the first place it is desirable that the acts should serve **to enhance the specific characteristics of the species and individual and their abilities rather than their inabilities and weaknesses.**

Secondly, it is not appropriate for the animals to be dressed up or displayed as if they were stupid or handicapped human beings.

Thirdly, it is desirable that whips, goads and other indications of potential negative reinforcement in the animal acts should be done away with or reduced substantially. The animals should show signs of pleasure in performing and no reluctance to enter the ring or fear of applause.

Displays which tend to enhance the 'courage' and 'greatness' of the presenter rather than the unique abilities and thus respect for animals should be discouraged; for example, attack-trained lions and tigers. An image of harmony and constructive cooperation between the animals and their presenters or trainers would be more admirable and display the potentially important aspect of the circus better.

It is desirable that the animal acts are innovative and aesthetically pleasing if they are to hold the attention of the audience and educate and entertain them.

There may be a place for demonstrating the tradition and history of circus, but it is unlikely that the possibly constructive aims of the circus in relation to animals will be enhanced by an emphasis on this.

Fig. 77. An appropriate act for the big cats, emphasising their ability to balance, their litheness, beauty and grace. Could they invent and develop acts for themselves, having learnt the technical building blocks? Do they have no aesthetic sense, no creativity, no ability for innovation?

The winter quarters

The winter quarters of almost all the circuses need severe attention. The same criteria for keeping the animals on tour must be adhered to and they should be inspected regularly (inspectorate run by the Association of Circus Proprietors perhaps). The period in the winter quarters should be regarded as a 'holiday' for the older trained animals that have been on tour - who should be allowed more freedom of movement, choice of environment and social contact during their period there. Any buildings should be adequately constructed and properly designed to maximise light, optimise ventilation, and heat conservation. It is possible to design buildings/tented accommodation which minimises labour and maximises the animals, choices and freedom.

Quo vadis circi?

Some have stated that they regard the circus as medieval (e.g. Desmond Morris in the Mail on Sunday 1989), implying that their attitude to animals is medieval, whatever this means. It is interesting to note that it was in this period that animals were considered to have rights and be responsible for their actions, they were even tried for criminal acts and sentenced [56].

Be this as it may, where do circuses go from here? Should they remain guardians of 'traditional entertainment' if they manage to fulfil the conditions and improvements outlined here, or should they and could they progress further? And if so, where?

I believe, as I have pointed out, that circuses could play a very important and exciting role in our advancement and understanding of animals, and of animal cognition. Yet further, they could perhaps if they developed appropriately and thought seriously about these ideas be a pivot in making us think more about the possible aesthetic appreciation, creativity, and innovativeness that various individual animals may be capable of. Would it not be possible to work towards a new inter-species art form: multi-species opera/ballet/theatre? Is this just fancy-free lunacy - for the fairies?!

Chapter 11

Conclusions

There are approximately 20 circuses operating in Britain at present, of which approximately 14 are members of the Association of Circus Proprietors'. Each circus with animals has from three to eight animal acts. In the larger circuses 1-4 groups of animals are owned by the proprietors and are semi-permanent. Sometimes even these acts may be hired to another circus. All the other animal acts are hired, usually for the season. Acts travel worldwide and there is much exchange between circuses throughout the world. There is a total of approximately 513 animals in British circuses.

The most common wild animals represented in circuses are the elephants and the big cats. Others, such as bears, zebras, camelids, various types of cattle, snakes and primates, go through periods of being popular. The most numerous and popular animal in circus is the horse. Dogs are also well represented.

There are 31 Indian and 6-10 young African elephants in British circuses. The majority of these are female, but there are now males standing at stud. For the other species, there is a slight bias in favour of males in the circus animals, particularly in the horses. The circuses sometimes act as a market for extra males bred by zoos which would otherwise be euthanised (Chapter 3).

Of the carnivores 54% were circus bred - 40% from zoos; 68% of the ungulates were circus born - 14% from zoos. All but two of the elephants were wild caught although the Indians are now between 28-35 years old.

The carnivores, except the dogs, were housed in beast wagons and now have exercise yards when encamped. The space allowance varied from 0.17 - 4.5 cubic metres for an adult lion in the beast wagon. The beast wagons rarely had any cage furniture although shelves are currently being introduced in some. The ungulates were housed in stalls, looseboxes or loose yards in tents. Some were tethered outside and some could run free some of the time. The elephants were shackled habitually in tents, although during my study electric-fenced yards were introduced and some elephants spent the majority of the day in them. Half of the elephants were allowed to move around freely with their handler for approximately 1 hour per day.

Because a circus might have only one of a species, some animals were isolated from conspecifics. However the nature of a moving circus is such that it was not possible for animals or people to be completely isolated. In the zoos and static circuses and winter quarters this was not always the case.

The animals were transported in either their living quarters or horse boxes and converted lorries. No evidence for distress or trauma as a result of transportation was seen as the animals become very used to this.

The animals were adequately fed and they had on the whole good veterinary supervision from the circus and zoo veterinarians. The majority of the animals were in good condition: 90% on tour. However, at the winter quarters 70% of animals were considered not to be in peak condition.

During the past two years 5.4% of the animals had had reported sickness. There was a 0.97% mortality reported to me. These figures are low when compared to farms, zoos and stables.

Drugs and surgery were not used to maintain the system.

The longevity of the animals compared favourably with zoos and domestic animal husbandry systems.

The stockmanship was not always skilled. The stockpeople spent from 1/2 hour to 3 hours per animal per day. The handling of the stock varied from adequate to good.

The training of the animals was generally professional and of high standard and skill. There was, however, insufficient training of the animals going on in many circuses. Some animals had been performing the same routine for some years with no effort to teach them new things. There was no evidence for cruelty, or prolonged pain and suffering during the training of any of the animals I witnessed. Most of the training was done with the aid of positive reinforcement. Negative reinforcement (a whip or verbal scolding) was used sometimes, but no more than is usual with a good horse or dog trainer.

There was some evidence for prolonged or acute behavioural distress in some of the animals in some housing conditions. In general, there was not significantly more of this in the circus animals than in zoos or other animal husbandry systems. There was, in the case of the horses, slightly less. However it can be suggested that if the animal husbandry is appropriate and ethologically and ethically sound, there should be **no** evidence of this. This should be possible to achieve in the next generation of animals with the increasing knowledge of the etiology of abnormalities in behaviour, increasing aggression, neuroses and other behavioural pathologies (Chapter 6).

Certain housing conditions (such as being semi-permanently confined to beast wagons, stalls or shackled) severely behaviourally restricted the animals. Such practices are unnecessary and should and can be eliminated.

Animal welfare organisations have argued that circuses **by their nature** cause suffering and distress to animals. They have also argued that, even if this were shown not to be the case, animals should not be used to entertain human beings, particularly if they are in the process made to look absurd as this undermines humans' respect for them. These are points that have been considered carefully (Chapter 7). The conclusion is that they are invalid, although the campaign against circuses has had a very salutary effect on the circuses themselves and has encouraged them to examine their motives and ideas concerned with the keeping, training and performing of animals.

On the other hand, not all the effects of the campaign to ban animals in circuses have benefited the welfare of the animals. One example of this that I encountered on three separate occasions was that because the council had banned the circus on its grounds, the circus had hired inferior grounds with inferior facilities (less space, very muddy, difficulties in being able to take the animals out etc.).

Much harm was also done to the cause of improving animal welfare as a whole by groups of violent activists (e.g. they smashed up the glass houses of a market gardener in Kent who had been host to a circus the previous week).

This study shows that the welfare of the animals in British circuses, as judged by physical and psychological criteria, is not as a rule inferior to that of other animal husbandry systems such as in zoos, private stables and kennels. It also points out that even if this were to be the case, there is no reason why it should be a **necessity** of the circus way of life.

It is therefore irrational to take a stand against circuses on grounds that the animals in circuses necessarily suffer, unless they are to take the same stand against zoos, stables, race horses, kennels, pets and all other animal-keeping systems.

There is, however, an argument to be made against the use of animals at all by human beings. This has three major objections. Firstly, it is unrealistic and would require a complete rethink of all of human society, and secondly, it would inevitably result in an even more anthropocentric world and further rapid animal extinctions because of conflicting interest of land use with humans. There is a third, and to my mind major, objection to this approach, and this is that many humans' lives would be substantially impoverished if they were not able to associate with, and even live with animals. It can also be argued that many animals' lives may well be impoverished equally because they have no contact with human beings.

The arguments for wild animals having special status have been examined, and it is concluded that there is no reason to assume that this should be so, or that only 'natural' behaviour is good. The individual's past experience is much more important to consider in designing the environment rather than the species' traditional character of being 'wild' or 'domestic'.

It is relevant here to point out arguments for circuses in terms of animal welfare. Here we are examining what circuses **could** do, not necessarily what they do do.

Circuses ensure a close relationship between individual animals of different species and individual human trainers and stockpeople. This is because when on the road they must effectively live together 24 hours a day in close encampments, and secondly the animals are trained to perform, which inevitably ensures direct contact between the species. At its best this working relationship does not necessitate domination of one species over the other and could and should leave room for the animal's innovative abilities and self-expression. In this way, the training and performance of the animal can emphasise both the particular species and individual characteristics and can educate the human audience in the cognitive abilities and uniqueness of the species; while at the same time, respecting the individual.

There is little doubt that the close association with individual animals that is possible in the circus is of considerable value to the people directly concerned. It is also possible that the animals themselves may find the training or 'educating' intellectually interesting and gain from it. This may be a reason why there is not more evidence of distress in circus animals kept in restricted and confined conditions. It is nonsense to say that circuses **cannot** play a role in conservation. To date they have not been active in this direction, but then nor had zoos until Jersey Zoo pointed out the possible role in breeding endangered species. There is however dispute as to whether this is a worthwhile aim.

It should be remembered that the reason why the dolphins and whales are receiving so much of the conservationists' attention is because of their demonstrated cognitive abilities, and their popularity often as a result of the public seeing them performing feats in aquaria. There are many other animals which are equally or more seriously threatened (e.g. the black rhinoceros, or the Orinoco crocodile) but which have not come to the public's attention because they have not **demonstrated** their cognitive abilities in the same way... they are not considered 'as intelligent'.

Circuses could have an important role to play here, particularly in relation to the elephants and some of the threatened big cats. I see this role not only in breeding the endangered species (which as in the case of the snow leopard they have already had some success with) but in raising public interest to the plight of species by demonstrating their special cognitive abilities.

Circuses are perfectly placed to do research on cognition: how and what different species can learn; how and what they think, and how they perceive the world: their 'telos'. They are well placed to do research on the effect of past experience and imprinting since they breed and rear several wild and domestic species. They can also collect much information on individual differences within species, and personality profiles.

Finally, they are uniquely placed to be able to do research on the human-animal relationship with both wild and domestic animals, and to learn much from the close association and familiarity from the animals about both humans and animals.

In this way they could have an important role to play in educating the public and heightening the respect for individual animals, their unique intelligences and amazing abilities.

On balance, I do not think that the animals' best interests are necessarily served by money and activities diverted to try and ban circuses or zoos either locally or nationally. What is much more important is to continue to encourage the zoos and circuses to improve their animal welfare along the lines pointed out in Chapters 9 and 10, and to back some inspection to ensure certain criteria are met in the animal keeping and training. In this it is important to mention that there should be no discrimination in favour of the larger zoos and circuses; some of the small ones were found to have high standards.

There is no doubt that this project has had a considerable effect on the upgrading of the animal husbandry in circuses at least, and on making the circus people think about the problems. For example, during this time the circus veterinarian introduced a series of requirements for inspection (see Appendix 1), which has been updated subsequently. Electric-fenced enclosures were introduced for the elephants. Exercise yards became necessities for the carnivores. The proprietors are now considering electric-fenced enclosures for more of the hoofed stock and horses, and one proprietor is consulting me on how to integrate previously stalled horses into a social group. Some further thought is going into the animal acts in order to display the species' particular characteristics.

Animal training sessions have become open to the public in a couple of circuses, and some educational material for the public on species and individuals is in preparation. The training of trainers and stockpeople is being considered but a more thorough training certificate for zoo and circus staff is essential.

There are still many improvements that could be made, particularly at the winter quarters. One constructive approach would be for the animal welfare organisations to offer an annual award, with accompanying publicity, for the circus which has the 'best' animal husbandry and most appropriate animal acts to enhance the species and display the animals' abilities. This has already been instigated for zoos [171].

Finally, let me reemphasise that the animal husbandry and environmental design for the animals in zoos and circuses **needs to be improved**, along the suggested lines. Let us hope that this occurs over the next decade and thereafter we continue to develop in our understanding and development of Animal Rights, as we continue to keep a watch on Human Rights. Ethically, ecologically and ethologically acceptable ways of inter-species associations are possible and desirable, and they **could** develop even in zoos and circuses. For this to happen, though, such institutions must change, not be banned.

Appendix 1

Veterinary requirements of the Association of Circus Proprietors of Great Britain

This paper sets out the details of the Association's Veterinary Scheme for the year 1989 which have been recommended by Messrs. Taylor and Greenwood, the international zoo vets, and accepted by all members as a condition of membership.

It should be noted that these requirements are not of a permanent nature, but form part of a continuously self-improving programme. They are, therefore, reviewed annually following the advice of the Association's Consultant Veterinary Officers.

In all matters, these standards are mandatory and failure by any member to comply results in a membership certificate being withdrawn.

Inspections
Each member shall be the subject of four inspections in each calendar year, one of which will be carried out at a circus winter quarters. Each member is then subject to spot checks as and when the Consultant Veterinary Officers shall require.

The General Principles
1. A member may not travel with sick animals or those which become ill *en route*. Permanent accommodation for housing such animals away from the circus must be available at all times.
2. Members may not travel with more animals which, in the view of the Consultant Veterinary Officers, they can readily cope with in the light of the staff and other facilities available. No member may travel animals which are not working. Animals in the course of training may be travelled, but not those which are trained but not working. Animals being hand reared or young with their mothers are acceptable.
3. Each member must have sufficient staff not only to care for the animals, but to provide them with extended periods of exercise and activity. The Consultant Veterinary Officers are to give individual advice as to the necessary inspections when making inspections.
4. Members must plan their routes so that the circus sites are suitable to accommodate the animals under expected weather conditions and their is sufficient open ground for exercise.
5. Except in isolated circumstances, the minimum length of stay on any one site should be one week so as to minimise the amount of travelling involved and to allow appropriate use of exercise facilities.
6. Members must keep individual records of every animal, particularly on veterinary items. This should be made available to every vet or other official who inspects the animals in order that further comments and recommendations may be added.

7. Members' staff should be trained and encouraged to undertake available animal management courses. They must be able to demonstrate to the Veterinary Officers their knowledge of the special requirements of each species they keep.

8. Members who take animals from outside their own resources must assume full responsibility for their care and veterinary attention. The employing circus is responsible for all aspects of this veterinary scheme.

9. Permanent circuses must have available exercise fields for all animals and those which cannot be exercised outdoors with reasonable frequency for practical or legal reasons should not be booked.

Specific requirements for each species

1. Sea lions. These should not be travelled and if kept in permanent sites, they should be provided with swimming water which is changed daily or filtered, and at least one metre deep. The size of all pools must be provided in advance by the Veterinary Officers and appropriate food storage and preparation facilities must be provided.

2. Apes (chimpanzee, oran-utan). These should not be in circuses over the age of seven years. After this age, the provision of sufficient accommodation, space and safety arrangements is impossible.

3. Primates. No monkey can be used whose activity has to be restricted because it is other than completely tame, unless very large accommodation and companionship is available.

4. Elephants. These must have a covered tent available which provides complete wind protection and incorporates clear panels which facilitate sufficient ingress of daylight. All elephants should be stood off the ground and boards and chains should be in 'as new' condition. Chains must be covered where they go round the leg and the covering must be kept well maintained. These chains must be lubricated daily. Board sizes should be a minimum of eight feet by six feet (seven feet by five feet for animals up to six years of age). Elephants standing on wet ground shall be reason for refusal of a certificate.

Elephants must be gently exercised for the majority of the day. The Veterinary Officers will require a system whereby elephants are enclosed within a barrier of an acceptable size depending on the number and size of the elephants, and are allowed to exercise within the circus site either on a tether of acceptable length or without restraint. Elephants may not be restrained by two legs for the greater part of the day, and must be able to roam throughout most of the day, except where severe weather prevents this. In long periods of severe weather, elephants must be exercised in the ring.

5. Cats. All cats must have an exercise area to approved standards and sizes which is to be available throughout every day. The exercise cage must be of minimum dimensions of twenty feet by forty feet (or forty feet diameter) and one cage will be acceptable where there are two groups of animals. Two cages are required where there are three groups of animals. In addition, there should be an exercise prop or other toy in the exercise cage. The wagons in which the animals are transported and to which they retire at night must be a minimum of eight feet wide and provide a minimum of ten feet in length for an individual animal and a minimum of seven

feet in length per animal where two or more animals are kept together. Shelves should be provided for leopards etc. Absence of an exercise cage shall be reason for refusal of a certificate.

6. Bears. These shall have the same accommodation as lions and tigers and an exercise cage shall be available with suitable furniture.

7. Dogs. These are generally kept as household pets, but where they are housed in a group they must be exercised twice daily as well as in the performance.

8. Horses. These shall be kept on standard cavalry lines. Suitable tents should be constructed so as to allow fresh air as well as protection, and the ground underfoot must be dry or covered with rubber matting or a **thick** layer of fresh straw. Horses which are tethered through the day must be exercised properly at least once in addition to the performance; and allowed other gentle exercise when not working. There must be a sufficient staff/horse ratio to make this possible.

9. Hoofed stock (exotics). These should be tethered or enclosed on open ground as far as possible and there must be sufficient space for this. They should be housed in tents on dry ground, mats or thick straw. Enclosures must be purpose-built and not makeshift.

10. Other animals. These may be used unless they have exercise or housing needs which cannot be met. Members must submit to the Veterinary Officers a list of animals which they intend to travel well in advance in order that appropriate recommendations can be made.

The aim of these requirements is to make all members consider seriously which animals they use and to ensure that they do not take on those with which they cannot adequately cope. They are designed to ensure that all circus animals receive adequate fresh air and exercise.

Appendix 2
Methods

Over a period of 18 months, 15 circuses in Britain (and one in Switzerland) were visited for a period of between 2 and 10 days each. Most circuses were visited more than once: at their winter quarters, while pulling down and during build up, and at their campsites. Performances were watched in all the circuses, some many times, with particular attention paid to animal acts. While we were with the circus, any training sessions, practices, exercise sessions, parades and educational activities for the public involving the animals, were also watched and recorded.

Understandably, since circuses have recently been under heavy attack from animal welfare organisations, the circus proprietors were highly suspicious initially of us visiting. Unlike the case of zoos which are open to the public much of the time, it would not have been possible to conduct this research without the cooperation of the circus people. Convincing the circus people that I was conducting a disinterested scientific study was difficult, but was achieved eventually. I addressed the Association of Circus Proprietors by invitation and since then circus people have shown us nothing but friendship, cooperation and an intense willingness to listen to criticisms and comment. Visits by us to the circuses have either been by prior arrangement, or surprise visits. There is no doubt that the fact that I am doing this study, coming and going and talking to all the circus people from the grooms to the proprietors, presenters and trainers, about all aspects of their animals and their husbandry has had some effect on the treatment of animals in circuses; if only to make the circus people think seriously about it rather than confronting hostility (and often violence from animal welfare interested groups) with hostility and violence. There have, however, been some obvious improvements to the husbandry of specific species as a result of suggestions I have made and these are discussed in the appropriate sections.

If, when I was with a circus, I found that there were animals which in my view required veterinary attention as a result of physical disease, or I could help with the treatment of psychological disease, the case was discussed with the circus proprietor and suggestions made.

Five zoos were visited. A period of at least 8 hours was spent at each, during which the mammals in particular were visited and observed. In addition, appointments were made to discuss the zoo and its policy with the director or a decision-making member of the zoo staff wherever they were interested.

An inventory was made of all the non-pet animals in the circuses visited, together with details of their husbandry, including their veterinary care and disease incidence, species, ages, sexes; the number of stockpeople, and their reasons for being with the circus; what and how often the animals were fed and watered; their keeping conditions including size of enclosures; their group's size and composition; amount and type of exercise; movement around; contact with the public; training and performing frequencies; and any other management practices such as routine foot care, transportation and so on were also recorded.

An attempt was made to assess the way the animals were handled, and the relationship between stockpeople, trainers and presenters and their animals.

Because we were with the circuses for some days, living as members of the circus and were allowed access freely around at all times, we were able to check any information we had been given against what we saw happening. At no time, once we had been given permission to visit the circus, were we prevented or discouraged from wandering around at will where we wished, with the exception of watching the elephants at night which a couple of circuses were anxious about as they were frightened that we might disturb them too much. It was not possible to watch the large cats at night either as they had their shutters lowered over the beast wagon fronts. This was done for security reasons as well as to reduce disturbance to the animals.

The circuses are not identified by name as at the Association of Circus Proprietors' meeting I promised that names would not be disclosed. An inventory of each circus's animals and their acts are not given for the same reason. In addition, the animal acts change each season, so it would be of little value.

During our time with the circus we had a tent or a caravan on the site with all the others and lived with the circus, usually within view of the stable tents. We made a total of 25 expeditions to circuses, spending a total of 79 nights and 115 days with the circuses.

The training sessions, if there were any, were assessed carefully in terms of the relationship of the trainer to the animals, the use of positive and negative reinforcement, the speed of learning new movements and 'tricks', and what these were. In relation to this, it was arranged for three individuals to work as grooms for one month each during the winter season in Circus Knie's winter quarters at Rapperswil in Switzerland, where they work full time on training the next year's acts. As a result, it was possible to monitor the training of a group of 12 Arab stallions over a nine-month period, the introduction of new acts for the elephants, and the training of a group of farm animals in a new act.

The behaviour of the animals in circuses and zoos was recorded on detailed sheets for one-hour periods. 124 different activities were recorded for 28 different species in a total of 2988 animal hours of observation. The majority of the observations were between 08.00 and 17.00 hours, but three 24-hour periods were observed on elephants, and two on horses, ponies and llamas. Other variables such as the place, the type of husbandry condition, the weather, the date and time were also recorded.

Behaviours which normally continued for more than 5 minutes, such as eating, standing, lying and so on were recorded in the number of five-minute periods in which the activity occurred for the hour. Activities which are of short duration, such as vocalisations or sniffing objects, and which usually occurred for less than 5 minutes, were recorded as occasions, and the total number for the hour's observation summed.

The information from the observation sheets was fed into a computer, and a programme written for analysing it. The behaviours were then batched into:

Maintenance behaviour: eating, drinking, urinating, defaecating, standing, lying, dozing and sleeping, moving and ruminating (if relevant).

Self-directed behaviour: ear twitch, groom self, head shake, rub self, roll, stretch, scratch, sneeze, etc.

Object directed and manipulative: lick or smell object, play with object, investigate object, reach for object, etc.

Social affiliative: rub or sniff another, touch another, close contact, call, etc.

Aggressive: bite or kick, growl, attack, ear flatten (where relevant) etc.

Attention getting: certain vocalisations and other specific behaviour, such as trunk to floor banging in elephants.

Vocalising

Behavioural indices of fear: such as running away, increasing body tension, shivering and sweating.

Frustration behaviour: bar biting, chain pulling, head shaking (sometimes), pawing, tail wagging (some species), run at bars etc.

Abnormal behaviour

a) neuroses, in the stable or training

b) pathologies

c) high levels of aggression directed either at humans or other animals

d) stereotypies which are defined as repeated actions not normally in the repertoire which are fixed in all forms and apparently purposeless: weaving, head nodding, head twisting.
e) self-destructive behaviour, e.g. licking and biting parts of the body until they are raw
f) other abnormal and apparently purposeless behaviours, such as bar biting, pacing, running at bars etc.

Pleasure or excitement: playing, certain vocalisations, greeting, leaping around.

These categories are not mutually exclusive, certain behaviours may fall into several categories, and the inclusion of some behaviours in certain categories, such as those in frustration and pleasure, has little empirical basis although it does have some *a priori* base.

In this study it was important to try to assess categories such as 'distress' and 'pleasure' in animals in different husbandry systems as these indices are crucial in the assessment of their welfare. These categories, which have been discussed, attempt to do this.

The large number of species, and the different conditions in which the animals were recorded, indicates that the information accumulated is only useful for developing an overview of patterns of behaviour. It would be more satisfactory to have more time to develop this work further. Many activities did not occur often, and thus the total figures for the number of hours recorded are not large enough to warrant statistical treatment. Where statistics are relevant they have been applied, for example, test for significant differences in behaviour and how time is spent in the different husbandry conditions and to test for any significant difference between the behaviour of animals in zoos and circuses. More observations are required on certain species and conditions, particularly in zoos, to obtain more meaningful quantitative results. The results are presented in tables as this allows a more direct and accurate comparison than histograms, pie diagrams or other visually appealing representations. The statistical tests and the value of 'p' where there is a significant difference are given.

The information on the presence or absence of physical disease and evidence for distress and pleasure of the animals in zoos and circuses and all other types of husbandry systems invented by humans - can help with environmental design or the disbanding of certain types of husbandry systems. One example of the latter was the banning of crated veal calves in 1987. This decision was taken on the grounds that the calves being young, and being unable to perform large numbers of the behaviours within their repertoire, including moving around, scratching themselves and interacting with others.

However, there are many who would still be opposed to certain husbandry systems, even if there were no evidence of behavioural distress in the animals involved. The animal welfare arguments here are philosophical, and it rapidly became apparent that a thorough investigation of animals in circuses, recording the physical health and behaviour of the animals, whatever the conclusions, would have little constructive effect on the debate, and ultimately would be unlikely to benefit the animals themselves.

Thus it was necessary to investigate all the arguments for or against circuses and zoos. By invitation from Professor B. Rollin, and with the help of a Welcome Foundation travel grant, I spent six weeks at Colorado State University, Colorado, USA, where they have a large and stimulating department of Applied Philosophy with strong links to Animal Science, Veterinary Science, Environmental and Development issues. I do not pretend to have learnt all the philosophy pertaining to the debates during such a short time, but perhaps have learnt how little I do know.

At each circus and zoo visited, various people owning, working in or speaking for the circus or zoos were interviewed and discussions on the various arguments for and against zoos and circuses were conducted to assess their attitudes, justifications and motivations. Without exception, all the circus proprietors, partners or spokespeople were very cooperative in this, open to suggestion and to consider new ideas. This was not always the case for zoos, some of whom showed little or no interest and gave the impression that there was nothing to discuss!

The RSPCA, Zoo Check and other animal welfare organisations in their publications state the case against captive and performing animals. These arguments have been considered carefully, as have the arguments of the zoo and circus people for performing animals in zoos and circuses.

There has been some discussion about having circuses without animals, and there has even been a clown school set up (which has had remarkably little contact with circus clowns!). Two circuses have tried to run without animals, one ironically enough in the grounds of a zoo but neither of these were economically successful. We decided to find out what the circus audiences at performances felt about the circus, and in particular the presence of the animals in circuses. To do this we conducted a questionnaire survey with the cooperation of the circus personnel at circus performances where forms were completed and later analysed.

It is extremely important for a constructive approach to welfare debates that the participants from different areas of specialism understand, and indeed are conversant with each other's arguments. This has not often been the case. My aim is to further the debate on the existence of circuses and zoos, on how their animals are kept and on how the humans relate to them, **in a constructive way.**

Statistics

Because of the number of different behaviours, species and variation in conditions, the reliability of the statistical comparisons must not be over emphasised. In addition, the number of hours of recorded behaviour in certain conditions is relatively small (for example, more recordings should be made in zoos), and many of the behaviours were relatively infrequent. They may, however, be particularly important as indicators of husbandry conditions, or of individual differences, and thus are analysed although the results should not be too heavily relied upon.

Behavioural differences under different conditions were analysed using the following methods:

1. The length of time a behaviour was recorded as the number of minutes/hour performed (laying, standing, moving, etc.) was compared for different conditions using the Mann Witney test.

2. A X2 test was conducted to test for significant differences in the occurrence of behaviours that were recorded as occasions, and were often not very frequent.

3. Behaviours were batched into categories to test for possible differences in these batches of behaviour between conditions (e.g. manipulation of objects in the environment or vocalising). In some cases the batching is somewhat arbitrary and experimental, such as in the case of behaviour related to frustration, distress and pleasure. Many of the behaviours are represented in several of these batches. The difference in the occurrence of these groupings were tested using a sign test.

List of behaviours recorded

aggressive bite	head twist	sit
attack	hitwall	sleep
attack leopard through bars	human contact	smell other
avoid	in run	snarl
bang trunk on floor	investigate object	sneeze
bark	lean	sniff ground
bite	leap up	snore
bite bars	lick lips	snort
blow	lip move	spit
carry meat	look over door	spray
chain playing	lying	squeak
chase pounce	manipulate with trunk	standing
claw cage	mounting	stand on hind legs
claw floor	move constantly	stretch
climbing	move in bed	strutt
contact mum	mutual groom	suckling
copulate	pace	sway
crib bite	pant	tail up
curl	pawing	tail wag
defaecate	play	touch other
door kick	play bite	touch other constantly
doze	play with food	trumpet
drink	purr	trunk out
eat	push	trunk reach
ears back	reach for food	trunk swing
ear flap	reach to human	trunk to bars
eat straw bed	rest	trunk to ground
eat wood	roar	trunk to mouth
erection	roll	trunk to other elephant
fidgets	rub bars	trunk to pig
flehmen	rub other	trunk to trunk
fly	rub self	trunk up
foot rub on floor	rub self on wall	urinate
foot stamp	rub tusks	vocal
foot to bars	rumble	wash
grimace	run	watch
groom self	run at bars	weave constantly
growl	scratch self	wrestle on hind legs
grunt	shake body	yawn
head nod	shiver	
head shake	sigh	

Appendix 3

Results of questionnaire
to circus audiences

Whilst with the circuses, we made a point of talking to Animal Liberation supporters who were demonstrating against circuses. It is worth noting that the Animal Welfare lobby had often never visited a circus and had, almost without exception, never witnessed any training. This despite being invited to attend at least two of the circuses we visited, including being allowed behind the scenes.

We also talked to many circus people.

We thought it would be useful to see what the circus audience thought of the performance and animals in circuses. We realised that to attend the circus meant that those completing the questionnaire would be biased towards circuses but felt that their opinion would still be of interest.

The results of 550 returned forms were:

1) 99.4% enjoyed the performance.
2) 57.3% of the audience liked the animal acts best,
   16.6% liked the human acts best and 25.3% liked both equally.
3) 60.2% of the audience would not attend if there were no animal acts.
4) 91.6% of the audience would like to see the training
5) 93.6% of the audience like to be able to meet the animals after the show.

The large percentage of people who wished to see the training and to meet the animals after the show indicates the potential educational value of the circuses.

List of circuses and zoos visited

Circuses

Name	Winter quarters/ permanent site	Tented camp/ circus building	Perfor- mance	Training	Build-up & down
Austen Brothers*	X	X	X	X	
Chipperfield Brothers*		X	X	X	
Chipperfield Organisation*	X		X	X	
Circus Fiesta		X	X	X	X
Circus Knie	X	X	X	X	X
Circus de Reszke		X	X	X	
Clubb-Chipperfield*	X		X	X	
Gandey's*		X	X	X	
Gerry Cottle's*	X	X	X	X	
Hoffman's*	X	X	X	X	
Paulo's		X	X		X
Peter Jay's Great Yarmouth*		X	X		
Peter Jay's Blackpool Tower*		X	X		
Roberts Bros. Super Circus*	X	X	X	X	X
Robert Bros. Famous Circus	X				

Zoos

Name	Winter quarters/ permanent site	Tented camp/ circus building	Perfor- mance	Training	Build-up & down
San Diego Sea Life Centre	X		X	X	
Bronx, New York	X				
Chester	X				
Edinburgh	X				
London	X				
San Diego, California	X				
Twycross	X				
Woburn Safari Park	X				

* member of the Association of Circus Proprietors at the time of the study.

Bibliography

1 Kiley-Worthington, M. **Behavioural problems of farm animals.** Oriel, Stockton, 1977.

2 Wiepkema, P.R., Pain and stereotypes in **Assessing pain in animals.** Ed. I.J.H Duncan and V. Molony, EEC, EUR 9742, 1986.

3 Wiepkema, P.R., On the significance of ethological criteria for the assessment of animal welfare in **Indicators relevant to farm animal welfare.** Ed. D. Smidt. Martinus Nijhoff, 1983.

4 Stamp-Dawkins, M. **Animal suffering. The science of animal welfare.** Chapman Hall, London, 1980.

5 Kiley-Worthington, M. The behaviour of confined calves raised for veal. Are these animals distressed? **International Journal of Stud Anim. Prob.** 4.198-213, 1983.

6 Selye, H. **The story of the Adaption Syndrome.** Acta, Montreal, 1952.

7 Tzchanz, B. Reaktionsnormen und Adaptation, in **Das tier im Experiment.** Ed. Wiehe W.E. Hans Huber, Bern, 1978.

8 Beilharz, R.G. & Zeeb, K. Applied ethology and animal welfare in **Applied. Animal. Ethology** 3.10. 1981.

9 Luoma, J.R. **A crowded ark. The role of zoos in wildlife conservation.** Mifflin, Boston, 1987.

10 Universities Federation of Animal Welfare. **Why Zoos?** UFAW, Potters Bar, 1988.

11 Smidt, D. (ed) **Indicators relevant to farm animal welfare.** Martinus Nijoff, 1983.

12 **Behavioural needs of farm animals.** Proceedings of Workshop Sponsored by the Farm Animal Care Trust and the Universities Federation of Animal Welfare. Appl. Animal. Behav. Sc. 19, 339-386, 1988.

13 Thorpe, W. in **Report of the Technical Committee on the Welfare of Animals under Intensive Husbandry Systems.** Ed. Brambell, H.M.S.O., 1965.

14 Rollin, B. **Animal consciousness, animal pain and scientific change.** OUP, 1989.

15 Dawkins, R. **The blind watchmaker.** Longman,1986.

16 Clarke, S.R.L. How to believe in fairies. **Inquiry.**320.337-55, 1987.

17 Broom, D.M. Animal welfare in **Vet. Annual 29.** Ed. C.S.G. Grunwell, M.E. Raw & F.G.Hill, Wright, London, p9-14, 1989.

18 Broom, D.M. Stereotypies as animal welfare indicators in **Indicators relevant to farm animal welfare.** Ed. D.Smidt, p81-87, 1983.

19 Sheldrake, R. **A new science of life.** Paladin. 1981.

20 Clarke, S.R.L. **The moral status of animals.** OUP, 1976.

21 Singer, P. **Animal Liberation.** Jonathan Cape, London, 1976.

22 Midgley, M. **Animals and why they matter.** University Press Georgia, Athens, 1983.

23 Rollin, E.B. **Animal rights and human morality.** Prometheus, 1981.

24 Regan, T. Animal rights. Human wrongs in **Ethics and Animals.** Ed. H.B. Miller & W.H. Williams pp 19-44, Humana Press, Clifton, 1983.

25 Sapontzis, S.F. **Morality, reason and animals.** Temple press, Philadelphia, 1987.

26 Dunphy, F. Elephants and their management in Sri Lanka. Talk to Elephant Keepers' Association, Bristol, 1989.

27 Moss, C. **Elephant memories.** Elm Tree, London, 1988.

28 Eltrtingham, K. **Elephants.** Blandford Mammal Series, 1980.

29 Kiley-Worthington, M. **The behaviour of horses in relation to management and training.** J.A. Allen, 1987.

30 Wood-Gush, D. **Elements of ethology.** Chapman Hall, 1983.

31 Duncan, I.J.H., & V.Molony (eds). **Assessing pain in farm animals.** EEC Commission Report EUR 9742.EN. 1986.

32 Cregier, S.E. **Transporting horses.** Ph.D. thesis, Univ. of Prince Edward Island, 1983.

33 Hughes, B.O., and Duncan, I.J.H.. The notion of ethological 'need'. Models of motivation and animal welfare. **Anim. Behav.** 36. 1696-1707, 1988.

34 Frey, R.G. **Rights, killings and suffering.** Blackwell, Oxford, 1983.

35 McKenna, V., Travers, W. & Wray, J. **Beyond the bars: the zoos dilemma.** Thorsons, Wellingborough, 1987.

36 **Animals in Circuses.** RSPCA, Horsham, Sussex.

37 **Performing animals.** RSPCA, Horsham, Sussex.

38 Thelestram, M., and A. Gunnarsson. **The ethics of animal experimentation.** Proc. 2nd CFN Symposium, Stockholm, Acta physiol. Sc., 1986.

39 Sharp, R. The cruel deception in **Advances in Animal Welfare Science,** 1986-1987, ed. M.W. Fox and L.D. Mickley, p9-19, Martinus Nijoff, Boston, 1987.

40 Jensen, P. Normal and abnormal behaviour of animals in **Ethics of Animal Experimentation.** Ed. Thelstram, M. & A. Gunnarsson. Acta Physiol, Sc. 128, p11-23, 1986.

41 Capra, F. **The turning point. Science, society and the rising culture.** Flamingo, London, 1983.

42 Rolson, S.L. Feeding problems in **Current therapy in euqine medicine.** Ed. Robinson, N.E.,. Saunders, Philadelphia, 1987

43 Baker, G.J. Surgery of the head and neck in **Equine medicine and surgery.** 2nd edition. pp 758-9. American Vet. Publications, USA. 1980

44 Fraser, A.F. **Farm animal behaviour.** pp 88-97. Balliere Tindall, London, 1974

45 Hartley-Williams, Vices in **Horse and Rider,** August. 1989.

46 Allen, W.E. **Fertility and Obstetrics in the horse.** Blackwell, London, 1988.

47 Shane, D. Assault on Eden. Destruction of Latin American rain forests in **Advances in animal welfare science 1986-87.** Ed. M.W. Fox and L.D. Mickley, p149-162, Martinus Nijoff, Boston, 1986.

48 Hediger, H. **Animals in zoos and circuses.** Butterworth, London, 1959.

49 Desmond, A. **The ape's reflexion.** Quartet Books, London, 1979.

50 Linden, E. **Apes, men and language.** Penguin, London, 1981.

51 Stamp-Dawkins, M. From an animal point of view. Consumer demand theory and animal welfare. **Behaviour and Brain Science.** 1990.

52 Petherick, C., Rutter, S.M. & Duncan, I.J.H. Push-door for measuring motivation. SVE meeting, Bristol, 1989.

53 Crandall, L.S. **Management of wild animals in captivity.** University of Chicago Press, p227, 1964.

54 Travers, W. Inadmissible evidence in **Beyond the Bars. The Zoo Dilemma.** Eds. V. McKenna, W. Travers & J. Wray. Thorsons, Wellingborough, 1987.

55 Hale, E.B. Domestication and the evolution of behaviour in **The behaviour of domestic animals.** Ed. E.S.E. Hafez, Balliere Tindall & Cox, p21-53, 1962.

56 Thomas, K. **Man and the natural world.** Penguin, London, 1984.

57 Broom, D. The scientific assessment of animal welfare. **Applied Animal Behaviour Science.** 20, pp 5-19, 1988.

58 Hinde, R.A. **Animal behaviour.** McGraw Hill, 1970.

59 Hutt, C. & Hutt, S.L. The effect of the environment on steroetypic behaviour of children. **Animal Behaviour.** 13, 1-4, 1965.

60 Fox, M.W. (ed.) **Abnormal Behaviour in Animals.** Saunders, London, 1968.

61 Danzer, R., Mormede, P. & Henry, J.P. Significance of physiological criteria in assessing animal welfare in **Indicators relevant to farm animal welfare.** Ed. Smidt, D., Martinus Nijhoff, 1986.

62 Donald, S.L., Albright, J.L. & Black, W.C. Primary social relationships and cattle behaviour. **Proc. Indiana Acad. Sci.** Vol. 81, 1972.

236

63 Horsman, P. **Captive polar bears in the UK and Ireland.** Report for Zoo Check. 1985

64 Ulrich, R. Pain as a cause of aggression. **American Zool.** 6, 643-662, 1966.

65 Bindra, D. **Motivation, a systematic reinterpretation.** Ronald Press, NY, 1966.

66 Berlyne, D.G. **Conflict, arousal and curiosity.** McGraw Hill, 1960.

67 Jensen, P.A.J., Jagneau, A. & Ienegeers, G.T.E. The effects of various drugs on isolation-induced fighting behaviour of male mice. **Pharmacol. Expt. Therapy,** 129, 471-475, 1960.

68 Mason, W.A. Effect of social restriction on monkeys. **J. Comp. Physiol. Psychol.** 53, 582-589, 1960.

69 Van Lawick-Goodall, H & J. **Innocent Killers.** Collins, London, 1970.

70 Frijlink, J.L. **In hetspoor van de wolf.** Stringholt, 1976.

71 Bertram, C. The behaviour of lions in the Serengeti. **Anim. Behav. Monograph.** 1971.

72 Schaller, G.B. **The deer and the tiger.** Univ. Chicago Press, 1967.

73 Kiley-Worthington, M. & S. de la Plain. **The Behaviour of Beef Suckler Cattle.** Verlag Birkhauser, Basel, 1983.

74 Douglas-Hamilton, I & D. **Among the elephants.** Collins & Harvill. 1975

75 Redford, I. A talk to the Elephant Keepers' Association, Bristol, 1975.

76 Sheldrick, D. quoted letter in **Beyond the Bars.**[35], p 179.

77 Tinbergen, N. **The study of instinct.** OUP, 1962.

78 Macfarland, D.J. On the causal and functional significance of displacement activities. **Zeit fur Tierpsychol.** 23, 217-235, 1966.

79 Morris, D. Typical intensity and its relation to the problem of ritualisation. **Behav.**11. 1-12.

80 Singer, P. The significance of animal suffering in **Behav. & Brain Sci.,** 1989.

81 Cannon, W.B. **Bodily changes in pain, hunger and rage.** N.Y., Appleton, 1929.

82 Campbell, W.E. **Behaviour problems in dogs.** Amer. Vet. publ. Santa Barbara, 1975.

83 Kiley-Worthington, M. DPhil theseis, University of Sussex. **Some displays of ungulates, canids & felids with particular reference to causation.** 1969

84 Bostock, S. **Ethical justification for zoos.** DPhil thesis, University of Glasgow, 1988.

85 Leyhausen, P. Verhaltstudien an Katzen. **Zeit. fut Tierpsychol.** Beiheft.2, 1956.

86 Gardner, R.A. & B.T. Teaching sign language to a chimp. **Sci.** 165, p618, 1969.

87 Grandin, T. Innovation in pre-slaughter handling. SVE. Bristol. 1989.

88 Mumford. Dogs manipulating people. SVE. London. 1988.

89 Decartes, R. **The philosophical works.** Translated by E.S. Haldane and G.R.T. Rose, N.Y., Dover, 1955.

90 Griffin, D.R. **Animal Thinking.** Harvard Univ. Press, Mass., 1984.

91 Dickinson, A. **Contemporary animal learning theory.** CUP, 1980.

92 Erlich, P.R., Erlich, A.H., & Holdren, J.P. **Ecoscience. Population, resources and environment.** W.H.Freeman, San Francisco, 1977.

93 Kiley-Worthington, M. **Food First Ecological Agriculture.** In press, 1990.

94 Cregier, E.E. Horse breakers, tamers and trainers in Advances in **Animal Welfare Science** 1986-87. Ed. M.W. Fox and L.D. Mickley, Martinus Nijoff, Boston, 1987.

95 Markowitz, H. **Behavioural enrichment in the Zoo.** Van Nostrand, Rheinhold, NY. 1986.

96 Syme, G.J & Syme, L.A. **Social structure in farm animals.** Elsevier. Amsterdam. 1974.

97 Sheppardson, D. Environmental enrichment in the zoo. SVE, Dec. 1989.

98 Mullan, B. & Marvin, G. **Zoo Culture.** Weidenfeld & Nicholson, London, 1987.

99 Harrison, R. **Animal machines.** Vincent Stuart, London, 1964.

100 Mason, J. & Singer, P. **Animal factories.** Crown Publications, N.Y., 1980.

101 Kiley-Worthington, M. Ecologically, ethologically and ethically sound environments for animals. Towards symbiosis. **Agric. Ethics,** in press, 1990.

102 Salt, H.S. **Animal's rights considered in relation to social progress.** Centaur Press, 1892, (reprinted 1980).

103 Midgeley, M. 'Keeping species on ice' in **Beyond the Bars** [35] pp. 55-65.

104 Paton, W. **Man and Mouse, Animals in medical research.** OUP, 1984.

105 Iggo. Animals and pain. UFAW lecture, Edinburgh, 1987.

106 Griffin, D.R. **Question of animal awareness.** Rockefeller University Press, N.Y., 1976.

107 Hearne, V. **Adam's task, calling animals by name.** Heineman, N.Y.,. 1987.

108 Walker, S. **Animal Thought.** Routledge & Kegan Paul, 1983.

109 Roitblatt, H.L., Beaver, T. & Terrace, H.S., editors. **Animal cognition.** Laurence Golbaum Ass., 1987.

110 Sherpell, J. **In the company of animals.** Blackwell, 1987.

111 Morton, D. Contribution to workshop on ethics in Veterinary Medicine. Society of Applied Philosophy, Glasgow, March 1987.

112 Society for Companion Animal Studies.

113 **Man, animals and the environment.** Delta Soc., Boston, 1986.

114 Riding for the disabled.

115 **The evolution of man.** Time Life Books, 1979.

116 Sinclair, E.R.R. The social organisationof the East African buffalo in **The behaviour of ungulates and its relation to management.** Eds. Geist & Walther, IUCN, Morge, pp 676-689, 1974.

117 Federation of Zoos. Meeting on reintroduction of species to the wild, London Zoo, 1989.

118 Erlich, P.R., & Erlich, A.H. **Extinction.** Victor Gollancz, 1980.

119 Carol Gandey in **King Pole,** magazine of the Circus Fans' Association, p4, March 1989.

120 Althaus, T. A code of ethics for circus animal training? in **Living together. People, animals and the environment.** Delta Society, Boston, 1986.

121 Zayan, R. **Assessment of pain in animals.**1986.

122 Shumaker. **Small is Beautiful.** Abacus, 1980.

123 Odum, E.P. **Fundamentals of Ecology.** W.B. Saunders, London, 1971.

124 Int. Federation of Organic Agricultural Movements symposium publications, 1986 & 1988.

125 Shoard, M. **The theft of the countryside.** Temple Smith, 1980.

126 Furness, R.W., and Monyihan, P. **Seabird Ecology.** Blackie, Glasgow, 1987.

127 Wood-Gush, D. Personal communication.

128 Kiley-Worthington, M. Okologische ethologie und Ethic der Tierhaltung in **Theorische und Praktische Grundlagen fur die Biologische Landwirtschaft.** Eds. H.Sambraus & E. Boehncke, pp35-56. Verlag C.F. Muller, Karlsruhe, 1988.

129 Tattersall, F. The effects of environmental complexity on the behaviour of captive leopards *(Panthera pardus).* UFAW student report. 1988.

130 113 **Man, animals and the environment.** Delta Soc., Boston, 1986.

131 Kiley-Worthington, M. The social organisation of a small captive group of eland, oryx and other antelope with analysis of personality profiles. **Behav.** LXVI, p32-55, 1978.

132 Jenison, H. **Evolution of the brain and intelligence.** Academic Press, London, 1973.

133 Turnbull, C. **The forest people.** Paladin, London, 1980.

134 Aristotle. **Basic works.** Ed. R. McKeon, Random House, N.Y., 1941.

135 Passmore, J. **Man's responsibility for nature.** Charles Scribner's Sons, N.Y., 1974.

136 Attfield, R. **The ethics of environmental concern.** Basil Blackwell, Oxford, 1983.

137 Stolba, A. and Wood-Gush, D. Verhaltensgliederung und Reaction auf Neurreise als ethologische Kriterien zuer Beurteilung in **Angewandte Ethologie bei Haustieren.** K.T.B.L., Damstadt, 1981.

138 UFAW. **Alternatives to intensive husbandry systems.** Potters Bar, 1981.

Index